OCS Study
MMS 2001-004

Coastal Marine Institute

Fate and Effects of Barium and Radium-Rich Fluid Emissions from Hydrocarbon Seeps on the Benthic Habitats of the Gulf of Mexico Offshore Louisiana

I0423771

U.S. Department of the Interior
Minerals Management Service
Gulf of Mexico OCS Region

Cooperative Agreement
Coastal Marine Institute
Louisiana State University

OCS Study
MMS 2001-004

Coastal Marine Institute

Fate and Effects of Barium and Radium-Rich Fluid Emissions from Hydrocarbon Seeps on the Benthic Habitats of the Gulf of Mexico Offshore Louisiana

Authors

Paul Aharon
Dan Van Gent
Baoshun Fu
L. Max Scott

January 2001

Prepared under MMS Contract
14-35-0001-30660-19946
by
Coastal Marine Institute
Louisiana State University
Baton Rouge, Louisiana 70801

Published by

U.S. Department of the Interior
Minerals Management Service
Gulf of Mexico OCS Region

Cooperative Agreement
Coastal Marine Institute
Louisiana State University

DISCLAIMER

This report was prepared under contract between the Minerals Management Service (MMS) and the Louisiana State University, Coastal Marine Institute. This report has been technically reviewed by the MMS, and it has been approved for publication. Approval does not signify that the contents necessarily reflect the views and policies of the MMS, nor does mention of trade names or commercial products constitute endorsement or recommendation for use. It is, however, exempt from review and compliance with the MMS editorial standards.

REPORT AVAILABILITY

Extra copies of this report may be obtained from the Public Information Office (Mail Stop 5034) at the following address:

> U.S. Department of the Interior
> Minerals Management Service
> Gulf of Mexico OCS Region
> Public Information Office (MS 5034)
> 1201 Elmwood Park Boulevard
> New Orleans, Louisiana 70123-2394
>
> Telephone: (504) 736-2519 or
> 1-800-200-GULF

CITATION

Suggested citation:

Aharon, P., D. Van Gent, B. Fu, and L. M. Scott. 2001. Fate and effects of barium and radium-rich fluid emissions from hydrocarbon seeps on the benthic habitats of the Gulf of Mexico offshore Louisiana. OCS Study MMS 2001-004. Prepared by the Louisiana State University, Coastal Marine Institute. U.S. Department of the Interior, Minerals Management Service, Gulf of Mexico OCS Region, New Orleans, LA. 142 pp.

ABOUT THE COVER

Cartoon showing composite images of submarine barite deposits and associated fauna from gas seeps occurring on the Gulf of Mexico slope. Original sketch by Paul Aharon; final drawing by Mary Lee Eggart.

ABSTRACT

The primary goals of this study were to document products and processes related to barium (Ba) and radium (Ra) -rich fluids seeping on the seafloor at bathyal depths and assess their impact on the benthic habitats on the Louisiana upper slope of the Gulf of Mexico.

Our strategy for deriving an inventory of Ba and Ra sources and sinks involved sampling of pore fluids at the points of exit, barite deposits consisting of chimneys and crusts, and fauna inhabiting the seepage sites consisting of sessile epifaunal mussels (Bathymodiolus spp.) harboring methanotrophic endosymbionts and vagrant heterotrophs such as galatheid crabs and starfishes. In order to establish the source of the emissions we fingerprinted the fluids using elemental chemistry tracers (Ca, Mg, Na, K, Sr, Ba, SO_4, Cl, Br), radioisotopes of Ra (^{226}Ra and ^{228}Ra), radiogenic Sr isotopes (^{87}Sr/^{86}Sr) and stable oxygen isotopes (δ^{18}O). The origin and nature of the barite deposits and their genetic link to the fluid emissions was established on the basis of micro-chemical analyses of their Ba, Ca and Sr contents, ^{87}Sr/^{86}Sr ratios and stable δ^{18}O and δ^{34}S compositions of the sulfate. Importantly, we exploited the anomalously high Ra content of the barites and the radioactive decay properties of its isotopes in order to derive a precise chronology of fluid emissions and barite deposition at seeps. Finally, we established the Ba and Ra flow into the fauna inhabiting the seeps by determining their contents in both soft tissue bodies and hard exoskeletons.

Our results indicate that the fluids advecting on the seafloor at barite-bearing seeps are typically highly saline (salinity up to 155°/oo) and anomalously enriched in Ra and Ba relative to bottom water values (by factors of 4.5x10^4 and 15x10^4, respectively). The chemical and isotope fingerprints show striking similarities to produced waters from offshore fields and point to a deep-seated source matched to Mesozoic-age formation waters. The barite deposits surrounding the seeps serve as an important sink for the Ba and Ra in the advecting fluids whereas their sulfate is derived primarily from seawater. Unlike the carbonate-bearing seeps which yield ages back to 200,000 years (Aharon et al., 1997) thus recording long-term hydrocarbon seepage, the barite deposits are remarkably young. Barite chimneys are 0.5 to 6.5 years old and their estimated growth rates vary from 4.4 cm/yr to 9.1 cm/yr, whereas the crusts are 9.0 to 23.1 years old. The fauna around the barite-seeps have the ability to concentrate Ba and Ra to varying degrees. In general, the heterotrophs appear to concentrate Ra preferentially compared to the mussels, probably through ingestion of the highly radioactive barite particles.

On the basis of mass balances we established leakage rates of 250 L/yr and 2920 L/yr from point sources in Garden Banks and Mississippi Canyon, respectively. The areal extent of the barite-bearing seeps is not known with certainty but our estimates suggest they may be considerable, matching in size the fluxes of Ba and Ra delivered to the Gulf of Mexico from the Mississippi River.

TABLE OF CONTENTS

LIST OF FIGURES

LIST OF TABLES

ACKNOWLEDGMENTS

We thank C. W. Wheeler for assistance with analyses, drafting and document layout, Mary Lee Eggart for skillful drafting of the cover and R. Carney for a critical reading of an early draft of the report.

Samples analyzed in this project were acquired during submersible dives in 1990, 1993, 1995 and 1997. These submersible activities were funded by grants from National Oceanic and Atmospheric Administration/National Undersea Research Program. We thank the pilots of the submersibles Johnson-Sea-Link and Alvin, and the captains and crews of the surface support vessels R/V Edwin Link, R/V Seward Johnson and R/V Atlantis II for assistance with diving and collection of samples.

We thank our colleagues H. H. Roberts, P. LaRock, R. Carney, B. K. Sen Gupta and J. Larkin at Louisiana State University for sharing with us the excitement of deep-sea exploration during cruises and dives, and Mary Boatman and Gail Rainey from the Mineral Management Service in New Orleans for constructive reviews of an early draft of the report.

1. INTRODUCTION

1.1. Statement of the Problem

Northern Gulf of Mexico offshore Louisiana is a mature oil and gas exploration province where nearly 18,000 oil and gas wells have been drilled since 1947. Deepwater exploration and development are predicted to increase in the future such that by the first decade of the 21st. century, 45% of all domestic oil and gas will be produced from new offshore developments. A variety of wastes are generated in drilling and production from oil and gas wells but the discharges of drilling mud and produced water in the offshore Gulf of Mexico has generated the most attention (Costlow et al., 1983; Boothe and Presley, 1985; Clark and Patrick, 1987; Environmental Health Criteria 107, 1990; Rabalais et al., 1991).

Barite (BaSO$_4$) is the principal constituent of drilling mud (about 63%) used in oil and gas drilling operations. A previously estimated annual rate of 1.13x10^6 metric tons of barite discharged with the fluid muds in the Gulf of Mexico caused sufficient concern on its impact on the marine environment to prompt special inquiries by the National Research Council (Costlow et al., 1983), the National Academy of Sciences (Jarmul, 1984), and academic institutions (e.g., Boothe and Presley, 1985). In addition to elevated barium, discharged produced water is also anomalously enriched in radionuclides (Bloch and Key, 1981; Kraemer and Reid, 1984; Raloff, 1991) with radium levels exceeding by up to a factor of 3x10^4 the concentration in Gulf of Mexico waters (Rabalais et al., 1991). The Minerals Management Service has also funded a number of recent surveys aiming to assess the fate and effects of drilling fluids and cuttings (e.g., OCS Study MMS 93-0021) and produced water discharges in coastal environments (e.g., OCS Study MMS 91-0004, Rabalais et al., 1991).

During routine submersible dives in 1993 followed by additonal targeted dives in 1997, we discovered that in addition to hydrocarbons some of the seeps occurring at upper bathyal depths (510 to 657 m) in Garden Banks-382 (27° 37.77' N; 92° 28.08' W), Garden Banks-338 (27°37.79'; 92°28.12') and Mississippi Canyon-929 (28° 01.46'N; 89° 43.63'W) are also issuing copious amounts of barium and radium-rich fluids (Fig. 1.1). Upon their exit on the seafloor, these fluids were likely to constitute the primary source for the extensive radium-rich barite deposits of varied morphological shapes documented by us on the seafloor (Fig. 1.2). At the time of the submersible observations, the impact of the excess barium and radium on the benthic habitats was unknown but the mud volcanoes blanketed with thick barite crusts (Fig. 1.2. A & B), the barite chimneys occurring above point sources (Fig. 1.2 C) and the gullies filled with highly radioactive coarse barite sands engulfing fields of dead methanotrophic Bathymodiolus spp. mussels over extensive areas (Fig. 1.2 D) suggested that the phenomena may be widespread on the seafloor along the Louisiana slope.

The inference that hydrocarbon seeps may act as additional sources and sinks for barium and radium in the benthic environment of the OCS Gulf of Mexico throws a "monkey wrench" on the previous assessments concerning the fate and effects of offshore drilling which have assumed that the only external source for these toxic/radioactive elements is derived from the drilling muds and produced waters, respectively (Costlow et al., 1983; Jarmul, 1984; Boothe and Presley, 1985; Clark and Patrick, 1987; Rabalais et al., 1991).

2

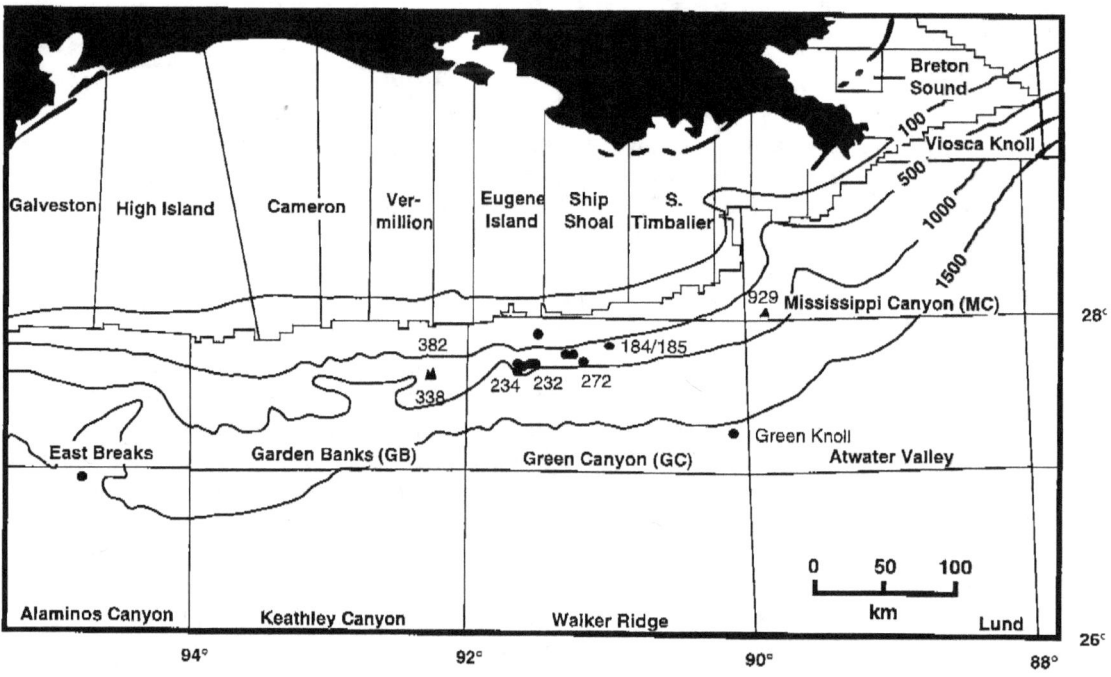

Figure 1.1. Base map of the study area on the Northern Gulf of Mexico slope and basin showing the location of hydrocarbon seep sites where cores, pore fluids, barites and fauna were acquired during submersible dives. Circles indicate carbonate-bearing seeps; triangles indicate barite-bearing seeps.

Therefore, in order to establish a technical basis for decisions concerning possible impact of deepwater drilling offsetting the subsurface hydrology and industrial discharges on the deepwater marine habitats, it was necessary to evaluate the contribution of barium and radium derived from seeps, their removal into the sediment and their uptake by the chemosynthetic communities associated with the seeps.

In contrast to the shelf area, where 50 years of drilling and production of hydrocarbons occurred (Clark and Patrick, 1987; Mendelssohn et al., 1990; Jackson et al., 1994; Manker and Rickman, 1994), the deepwater habitats along the slope are relatively pristine. However, as the oil and gas industry is moving its exploration and production main activities to deepwaters, their present pristine status is likely to change. It is therefore of importance to explore the natural processes occurring in deepwaters ahead of the anticipated anthropogenic complications.

1.2. Objectives and Questions Addressed in the Study

The primary objectives of this study were to document products and processes related to naturally occurring barium and radium-rich fluid emissions from hydrocarbon seeps, and assess their impact on the offshore habitats in deepwater Gulf of Mexico. The specific questions we have addressed are as follows:

(1) What are the levels of barium and radium in the pore fluids underlying seeps, in the barite deposits forming around the seeps, and the chemosynthetic communities?

(2) What are the nature and origin of barite deposits and the processes promoting their formation?

(3) What are the timing and duration of emissions? are these emissions altered or accelerated by anthropogenic activities?

(4) What are the fluxes of barium and radium from naturally occurring emissions on the benthic habitat?

(5) Do recently discovered radium-rich fluid emissions pose a significant internal and/or external radiation threat to the existing seep communities?

The first and second questions were addressed by a direct approach involving (i) specific determinations of barium, radium and selected chemical elements and their isotopes in pore fluids squeezed from sediment cores taken with the submersible robot arm from barite-bearing seep sites; (ii) measurements of barium, radium and selected chemical elements and their isotopes in solid barites, and (iii) determinations of radium and barium in both soft tissues and hard skeletons from methanotrophic mussels and heterotrophic fauna living in the proximity of the barite seeps. These results were compared and contrasted with radium and barium determinations from pore fluids and fauna from carbonate-bearing seeps which appear to represent natural, unperturbed, background radioactive and chemical emission sites. We found that pore fluids contain important information concerning their source and migration pathways and their chemical fingerprinting allowed us to identify their subsurface source/s with a fair degree of certainty.

The third and fourth questions are much more difficult to resolve definitively within the time-limited scope of this study. An indirect approach to the problem was taken, which involved inferences from spatial and temporal distribution patterns of barium and radium within the barite

4

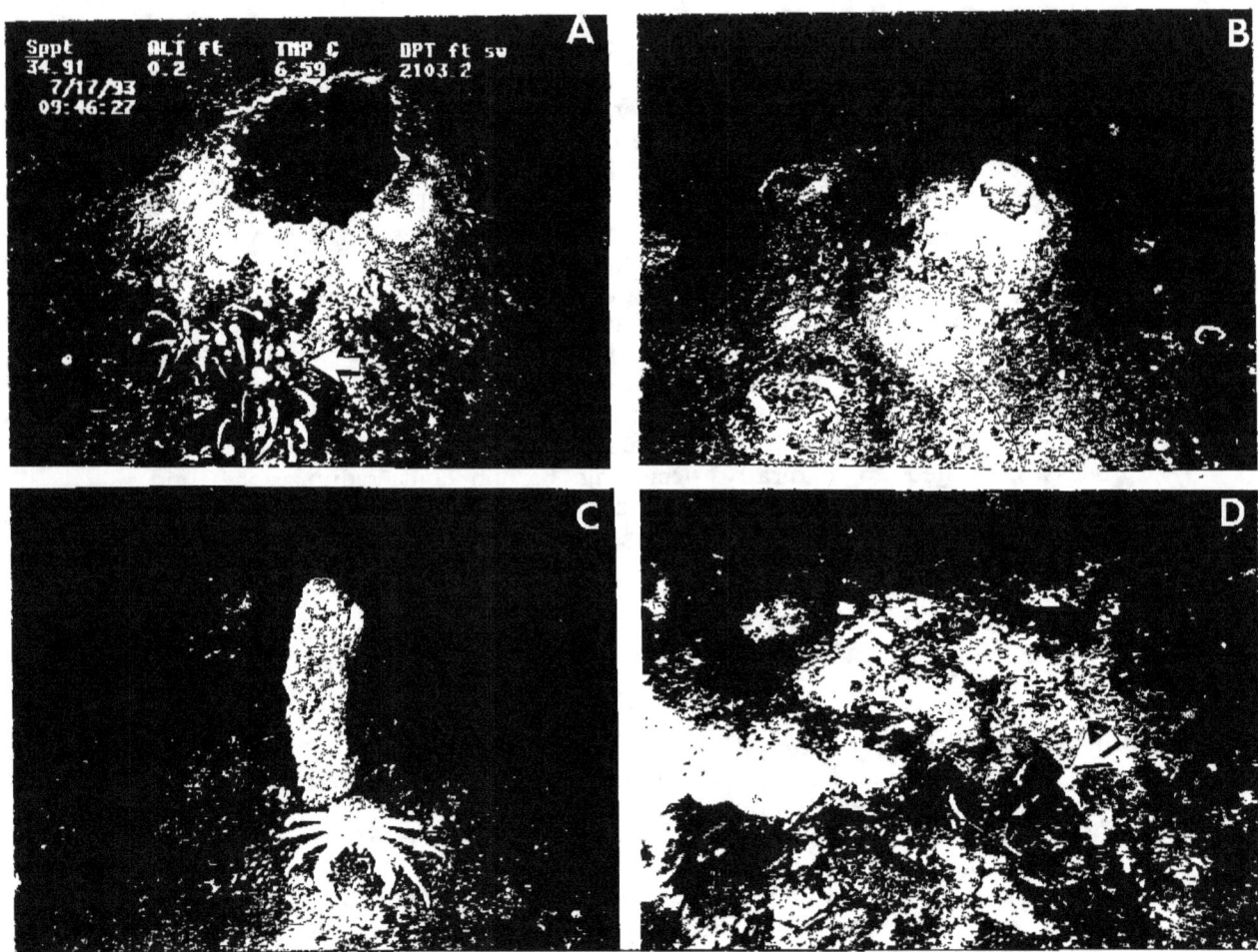

Figure 1.2. Occurrences of highly radioactive barite deposits associated with barium/radium/methane-rich fluid emissions in deepwater Gulf of Mexico (Garden Banks blocks #338 and #382 at 510 to 522 m depth and Mississippi Canyon block#929 at 640 m depth). Field of view in the photographs is 0.5 m. A: Dormant mud volcano with orange-white barite crust blanketing its flanks. Note the brine-filled caldera and the presence in the foreground of living methanotrophic <u>Bathymodiolus</u> spp. mussels. B: Cup-shaped barite deposits. Note the high density of fluid emission sites. C: Cylindrical-shaped barite chimney. Note the galatheid crab in the foreground and the incipient growth of chimneys in the backround. D: Dead methanotrophic mussel shells engulfed in coarse-grained barite sand infilling gulleys.

deposits. Radium and barium in growth increments from the barite chimneys were used as an archived history and record of episodic venting whose chronology was derived from the radium-decay series isotopes. The youthfulness of all the barite deposits may be taken as an indication of possible accelerated emissions from the seeps, implicating unusual nonuniform disturbances of the subsurface hydrology increasing formation water ascent to the seafloor through normal faults from deep reservoirs.

In order to resolve the fifth question, external gamma ray and internal alpha radiation (derived by ingestion of radioactive barite) exposure and dose to epifauna inhabiting the barite seeps, consisting of vagrant heterotrophs (galatheid crabs, starfishes) and sessile methanotrophic mussels, was estimated from measured radium-decay series specific concentrations by means of a computerized dose calculation program (Microshield 5.0).

1.3. Site Descriptions

The barite-bearing seeps which form the focus of this study have been documented and sampled during submersible dives in GB-382, GB-338 and MC-929 (Fig. 1.1). The sites are characterized by intense gaseous hydrocarbon and fluid mud venting occurring from numerous cone-shaped mud volcanoes (Fig. 1.2 A &B). Subsurface seismic data indicate that shallow salt diapirs are present under the three sites and seepage occurs through normal faults associated with the diapirs (Fu, 1998). These seeps are in the process of evolving from a state of rapid venting, which produces mud-prone features, to slow seepage which produces mineral-prone features (Roberts and Carney, 1997). Vast quantities of mud have been expelled from the Garden Banks circular expulsion centers, now encrusted with barite deposits, producing mudflows and fluid debris flows clearly recognizable on side-scan sonar data. A thin (<4 m thick) hemipelagic sediment drape occurs over much of the seafloor which is thinning toward young flow channels suggesting a very young age (Roberts and Carney, 1997).

Dense communities of methanotrophic mussels (Bathymodiolus sp.), neritid gastropods and galatheid crabs inhabit the flanks of these mud volcanoes. Other chemosynthetic biota such as tube worms, clams, and Beggiatoa mats that are common elsewhere on the Gulf of Mexico slope in association with hydrocarbon seeps (Carney, 1994) are conspicuously absent from these sites. The chimneys (Fig. 1.2 C) are engulfed in black-colored haloes consisting of fine anoxic sediment. Profuse trains of gas bubbles venting into the water column were noticed during the uprooting of the chimneys.

2. METHODOLOGY

Laboratory practices employed in this study can be conveniently grouped under three headings: (i) chemical and isotope methods applicable to pore fluids in seep sediments, particularly from barite seeps, to enhance our understanding of the source and nature of the Ba and Ra-rich fluid venting; (ii) petrographic, mineralogic, chemical and isotope methods applicable to barite deposits associated with seeps to provide insights on the mode, age and rate of barite deposition, and (iii) radiological and chemical methods applicable to chemoautotrophic and heterotrophic seep fauna to derive the uptake of radionuclides by both soft tissues and hard exoskeletons and to evaluate the consequences of radionuclide radiation on the benthic fauna. In the following sections the laboratory methods used in the fluid assays will be described first.

2.1 Pore Fluids

Figure 2.1 is a flow chart summary of the analytical assay types employed in this study for pore fluids.

Push cores, up to 40 cm long, were taken with the submersible robot arm during dives in the Gulf of Mexico at seep sites indicated in Figure 1.1. Immediately after recovery, the cored sediments were taken to the laboratory on the support surface ship where continuous pore fluid profiles were acquired with a squeezer modified from Jahnke (1988). The pore fluids were passed into plastic disposable syringes inserted into the core barrel at 3-4 cm depth intervals and were filtered through a 0.25 μm filter capping the syringe. After filtering, each pore fluid sample was divided into three aliquotes. One was used for determination of salinity, dissolved sulfide and sulfate concentrations immediately after recovery. The second was acidified with few drops of concentrated HNO_3 to pH<1 and stored in 5 ml size glass bottles with rubber stoppers and aluminum vacuum caps for subsequent elemental analysis. Mercuric chloride was added to the third to prevent bacterial activity and this aliquot was used for the analysis of oxygen isotopes ($\delta^{18}O$) of water.

Salinity was measured by a hand-held refractometer (model A366 ATC) having an accuracy of $\pm 1^o/oo$. Dissolved sulfide and sulfate concentrations were determined by the colorimetric method of Cline (1969) and barium gravimetric method (Presley, 1969), respectively. The analytical error (1σ) based on replicate analyses of standards was 4.5% for sulfide and 0.5% for sulfate determinations. $\delta^{18}O$ of water were determined with a Nier-type triple collector gas source mass spectrometer using the technique described by Graber and Aharon (1991). Accuracy and precision of $\delta^{18}O$ are within $0.1^o/oo$ based on standard repeats. Stable isotopes are reported in the delta (δ) notation in permil relative to SMOW standard for oxygen isotopes (Graber and Aharon, 1991).

Dissolved K, Na, Ca, Mg, Sr and Ba were determined using an inductively coupled plasma spectrometer (ICP-AES); Cl and Br were measured using an Ion Chromatograph (IC). Replicate analyses of standards and samples yield precisions of $\pm 0.5\%$ for the major and minor cations, $\pm 3\%$ for Cl and $\pm 3.5\%$ for Br. $^{87}Sr/^{86}Sr$ ratios of the pore fluids were measured on a Finnigan MAT 262 six collector thermal ionization mass spectrometer (TIMS). The results are

8

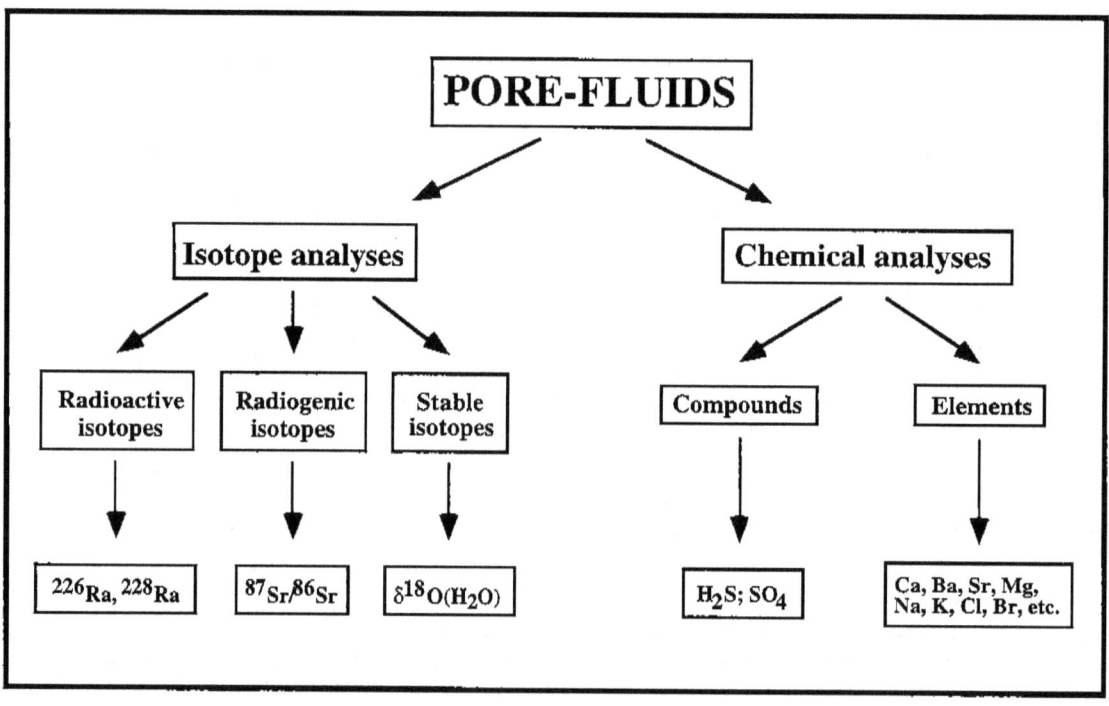

Figure 2.1. Flow chart of chemical and isotope analyses of pore fluids.

normalized to $^{87}Sr/^{86}Sr$ of NBS-987 = 0.71023 and to $^{86}Sr/^{88}Sr$ = 0.1194 with an estimated analytical error of $\pm 1 \times 10^{-5}$ (2σ).

^{226}Ra determinations in fluid samples were conducted with a modified scintillation technique developed by Prichard et al. (1980). A 5 ml aliquot of a fluid sample was injected under 10 ml of a toluene-based scintillation cocktail with Liquifluor® (New England Nuclear product) added as the scintillating agent. The entire two-phase aqueous-organic layer was sealed gas-tight with a polyseal cap in a 20 ml borosilicate-glass scintillation vial and stored for at least three weeks prior to analysis. The ^{222}Rn isotope (half-life 3.82 days, Broecker and Peng, 1982) resulting from alpha decay of ^{226}Ra, and in secular equilibrium with the parent isotope, was then assayed using a liquid scintillation counter with α-discrimination capabilities. The total activity of ^{226}Ra in the sample was calculated from the counting data and the detection efficiency was determined by measuring the ^{226}Ra blanks and standards. Based on multiple analyses of standards, the average conservative error (1σ) in the ^{226}R activity values is estimated to be $\pm 5\%$ or lower.

For ^{228}Ra determination, 5 ml of a fluid sample was acidified to 0.1 N with dilute hydrochloric acid. The acidified sample was aliquoted onto a mini-column of Dowex 50W-X12 cation exchange resin. The ^{228}Ra was allowed to decay to its first daughter product, ^{228}Ac, over a period of 36 hours. Subsequently, the ^{228}Ac was selectively eluted from the column with dilute lactic acid and collected in 10 ml of a water miscible liquid scintillation cocktail. The high energy beta particle emissions of ^{228}Ac are measured on the liquid scintillation counter by virtue of visible microflashes of light produced by interaction of the beta particles with the liquid scintillation cocktail. These samples were also compared to a NIST (National Institute of Standards and Technology) traceable ^{228}Ra standard which was carried through the identical procedure. Based on multiple analyses of standards, the average conservative error (1 σ) in the ^{228}Ra activity values is estimated to be $\pm 8\%$ or lower.

2.2. Barite Deposits

The types of imaging, chemical and isotope analyses applied to the barite chimneys and crusts from barite-bearing seeps are summarized in a flow chart in Figure 2.2.

2.2.1. Imaging, Chemical and Stable Isotope Assays

The soft and friable chimneys were hardened at room temperature using Araldite GY-506 water insoluble resin. Polished thin sections were made of chimneys and crusts. Mineral identifications and textural interpretations were made using reflected and transmitted light microscopes and a JEOL-840 scanning electron microscope (SEM) equipped with an EDS X-ray and back-scatter electron-detector units. Quantitative analyses for Ba, Sr, Ca, Na and Fe in barite were performed using an electron microprobe model JEOL-733, equipped for WDS X-ray spectroscopy. The instrumental conditions for the duration of the analyses were: 15 KV accelerating voltage, 2 nA beam current, and 60 second counting intervals. Sulfates and carbonates of known chemical compositions were used for the purpose of standardization using conventional

10

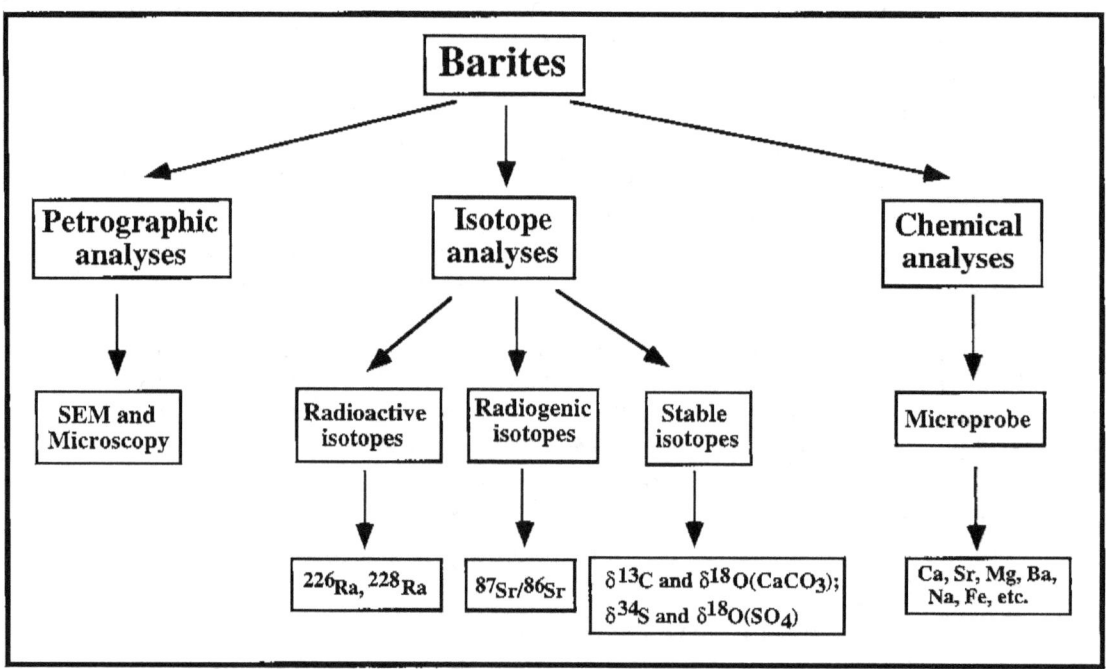

Figure 2.2. Flow chart of imaging, chemical and isotope analyses of barites.

electron microprobe techniques. Corrections for matrix effects used in the final computations followed Bence and Albee (1968).

For sulfur, oxygen and strontium isotope analyses of barite samples were purified with a modified procedure described by Church (1970). Samples were first treated with 6 N HCl to decompose calcite, dolomite, and iron oxide. Organic phases were then removed by reaction with warm (about 50 $^{\circ}$C) sodium hypochlorite. Silicate minerals were neglected due to their low concentrations (<1% by volume).

δ^{34}S was measured by graphite reduction of $BaSO_4$ to BaS, which was subsequently dissolved in water and precipitated as Ag_2S with 0.1 N $AgNO_3$. Ag_2S was then oxidized with Cu_2O (mixture 1:4 by mass) at 900°C to SO_2, which was analyzed with the mass spectrometer. The overall error ($\pm$ 1 σ) of δ^{34}S determinations is better than 0.2°/oo and the reference standard is troilite from the Canyon Diablo meteorite (CDT).

δ^{18}O of SO_4 were analyzed in the manner described by Rafter and Mizutani (1967) and Mizutani (1971). Intimate mixtures of $BaSO_4$ and spectrographically pure (99.999%) graphite (1:2 by mass) were decomposed in resistance-heated platinum boats near 1000 $^{\circ}$C. In addition to CO_2 some CO was produced, which was converted into CO_2 using a high-voltage electrical discharge between platinum electrodes in a trap assembly immersed in liquid nitrogen. Isotope measurements were made on a Nier-type triple collector gas source mass spectrometer. Accuracy and precision of δ^{18}O determinations is better than 0.3°/oo based on repeat standard analyses and the results are reported relative to the standard mean ocean water (SMOW).

For strontium isotope analysis pure barite was decomposed with sodium carbonate (Sr free Na_2CO_3) using the method modified from Breit et al. (1985). 0.1 g of barite, 1 g of sodium carbonate and 200 ml of triple-distilled water were combined in a Teflon beaker. The beaker was covered and heated at 95°C for 4 hours. After cooling the solid residue ($SrCO_3$ and $BaCO_3$) were separated by filtration. The residue is rinsed thoroughly with triple-distilled water to remove sodium and sulfate. The $SrCO_3$ and $BaCO_3$ obtained this way were dissolved with 6 N HCl and Sr was then separated using standard ion chromatography techniques. $^{87}Sr/^{86}Sr$ ratios were measured on a Finnigan MAT 262 six collector thermal ionization mass spectrometer (TIMS). The results are normalized to $^{87}Sr/^{86}Sr$ of NBS-987 = 0.71023 and to $^{86}Sr/^{88}Sr$ = 0.1194 and carry an estimated analytical error of $\pm 1 \times 10^{-5}$ (2σ).

For carbon isotope analysis of carbonates in the crusts, powders of barite crusts were dissolved at 50°C in 100% H_3PO_3 under vacuum, and δ^{13}C and δ^{18}O of the carbonates were determined on the cryogenically purified CO_2 using an automated Nier-type triple collector mass spectrometer. The isotope data are reported in the conventional "d" notation in permil relative to the PDB standard. Accuracy and precision for δ^{13}C and δ^{18}O are within 0.1°/oo .

2.2.2. Principles of Dating Methods

Barite deposits including chimneys and crusts were examined with a portable gamma-ray detector (μR meter) which indicated that they were unusually highly radioactive. These initial radioactivity measurements led to a more detailed gamma-ray spectrometric investigation which revealed that ^{226}Ra and ^{228}Ra were unsupported by their parents ^{238}U and ^{232}Th, and therefore can be considered "orphans". The apparent ages of the barite samples, therefore, can be determined using the Ra decay series isotopes.

The radionuclides used in this study for dating barites are ^{228}Ra, ^{226}Ra and their radioactive daughters ^{228}Th and ^{210}Pb, respectively (Fig. 2.3). Because Ra and Ba are chemically similar (both occupy the same column in the periodic table), Ra commonly coprecipitates with Ba during the formation of barites. Subsequently, both ^{226}Ra and ^{228}Ra, uptaken by the barites, decay with time as follows:

$$^{226}Ra \xrightarrow[1.62\times10^3 y]{\alpha} {}^{222}Rn \xrightarrow[3.82d]{\alpha} {}^{214}Pb \xrightarrow[26.8min]{\beta} {}^{210}Pb \xrightarrow[22.3y]{\beta} {}^{206}Pb$$

$$^{228}Ra \xrightarrow[5.75y]{\beta} {}^{228}Ac \xrightarrow[6.13h]{\beta} {}^{228}Th \xrightarrow[1.91y]{\alpha} {}^{220}Rn \xrightarrow[55.6s]{\alpha} {}^{212}Pb \xrightarrow[10.6h]{\beta} {}^{208}Pb$$

Since the longest-lived daughters of ^{226}Ra and ^{228}Ra decay series are ^{210}Pb and ^{228}Th, respectively, ^{210}Pb and ^{228}Th will accumulate with time. Therefore, the ^{210}Pb/^{226}Ra and ^{228}Th/^{228}Ra daughter/parent ratios in the barites can be used for age determinations.

The ^{228}Th/^{228}Ra method is based on the incorporation of ^{228}Ra into the barite, where it decays to ^{228}Th. The ^{228}Th/^{228}Ra present in the barite is dictated by the decay rates of these two isotopes and the time elapsed since ^{228}Ra was incorporated. Therefore the age of the barite can be determined according to the following equation:

$$(A_{228Th})/(A_{228Ra}) = [\lambda_{228Th}/(\lambda_{228Th} - \lambda_{228Ra})][1 - \exp(\lambda_{228Ra} - \lambda_{228Th})t] \quad (2.1.)$$

where A_{228Ra} and A_{228Th} are the measured activities of ^{228}Ra and ^{228}Th, respectively; t is the age of the sample in years; and λ_{228Ra} and λ_{228Th} are the decay constants for ^{228}Ra and ^{228}Th, respectively. The half lives of ^{228}Ra and ^{228}Th are 5.75 and 1.91 years (Broecker and Peng, 1982) and these translate to decay constants of 0.1205 yr^{-1} for λ_{228Ra} and 0.3628 yr^{-1} for λ_{228Th}, respectively.

Because the half lives of both the parent (^{228}Ra) and daughter (^{228}Th) are comparable, the ^{228}Th/^{228}Ra will first reach transient equilibrium (a ratio of 1) and will increase to approach a constant value with time. As shown in Figure 2.4, this constant value will reach 1.5 after 15 years. Therefore, the useful range of the ^{228}Th/^{228}Ra dating method does not exceed 15 years.

The successful application of the ^{228}Th/^{228}Ra method depends upon the following assumptions: (i) the ^{228}Ra must be orphan, namely no parents of ^{228}Ra exist in the barite, (ii) there must be no initial ^{228}Th in the barite, and (iii) the system must have remained closed with respect to both ^{228}Ra and ^{228}Th. As will be shown in the discussion, all these assumptions have been validated for the Gulf of Mexico barites.

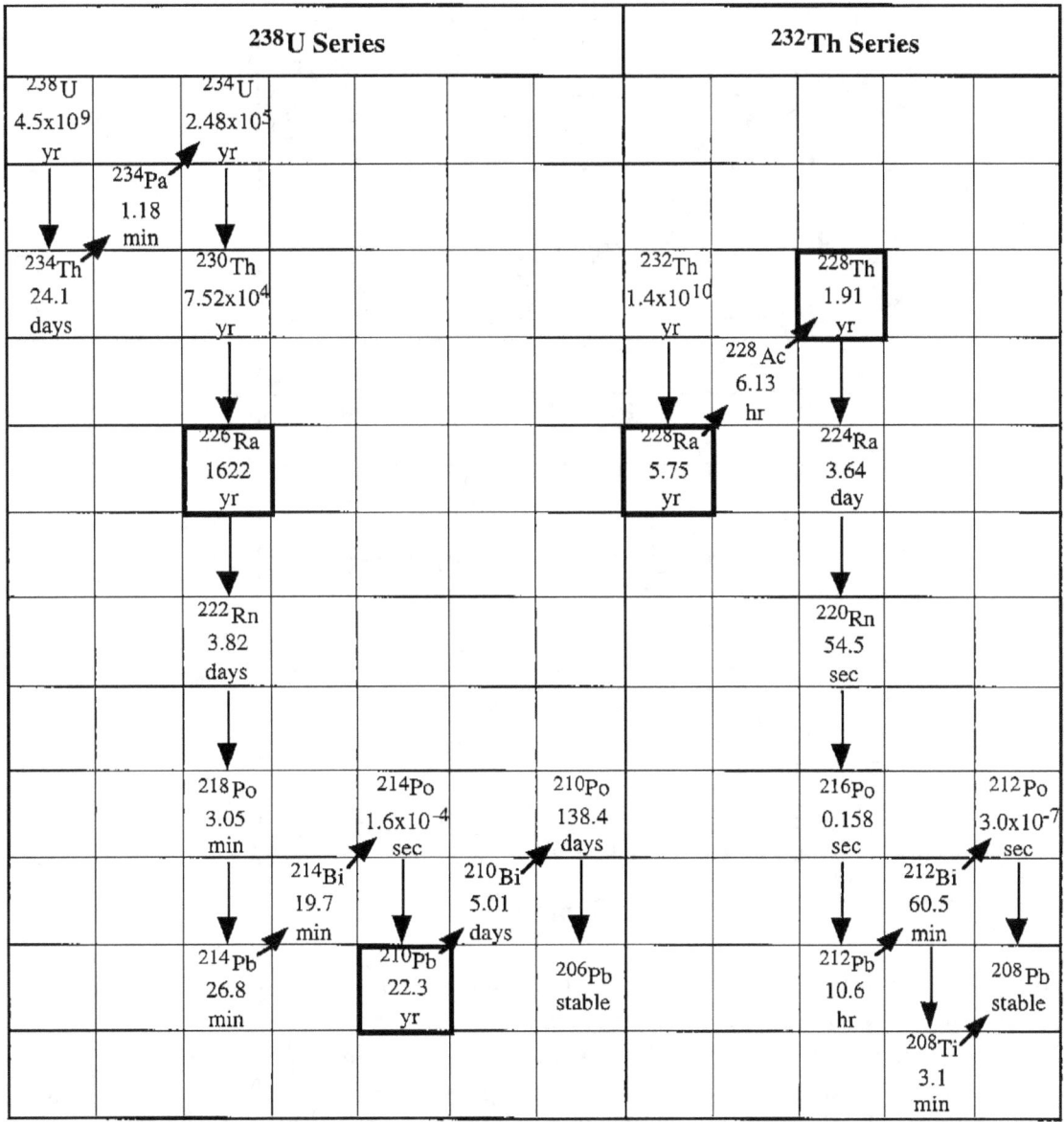

Figure 2.3. ^{226}Ra, ^{228}Ra and their parent and daughter radionuclides; the half-lives are listed below the radionuclides (adapted from Broecker and Peng, 1982).

14

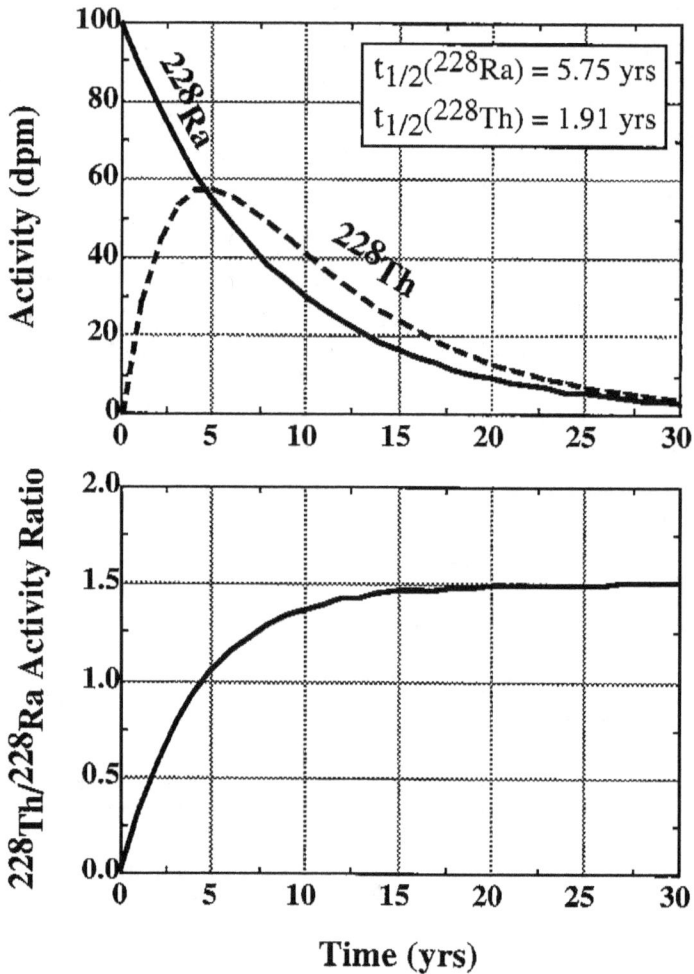

Figure 2.4. Radioactivity decay and growth in the system ^{228}Ra-^{228}Th. Upper: Decay of parent isotope ^{228}Ra and ingrowth and decay of daughter isotope ^{228}Th as a function of time. For illustrative purposes an activity of 100 dpm was assigned to ^{228}Ra whereas the ^{228}Th activity is zero at t = 0. The parent and daughter reach transient equilibrium at about 4.3 yrs from t = 0. Lower: Evolution through time of the ^{228}Th/^{228}Ra activity ratio approaching a maximum of 1.5. The useful range of the ^{228}Th/^{228}Ra dating methodology is 15 yrs or younger.

Since the useful range for $^{228}Th/^{228}Ra$ method is 15 years or less, $^{210}Pb/^{226}Ra$ method was also applied to date samples older than 15 years. This technique uses the ingrowth of the ^{210}Pb which is a decay product of ^{226}Ra in the barite. The technique mimics the $^{228}Th/^{228}Ra$ method and can be described by the following equation:

$$(A_{210Pb})/(A_{226Ra})=[(\lambda_{210Pb})/(\lambda_{210Pb} - \lambda_{226Ra})][1-exp(\lambda_{226Ra} - \lambda_{210Pb})t] \quad (2.2)$$

where, A_{226Ra} and A_{210Pb} are the activities of ^{226}Ra and ^{210}Pb, respectively; t is the age of the sample in years; and λ_{226Ra} and λ_{210Pb} are the decay constants for ^{226}Ra and ^{210}Pb, respectively. The half lives of ^{226}Ra and ^{210}Pb are 1,620 and 22.3 years, respectively (Broecker and Peng, 1982) and these translate to decay constants of $4.28 \times 10^{-4} yr^{-1}$ and $3.11 \times 10^{-2} yr^{-1}$, respectively.

Because the half life of ^{226}Ra is sufficiently greater than that of ^{210}Pb, the parent (^{226}Ra) does not appreciably decay during the period of ingrowth of the daughter (^{210}Pb). The $^{210}Pb/^{226}Ra$ will then approach a secular equilibrium (a ratio of 1) at about 120 years (Fig. 2.5), which is the upper age limit of the technique. This dating technique is therefore useful for dating barites younger than 100 years.

Similar assumptions as for the $^{228}Th/^{228}Ra$ method apply here, namely: (i) the ^{226}Ra must be orphan, (ii) there must be no initial ^{210}Pb in the barite, and (iii) the system must have remained closed with respect to ^{226}Ra and ^{210}Pb. As will be discussed later, all these assumptions are satisfied for the Gulf of Mexico barites.

2.2.3. Sample Processing for Dating

The samples used for dating are chimneys and crusts associated with barite-bearing seeps in the Gulf of Mexico. Whereas the chimneys are dominated by barite (>95% by volume), the crusts are composed of barite coexisting with various amounts of carbonate and sulfide. Three types of samples (raw barite sample, pure barite and hardened chimney sample) were analyzed in this study.

For the raw barite samples, the original barite chimney and crust fragments were air dried. Then, about 30 gm sample was taken from each fragment and ground to a fine powder. Pure barite was also prepared for each raw sample by chemical removal of carbonates, organic matter and sulfides using methods modified from Church (1970) and Cecile et al. (1983). Purification of a 1 gm sample was carried out by mixing it with 60 ml of 6N double-distilled HCl and gently heated for 4 hr. This step removes carbonates (calcite, aragonite and dolomite) and iron oxide. The sample is then thoroughly washed by centrifugation to remove all leachate. Immediately following this step, the sample is treated with warm (about 50°C) sodium hypochlorite (slightly acidified with HCl to produce Cl_2 gas) for 4 hours which removes the organic matter and oxidizes the fine sulfides to iron oxides. Next, the residue is washed and then leached with 0.02 M hydroxylamine hydrochloride in 25% acetic acid in order to remove transition metal oxyhydroxides. Finally, the residue is again reacted with 6 N double-distilled HCl and heated gently for 4 hr

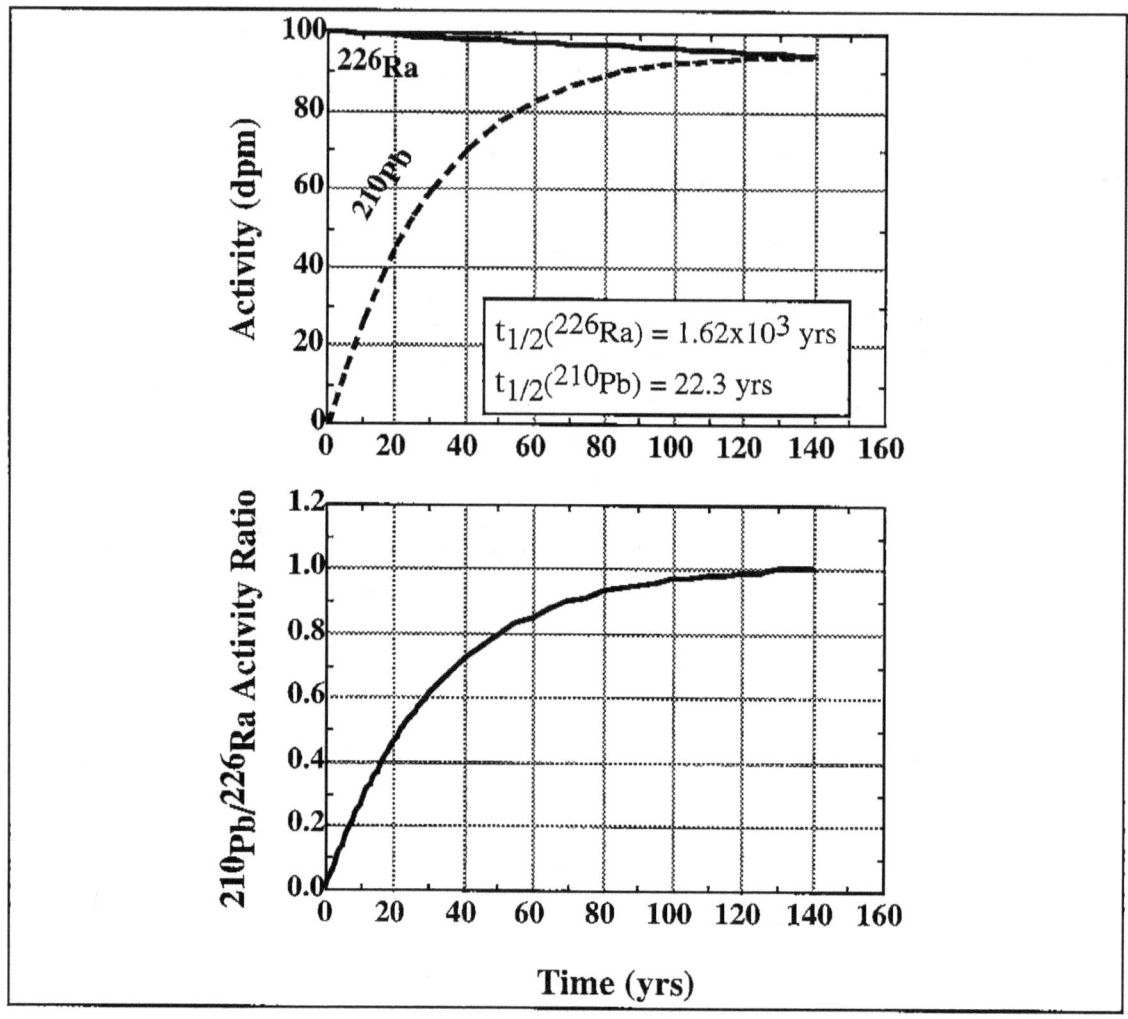

Figure 2.5. Radioactivity decay and growth in the system ^{226}Ra-^{210}Pb. Upper: Decay of parent isotope ^{226}Ra and ingrowth and decay of daughter isotope ^{210}Pb as a function of time. For illustrative purposes an activity of 100 dpm was assigned to ^{226}Ra whereas the ^{210}Pb activity is zero at t = 0. Lower: Evolution through time of the ^{210}Pb/^{226}Ra activity ratio toward secular equilibrium (^{210}Pb/^{226}Ra = 1). This ratio serves as an useful chronometer for samples whose age does not exceed 120 yrs.

to remove any Fe_2O_3 produced during the oxidation step. After this final step, the purified barite is dried and ready for analysis.

Because of their friable nature, most chimneys were hardened at room temperature using Araldite GY-506 water-insoluble resin to preserve their morphologies. Continuous suites of subsamples were sectioned from the base to the top of the hardened chimneys at intervals of 2 to 3 cm and each subsample, herein called hardened chimney sample, was also subjected to nuclide analysis.

In order to check the effects of sulfides on the age determination, sulfide concentrations of the chimneys and crusts were determined. Na_2CO_3 was used to dissolve barite and then 2N HCl acid was used to dissolve the carbonates. The residues are dominated by organic matter, sulfides and detrital minerals. The amount of organic matter in the barites was estimated by combustion of the residue and measuring the CO_2 pressure. Since the SEM (scanning electron microscopy) and microscope analyses reveal that the chimneys and crusts contain only a negligible amount of detrital minerals (<1% by volume), the sulfide concentrations were roughly estimated by subtracting the organic matter from the residue after Na_2CO_3 and HCl treatment.

2.2.4. Instrumentation and Analytical Methods

All the samples were non-destructively analyzed by using a high purity intrinsic germanium gamma detector (HPGe) in order to quantify the activities of the radionuclide occurring in the barites. The detector consists of a 98 cm^3 coaxial intrinsic germanium crystal with a 1 cm in diameter and 4 cm long well. The detector was coupled with a 8192 multiple channel analyzer (Ortec Buffer card). The resolution is 2.1 keV at 1332 keV.

For raw and pure barite samples, about 1 gm subsample powders were spread out evenly over a filter paper and made to conform as nearly as possible to the original mixed gamma planar geometry. The filter paper was placed on the detector head inside the shielding assembly. The hardened chimney samples (about 3x5 cm) were put in a plastic bag and placed with the bag directly on the spectrometer window. For all types of samples, gamma spectra were allowed to collect for up to 300,000 seconds.

The gamma ray from the decay of ^{212}Pb at 300.09 keV was used as a proxy nuclide to calculate the activity of ^{228}Th. To obtain the activity of ^{228}Ra, the peak at 911.21 keV from ^{228}Ac was used. Likewise, the ^{226}Ra activity was calculated by using the energy at 351.92 keV from the decay of ^{214}Pb. This is because these daughters (^{212}Pb, ^{228}Ac and ^{214}Pb) are in secular equilibrium with their parents (^{228}Th, ^{228}Ra and ^{226}Ra), therefore, AD (activity of daughter) is equal to AP (activity of parent). ^{210}Pb activity was directly measured from its 46.52 keV gamma ray peak.

Gamma spectra collected from the samples were subjected to an analysis scheme which allowed quantification of ^{214}Pb (proxy for ^{226}Ra), ^{210}Pb, ^{228}Ac (proxy for ^{228}Ra), and ^{212}Pb (proxy for ^{228}Th). GammaVision© Software by Ortec was utilized for peak search, identification, and quantification of the radionuclides. Nuclide libraries were created and optimized for accurate quantification of the isotopes by minimization of the possibility of interfering peaks. Since the ^{226}Ra series is pervasive throughout nature, a 300,000 sec background (bare detector) count was stripped from each spectrum prior to analysis. Each spectrum was subjected to an internal energy calibration secondary to that based on the mixed gamma standard. After peak search and identification of primary gamma peaks based on the energy calibration obtained from the mixed gamma standard were achieved, a range of peaks from naturally occurring radioisotopes inherent to the counting system shielding was used to obtain a customized energy calibration for each spectrum. This methodology significantly improved quantitative results since peak fitting algorithms are greatly dependent on the accuracy of the internal energy calibration. This technique is extremely useful for correcting minor energy calibration drift during long counting periods.

Potential problems such as self-absorption of the gamma rays by the sample were obviated by utilizing an "infinitely thin" planar counting geometry. This was accomplished by carrying out an efficiency calibration using a mixed gamma standard in the form of 1.0 gm of sandy loam. The sandy loam mixed gamma standard was spread out in a 4.5 cm diameter Whatman filter paper to a linear thickness less than 2 mm. The filter paper with mixed gamma standard was placed on the center of the detector head, and counted for 1 hour. The net area under 15 primary gamma and X-ray peaks was used to calculate fractional efficiency. The 15 peak centroid positions were used to calibrate the counting system at corresponding energies ranging from 31.8 keV to 1836.1 keV. Fractional efficiency was calculated by dividing net counts per second under each primary gamma peak by the absolute number of gamma photons emitted per second by the corresponding radionuclide. A continuous energy vs. efficiency function was derived by fitting a 5th order polynomial equation to the 15 data points obtained from the 1 hour count of the mixed gamma standard. The total uncertainty of the fit was 2.18%. This function was subsequently utilized to quantify gamma emitting radionuclides endogenous to 1 gm subsamples of barites.

Uranium and thorium ore reference materials (LSUO1 (U) and LSUO2 (Th)) were also measured for comparison. A 1.0 gm sample of uranium ore standard was ground to a fine powder and used for quality assurance of the analysis scheme. The $^{210}Pb/^{226}Ra$ for the ore standard as determined by the counting system and analysis scheme was not significantly different from 1.0 at the 95% confidence level throughout the experiment thus validating the methodology.

2.3. Seep Fauna

The flow chart illustrating the type of materials and methods employed in the analyses of seep fauna is shown in Figure 2.6.
Macrofauna were collected from barite-bearing seeps in Garden Banks (GB-382; GB-338) and Mississippi Canyon (MC-929), and carbonate-bearing seeps from Green Canyon (GC-184/185, also known as Bush Hill, GC-234, GC-272, MC-709) and Alaminos Canyon. Major faunal groups assayed for ^{226}Ra include the symbiont-bearing, chemoautotrphic, Bathymodiolus spp. mussels, and heterotrophic fauna living in the proximity of seeps including starfishes, galatheid crabs, and polychaetes. These samples were obtained during submersible dives from 1990 to 1997 on the outer continental shelf of the Gulf of Mexico (Fig. 1.1). The carbonate-bearing seep fauna were hypothesized a priori to contain less radium activity and barium levels relative to the radioactive barite-rich seep fauna.

All available seep fauna whole soft tissues and separated calcareous parts were oven-dried at 90 degrees centigrade, ground into a fine homogenous

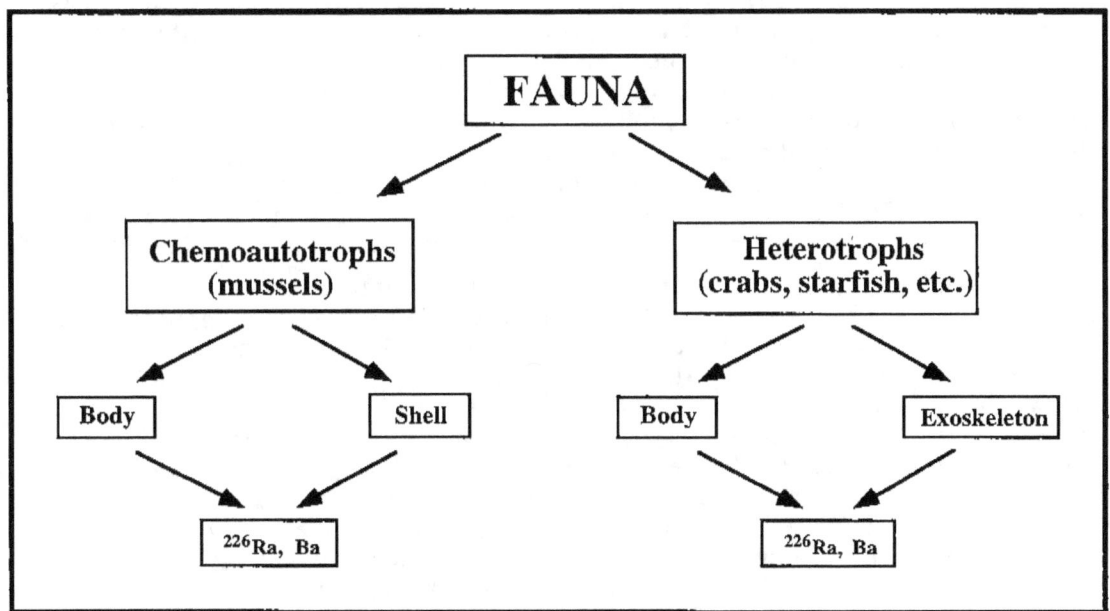

Figure. 2.6. Flow chart of chemical and isotope assays of fauna.

powder, acid digested and subsequently assayed for ^{226}Ra using a modified standard quantitative technique described in EPA-600/4-80-032 (EPA, 1980). This technique involves determination of ^{226}Ra by measuring its first decay product, ^{222}Rn, via radioequilibration ingrowth and emanation into Lucas Cells (EPA method 903.1, EPA, 1980). Since the half-life of ^{222}Rn is 3.82 days, an ingrowth period of approximately 24 days for each sample was sufficient for achieving 95% secular equilibrium with the ^{226}Ra parent nuclide before emanation analysis was carried out.

Following radium analysis, selected acid-digested whole soft tissue and calcareous exoskeleton samples from each site were subjected to stable barium analysis. This was carried out by means of standard ICP-AES elemental analysis in order to estimate seep fauna barium concentrations and compare the results with the corresponding radium values for each selected sample. Hydrochloric and nitric acid tissue digestion methods adapted from Horwitz (1980), for fish and other marine products, were utilized for biological sample dissolution in this study. Previously oven dried samples sealed in moisture proof vials were weighed (approximately 0.5 gram each sample) and placed into acid washed 10-ml PYREX test tubes. Five ml of concentrated hydrochloric acid brought to boiling temperature on a block digester was used to dissolve the calcareous mussel shells. Sample dissolution for counting ^{226}Ra and stable barium of all whole soft tissue and chitinous exoskeleton was accomplished by utilizing 5 ml of concentrated nitric acid and 1 ml of 30% hydrogen peroxide brought to boiling temperature with approximately 0.5 g of each sample.

Organic exoskeleton samples, such as powdered crab shells, required special care when adding acid so as not to lose sample due to initial exothermic foaming. Acid was added drop-wise into test tubes containing such samples, while all exothermically produced foam dissipated before the entire volume of acid was added for complete digestion. The samples were carefully brought to boiling temperature in a block digester and refluxed until the samples achieved optical clarity. In some instances, it was difficult to completely dissolve some of the body tissue and chitinous components because these body parts contain a considerable quantity of organic oils and waxes which were not completely soluble in inorganic acids. When this difficulty was encountered, the waxy residue was vacuum filtered onto a Gelman 0.45 micron membrane filter, and the filtered liquid was collected for ^{226}Ra and Ba assays. All acid digested samples were cooled, diluted to 10 ml with double-distilled deionized water, and sealed in radon bubblers for approximately three weeks before radon emanation.

Acid-digested samples were processed following the guidelines of EPA method 903.1 (EPA, 1980). Evacuated 150 ml Lucas scintillation cells were attached to an aged nitrogen gas cylinder and allowed to come to atmospheric pressure with the nitrogen gas. Each cell was subsequently counted for 1000 minutes on a Randam Model SC-5 Scintillation Counter, and the resulting values were used for background subtraction. Acid-digested samples were transferred to clean dry radon bubblers. A radon bubbler consists of three main components: scintillation cell, desiccant column, and bubble chamber. The sample was sealed airtight in the bubble chamber, and the start date and time of radon ingrowth was recorded. In order for ^{222}Rn to achieve near secular equilibrium with ^{226}Ra, a 24-day ingrowth period was required. After this ingrowth period, the samples were sparged with aged nitrogen gas in order to emanate the radioequilibrated radon into evacuated Lucas cells. This step required about 15 minutes of sparging in order for the gas in the Lucas scintillation cell to reach atmospheric pressure. Following the sparging process, the scintillation cell stopcock was closed, and a 3-hour equilibration period was allowed to pass in order for radon to reach transient equilibrium with its short-lived alpha emitting daughters, thus increasing the efficiency of the counting. The scintillation cell was then removed from the radon bubbler and placed inside the counting chamber of a Randam Scintillation Cell Counter. This instrument contains a counting chamber optically coupled to a photomultiplier. Alpha particles striking the zinc sulfide coating on the inside of the Lucas cell give off visible flashes of light which are detected and amplified into a signal by the photomultiplier and recorded on a digital readout.

After a three-hour equilibration period, scintillation cells were counted 1000 minutes to reduce counting error to acceptable levels. Total counts on the digital readout and counting time were recorded for each sample when the 1000 minute counting time had elapsed. The original background counts were carried out with nitrogen gas in the Lucas cell at atmospheric pressure because the alpha background inherent to the cells is higher in a vacuum than in nitrogen gas at atmospheric pressure. The background counting was done under the same counting conditions as those used for the samples and standards. Based on the sample weight and the total counts per 1000 minutes, an activity per unit weight was obtained. The data results were calculated using recommended formulas found in the EPA-600/4-80-032 procedure (EPA, 1980). Radioactivity was originally calculated in units of picocuries ^{226}Ra per sample unit weight. Picocuries of ^{226}Ra per unit weight of sample is calculated as follows:

$$A=(C_S-C_B)/[CF* D* I* Wt] \qquad (2.3)$$

Where,

A= picocuries of radon per gram of sample

C_S= Sample cpm

C_B= Background cpm

CF= cpm/pCi conversion factor

D= Decay Correction

I= Ingrowth Correction

Decay Correction (D)= EXP (-0.693*T_1/ $t_{1/2}$)

Wt= Sample weight in grams

Where,

T_1= Time in days from the emanation time to midpoint of counting time

$t_{1/2}$= Radiological half-life of ^{222}Rn, 3.82 days

I= [1- EXP (-0.693*T_2/$t_{1/2}$)].

Where,

T_2= Time in days from the sealing time to starting point of emanation time

$t_{1/2}$= Radiological half-life of ^{222}Rn, 3.82 days.

A reagent blank and an EPA ^{226}Ra standard were processed exactly as described above for each batch of approximately 10 environmental samples. The calculated values of ^{226}Ra were corrected for any background artifacts indicated by procedural and reagent blanks of typically 0.01 dpm level.

Elemental barium concentrations of acid-digested soft tissues and hard skeletal parts were obtained following the procedures described by Robinson (1980) and were measured with a Perkin-Elmer ICP-AES 6500. The elemental concentrations were corrected for systematic variations with the Topla reference dolomite (Schroll, 1987). Replicate analyses of the reference solution indicate an average Ba concentration of 55 ±3.0 ppm (1σ error).

3.0 RESULTS

3.1 Hydrocarbon-Rich Fluids

Fluids occurring in hydrocarbon seep sites at bathyal depths (Fig. 1.1) were assayed for isotopes and elemental chemistry according to the methods described in methodology. The fluids analyzed here can be conveniently grouped according to their mode of acquisition and their association with specific geologic deposits as follows:

(i) Pore fluids (n=34, Table 3.1) acquired from 40 cm long cores taken by the Johnson-Sea-Link submersible in carbonate-bearing seep sediments (Fig. 1.1) and squeezed on the support surface ship using a modified Jahnke device (Jahnke, 1988).

(ii) Pore fluids (n=34, Tables 3.1, 3.2 and 3.3) acquired from 40 cm long cores taken by the Johnson-Sea-Link submersible in barite-bearing seep sediments (Fig. 1.1) and squeezed on the support surface ship as above.

(iii) Fluids (n=6) from the crater of a barite-draped mud volcano drawn into the submersible through a thin probe (Tables 3.2 and 3.3).

Our geochemical surveys show that pore fluids from hydrocarbon seeps in the Gulf of Mexico offshore Louisiana can be clearly distinguished on the basis of their level of Ba and radioactivity ascribed to ^{226}Ra and ^{228}Ra. The pore fluids from carbonate-bearing seeps (Table 3.1), ranging in salinity from slightly higher than normal Gulf of Mexico deepwater values (35.0 ^{o}/oo) to highly saline (up to 182 ^{o}/oo), show universally low Ba concentrations (0.2 to 3.3 ppm) and Ra activity levels (<16 dpm/L, not reported in the Table) which are compatible with values previously reported in pore fluids from open ocean marine sediments (Cochran, 1982). Recent Ba assays in the water column of the Western Gulf by Buerket (1997) indicate levels of 7.9 ppb at 700 m depth and a maximum of 9 ppb at lower bathyal depths which are 3 orders of magnitude lower than the Ba concentrations in pore fluids from carbonate-bearing seeps (Table 3.1). In contrast, pore fluids from barite-bearing seeps (Table 3.3) display highly anomalous Ra activity levels that are a factor of about 200 to 40,000 times higher than that of the ambient Gulf of Mexico bottom water (0.132 dpm/L, Key, 1981), Ba levels higher by up to a factor of 130,000 and salinities substantially higher than normal marine seawater (45°/oo to 155°/oo).

3.1.1. Radium and Barium Assays in Barite-Bearing Seeps

This section reports the anomalously high Ra isotopes and elemental Ba in fluids advecting at barite-bearing seeps in cores retrieved by submersibles in MMS blocks MC-929, GB-382 and GB-338 (Fig. 1.1). These fluids belong to type III according to the clasification of their chemical fingerprinting reported below. Table 3.2 lists the exact locations of the material studied and core-sediment descriptions. The objectives here are to delineate the activity of the specific isotopes of ^{226}Ra and ^{228}Ra and Ba concentrations in order to provide insights on the source and origin of the fluids advecting on the seafloor in barite-bearing seeps. The following patterns emerge from the data listed in Table 3.3.

The fluids yield a wide range of salinities, from 45.5^o/oo to 155°/oo, which are higher than the ambient Gulf of Mexico deepwater at 600 m by factors of 1.2 to 4.1. The ^{226}Ra activities range from 27.2 to 3656 dpm/L and ^{228}Ra activities range from

Table 1.1. Chemical and isotope compositions of pore fluids from seeps and ambient Gulf of Mexico deepwaters.

sample name	depth (cm)	salinity (o/oo)	Br	H2S	Cl Conc.	Cl EF	SO4 Conc.	SO4 EF	Na Conc.	Na EF	K Conc.	K EF	Ca Conc.	Ca EF	Mg Conc.	Mg EF	Sr Conc.	Sr EF	Ba Conc.	Ba EF	SI	$\delta^{18}O$	$^{87}Sr/^{86}Sr$
Gulf of Mexico bottom water at 600 m depth seawater																							
	-	38	-	-	568		29.0		481		10.2		10.4		52.2		86.8		0.2		0.1	0.3	0.709917
Gulf of Mexico bottom water at 1938 m depth seawater																							
	-	37	-	-	566		30.5		499		11.4		10.0		52.0		86.8		-		-	-0.2	-
Salt areas at Green Knoll (1990 cruise).																							
2201-2-M 2H	-	150	1.3	-	8494	6.2	42.3	1.4	3298	6.6	29.6	2.6	25.9	2.6	31.3	0.6	67.4	0.8	1.6	8	0.2	-1.4	0.70707
2201-2-M V4	-	177	1.5	-	8804	6.7	44.6	1.5	3711	7.4	29.1	2.6	28.2	2.8	33.9	0.6	67.4	0.8	2.0	10	0.4	-1.1	-
2201-2-L 4/4	-	182	1.3	-	8901	6.9	43.7	1.4	8819	7.6	30.1	2.6	29.3	2.9	33.1	0.6	61.7	0.7	2.3	11	0.1	0.1	0.70875
2201-1-U 1/3	-	102	2.0	-	1646	2.9	42.5	1.4	1430	2.9	142.7	12.5	15.8	1.6	47.2	0.9	84.5	1.0	2.6	11	-0.3	-	-
2201-1-M 2/3	-	118	2.1	-	1898	3.4	40.5	1.3	1625	3.3	171.7	15.1	17.7	1.8	46.9	0.9	84.5	1.0	2.0	10	-0.1	-	-
2201-1-L V1	-	116	2.2	-	1918	3.4	41.4	1.4	1648	3.3	165.7	14.5	17.1	1.7	47.7	0.9	90.2	1.0	2.4	12	0.1	-0.1	0.70897
Brine areas, Mississippi Canyon block 929 (1991 cruise).																							
1559-2-14	-4.0	52	1.1	-	807	1.4	28.1	1.0	654	1.4	11.3	1.1	15.8	1.5	52.5	1.0	241.1	2.8	1.4	7	0.2	0.3	0.70865
1559 2-17	-7.0	65	1.3	-	1115	2.0	22.8	0.8	912	1.9	11.6	1.1	21.6	2.3	52.4	1.0	423.4	4.9	0.9	4	0.4	0.3	-
1559 2-30	-10.0	96	1.7	-	1704	3.0	13.6	0.5	1440	3.0	12.8	1.3	37.4	3.6	54.0	1.0	770.3	8.9	3.5	17	0.1	0.1	0.70855
1559 2-21	13.0	130	2.8	-	2780	4.9	4.2	0.1	2511	5.2	13.5	1.3	62.9	6.1	56.1	1.1	1413.1	15.1	14.4	72	0.6	-0.3	0.70847
1559-2-32	-22.0	155	3.2	-	3520	6.2	0.5	0.0	3138	6.9	14.8	1.4	76.0	7.4	59.5	1.1	1679.1	19.3	639.9	3299	0.6	0.1	0.70843
Brine areas, Garden Banks block 382 (1993 cruise).																							
1566-1 15	-7.0	134	2.7	70	2735	4.8	0.7	0.0	2357	4.9	10.7	1.0	86.0	8.4	42.5	0.8	7096.4	15.7	3996.1	19981	0.0	1.4	-
1566-1 18	-10.0	127	2.4	2	2666	4.7	0.6	0.0	2221	4.6	10.1	1.0	78.5	7.6	41.8	0.8	2972.1	34.2	3988.8	19944	1.0	1.5	-
1566-1-21	-11.0	139	2.6	2	2792	4.9	0.3	0.0	2485	5.2	10.6	1.1	84.4	8.2	43.2	0.8	3230.1	37.2	6101.4	305107	1.0	1.7	0.70854
1566-1-24	-16.0	135	2.4	1	2677	4.7	0.6	0.0	2280	4.7	10.6	1.0	79.8	7.7	41.6	0.8	3024.8	34.8	6740.6	33703	0.9	1.5	-
1566-1-27	-19.0	127	2.1	1	2465	4.3	0.8	0.0	2076	4.3	10.1	1.1	69.7	6.8	41.3	0.8	2566.5	29.6	7405.9	17030	1.0	1.3	0.70857
1566 1-30	22.0	40	2.2	1	2415	4.3	0.5	0.0	1981	4.1	10.7	1.1	67.6	6.6	44.9	0.9	2385.1	27.5	2115.3	10576	1.1	1.2	0.70858
1566 2 27	-1.0	45	-	2	906	1.6	22.1	0.8	730	1.5	10.8	1.1	22.1	2.1	51.9	1.0	106.4	1.2	2.1	11	0.5	0.8	-
1566 2 30	-4.0	51	1.0	2	922	1.6	22.9	0.8	724	1.5	11.2	1.1	20.8	2.0	54.8	1.1	99.9	1.2	1.7	9	0.5	1.1	0.70863
Chemosynthetic community areas, Green Canyon block 232 (1995 cruise).																							
2635-1-2	-5.0	40	-	8850			22.8	0.8	494	1.0	12.7	1.2	9.6	0.9	71.0	1.0	81.6	1.0	0.5	2	0.1	-0.4	-
2635-1-3	-8.5	40	-	4230			22.0	0.8	494	1.1	12.9	1.3	9.5	0.9	50.8	1.0	83.2	1.0	0.3	1	0.1	0.4	-
2635-1-4	-12.5	40	-	5170			21.1	0.7	498	1.0	13.0	1.3	9.3	0.9	50.9	1.0	83.8	1.0	0.2	1	0.1	0.6	-
2635-1-5	-16.0	40	-	7000			18.8	0.6	502	1.0	13.1	1.3	8.9	0.9	51.0	1.0	82.7	1.0	0.4	2	0.1	0.3	-
2635 1 6	-19.0	40	-	8600	582	1.0	15.9	0.5	494	1.0	13.1	1.3	8.1	0.8	50.0	1.0	78.8	0.9	0.4	2	0.4	0.9	0.70916
2635-2-1	-4.0	40	-	1670			26.1	0.9	504	1.0	12.9	1.3	9.9	1.0	52.0	1.0	86.4	1.0	0.4	2	0.1	0.8	-
2635-2-2	-7.0	40	-	2100			25.7	0.9	514	1.1	13.3	1.3	10.3	1.0	51.9	1.0	86.5	1.0	0.9	4	0.1	0.9	-
2635-2-3	10.0	40	-	1270			24.1	0.8	501	1.0	13.0	1.3	9.7	0.9	50.8	1.0	86.4	1.0	0.5	4	0.1	0.7	-
2635-3 11	-0.5	40	-	200			28.6	1.0	486	1.0	13.1	1.3	10.6	1.0	51.5	1.0	86.3	1.0	0.9	4	0.1	0.8	-
2635-3-2	-3.5	40	-	1000			27.3	0.9	491	1.0	12.6	1.2	10.1	1.0	51.2	1.0	85.2	1.0	0.7	4	0.1	1.1	-
2635-3-3	6.5	40	-	1000			26.9	0.9	497	1.0	12.3	1.2	10.1	1.0	50.9	1.0	84.8	1.0	1.2	5	0.2	1.2	-
2639-2-2	-2.5	38	-	4900	558	1.0	19.4	0.7	466	1.0	12.3	1.2	9.3	0.9	50.2	1.0	78.0	0.9	1.5	5	0.2	0.9	-
2639-2-3	-5.0	39	-	8650	571	1.0	17.7	0.6	485	1.0	12.9	1.3	8.7	0.8	50.4	1.0	78.7	0.9	0.6	3	0.1	0.6	-
2639 2 4	-8.0	40	-	10010	580	1.0	15.2	0.5	481	1.0	12.6	1.2	8.9	0.9	50.5	1.0	75.2	0.9	1.1	6	0.2	0.4	-
2639 2 5	-11.0	40	-	10620	578	1.0	14.8	0.5	476	1.0	12.7	1.2	8.4	0.8	50.1	1.0	76.8	0.9	0.9	5	0.2	0.6	-
2639-2-6	14.5	40	-	13180	585	1.0	10.8	0.4	481	1.0	12.6	1.2	8.0	0.8	50.1	1.0	71.3	0.8	0.9	5	0.1	0.5	-
2639-2-7	-18.0	40	-	15150	581	1.0	8.7	0.3	478	1.0	12.8	1.2	7.5	0.7	49.0	0.9	71.0	0.8	0.9	5	0.1	0.7	-
2639-2-8	-21.0	40	-	16340	581	1.0	7.8	0.1	482	1.0	12.9	1.3	7.1	0.7	49.6	0.9	68.4	0.8	1.0	5	0.1	0.3	0.70917
Chemosynthetic community areas, Green Canyon block 184/185 (1995 cruise).																							
2647-2-1	2.0	40	-	7660	575	1.0	14.3	0.5	488	1.0	12.4	1.2	8.8	0.9	51.2	1.0	80.1	0.9	1.0	5	0.3	0.7	-
2647-2-2	4.0	40	-	17320	567	1.0	5.1	0.2	497	1.0	13.2	1.3	7.7	0.7	47.5	0.9	80.2	0.8	2.1	11	0.3	1.0	-
2647-2-3	-6.0	40	-	19400	576	1.0	2.6	0.1	489	1.0	12.8	1.3	7.7	0.7	47.1	0.9	70.1	0.8	1.5	8	0.2	0.6	-
2647 2 4	-9.0	40	-	14690	578	1.0	0.4	0.0	495	1.0	14.0	1.4	7.5	0.7	46.8	0.9	68.7	0.8	1.8	9	0.2	0.7	-
2647-2-5	-12.0	40	-	19690	575	1.0	0.3	0.0	490	1.0	13.7	1.3	6.9	0.7	46.5	0.9	65.1	0.7	1.1	15	0.3	0.7	-
2647-2-6	-15.0	40	-	19890	570	1.0	0.3	0.0	493	1.0	13.6	1.3	6.2	0.6	46.2	0.9	59.6	0.7	1.0	15	0.2	1.1	-
2647-2-7	-18.0	40	-	20280	577	1.0	0.4	0.0	489	1.0	13.8	1.3	5.8	0.5	46.1	0.9	57.3	0.7	1.1	5	0.2	1.0	-
2647-2-8	21.0	40	-	573	-	-	4.2	0.0	492	1.0	13.8	1.3	5.8	0.6	46.1	0.9	56.6	0.7	2.9	14	0.3	1.0	-
2647-1-1	-2.0	40	-	11400	-	-	11.3	0.4	501	1.0	11.9	1.2	10.2	1.0	52.2	1.0	78.3	0.9	2.4	12	0.1	0.9	0.70917
2647-1-2	6.0	40	-	14960	-	-	4.4	0.2	497	1.0	11.4	1.1	10.1	1.0	51.5	1.0	76.1	0.9	2.6	13	0.1	0.9	-

Note. Concentrations for H2S, Ba, and Sr are in $\mu M/L$, and other compounds are in mM/L, $\delta^{18}O$ is in permil (SMOW). Estimated analytical precision and definition of the the enrichment factor (EF) are given in text. The charge balance in meq/L is lower than 2% for analyses listed here. Samples from 1995 dives are pore fluids type I; samples from 1993 dives are pore fluids type II; samples from 1990 dives are pore fluids type III.

Table 3.2. Description of push cores taken in barite deposition sites whose pore waters have been analyzed in this study.

Push Core No.	MMS Block	Lat./Long.	Water Depth (m)	Core Length (cm)	Description
93-3559-2	MC-929	28°01.471/ 89°43.651	640	28	Flank of a mud volcano draped with orange-stained barite crusts. Silty sediment changing downcore color from orange (2 cm), to black (4 cm) to grey (24 cm).
93-3562-1	MC-929	28°01.509/ 89°43.572	657	13.5	Base of dormant mud volcano draped with clusters of methanotrophic mussels.
93-3566-1	GB-382	27°37.771/ 92°28.076	513	30	Black, anoxic, silty sediment at the base of twin barite chimneys.
93-3566-2	GB-382	27°37.747/ 92°28.108	513	8	White sand to silt-size barite (probably transported) infilling a small depression.
97-2897-1	GB-338	27°37.794/ 92°28.123	510	35	Shoulder of an active mud volcano draped with orange-stained barite crusts. Silty sediment with downcore change of color from black (6 cm) to grey mud (12 cm) to black mud with vertical stripes (18 cm).
97-2897-3	GB-338	27°37.794/ 92°28.123	510	15.5	Flat black surface next to an incipient mud volcano. Upper part is missing (removed during coring). Downcore change from black silt (3 cm) to grey mud (12.5 cm).
97-2897-4	GB-338	27°37.794/ 92°28.123	510	36	Chimney site after sampling the chimney. Uniform grey mud. Profuse gas release during punching of the core.

Table 3.3. Salinity, Barium Concentration and Ra Isotope Activities in Pore Fluids from Barite-Bearing Seeps.

Sampling Year	Sample Code	Core Depth (cm)	Dive No.	MMS Block No.	Water Depth (m)	Salinity (ppt)	Ba (mg/L)	^{226}Ra (dpm/L)	^{228}Ra (dpm/L)	228/226 AR
1993	3559-2-14	-4	JSL-3559	MC-929	640	52	0.19	190.1±26	106.8±8	0.56±0.09
1993	3559-2-17	-7	JSL-3559	MC-929	640	65	0.12	27.2±14	——	——
1993	3559-2-20	-10	JSL-3559	MC-929	640	96	0.48	——	——	——
1993	3559-2-23	-13	JSL-3559	MC-929	640	130	1.98	——	——	——
1993	3559-2-32	-22	JSL-3559	MC-929	640	155	90.60	738.7±44	490.5±26	0.66±0.05
1993	3562-1-20	-6	JSL-3562	MC-929	657	64		106.1±20	63.3±5	0.60±0.12
1993	3566-1-15	-7	JSL-3566	GB-382	513	134	548.80	1731.4±82	1327.1±90	0.77±0.06
1993	3566-1-18	-10	JSL-3566	GB-382	513	127	547.80	1381.3±58	1239.6±65	0.90±0.06
1993	3566-1-21	-13	JSL-3566	GB-382	513	139	838.00	2491.5±88	2137.8±91	0.86±0.05
1993	3566-1-24	-16	JSL-3566	GB-382	513	135	925.80	2829.3±74	2452.8±165	0.87±0.06
1993	3566-1-27	-19	JSL-3566	GB-382	513	127	467.80	1314.2±64	1060.2±83	0.81±0.07
1993	3566-1-30	-22	JSL-3566	GB-382	513	119	290.50	701.8±48	606.2±46	0.86±0.09
1993	3566-2-27	-1	JSL-3566	GB-382	513	45	0.29	——	——	——
1993	3566-2-30	-4	JSL-3566	GB-382	513	51	0.23	42.7±17	——	——
1997	97-2897-1-1	-12	JSL-2897	GB-338	510	154	616.30	2451.4±71	942±76	0.38±0.03
1997	97-2897-1-2	-15	JSL-2897	GB-338	510	154	756.72	1970.7±65	828.8±59	0.42±0.03
1997	97-2897-1-3	-18	JSL-2897	GB-338	510	154	936.32	3655.9±87	834.6±52	0.23±0.02
1997	97-2897-1-4	-21	JSL-2897	GB-338	510	152	913.13	2757.3±86	698.4±57	0.25±0.02
1997	97-2897-1-5	-24	JSL-2897	GB-338	510	152	891.51	2270.7±69	779.7±43	0.34±0.02
1997	97-2897-1-6	-27	JSL-2897	GB-338	510	153	750.07	3250.0±85	695.5±43	0.21±0.01
1997	97-2897-1-7	-30	JSL-2897	GB-338	510	150	797.37	2179.5±74	664.7±46	0.31±0.02
1997	97-2897-1-8	-33	JSL-2897	GB-338	510	150	689.50	2722.9±85	958.2±64	0.35±0.03
1997	97-2897-3-1	-16	JSL-2897	GB-338	510	50	0.28	773.8±61	491.3±45	0.63±0.08
1997	97-2897-3-2	-19	JSL-2897	GB-338	510	53	0.32	287.3±27	172.5±18	0.60±0.09
1997	97-2897-3-3	-22	JSL-2897	GB-338	510	58	0.64	214.3±49	——	——
1997	97-2897-3-4	-25	JSL-2897	GB-338	510	60	1.57	607.1±69	292.4±28	0.48±0.07
1997	97-2897-4-1	-12	JSL-2897	GB-338	510	78	0.24	224.9±49	——	——
1997	97-2897-4-2	-15	JSL-2897	GB-338	510	88	119.34	789.8±42	241.1±35	0.30±0.05
1997	97-2897-4-3	-18	JSL-2897	GB-338	510	104	246.06	1261.3±52	281.1±37	0.22±0.03
1997	97-2897-4-4	-21	JSL-2897	GB-338	510	115	436.36	1609.3±58	316.1±37	0.20±0.02
1997	97-2897-4-5	-24	JSL-2897	GB-338	510	122	732.19	2002.5±64	350.7±50	0.18±0.03
1997	97-2897-4-6	-27	JSL-2897	GB-338	510	132	883.74	2748.5±82	589.2±65	0.21±0.02
1997	97-2897-4-7	-30	JSL-2897	GB-338	510	146	1125.48	3023.3±79	819.6±97	0.27±0.03
1997	97-2897-4-8	-33	JSL-2897	GB-338	510	144	1173.27	2778.4±75	393.9±43	0.14±0.02
1997	97-2897-MV-1		JSL-2897	GB-338	510	45.5	0.57	80.4±17	——	——
1997	97-2897-MV-2		JSL-2897	GB-338	510	138	9.80	302.2±28	——	——
1997	97-2897-MV-3		JSL-2897	GB-338	510	132	4.25	240.2±25	——	——
1997	97-2897-MV-4		JSL-2897	GB-338	510	146	17.48	390.5±30	263.6±30	0.67±0.09
1997	97-2897-MV-5		JSL-2897	GB-338	510	141	93.43	474.0±32	241.9±44	0.51±0.10
1997	97-2897-MV-6		JSL-2897	GB-338	510	140	162.55	840.2±43	522.6±51	0.62±0.07

Note: Barium determinations by ICP carry an estimated error of ±0.5%.

63.3 to 2453 dpm/L. These values are considerably higher than the ambient Gulf of Mexico bottom water (13.2x0^{-2} dpm/L for ^{226}Ra and 0.45x10^{-2} dpm/L for ^{228}Ra, Key, 1981; Orr, 1988). Barium concentrations range from 0.12 mg/L to as high as 1173.3 mg/L which is up to 15x10^4 times higher than the upper bathyal waters in the Gulf of Mexico (i.e., 7.9 x10^{-3} mg/L, Buerket, 1997).

Typical depth profiles for ^{226}Ra and ^{228}Ra activities and Ba and salinity in pore fluids from a core in Garden Banks (GB-382) are shown in Figure 3.1. The salinity, Ba, ^{226}Ra and ^{228}Ra activities reach maximum values of 139 ^{o}/oo, 926 mg/L, 28.3x10^2 dpm/L and 24.5x10^2 dpm/L at 13 to 16 cm depth below sediment surface, respectively, followed by a decrease of values of 119 ^{o}/oo, 291 mg/L, 7.0x10^2 dpm/L and 6.0x10^2 dpm/L at 22 cm depth.

The ^{226}Ra and ^{228}Ra activities analyzed here, of up to 3.7x10^3 dpm/L and 2.5x10^3 dpm/L, respectively, are by far the highest values reported so far from fluids advecting through marine sediments. The positive relationships observed between salinity and Ba (Fig. 3.2 A) and between salinity and ^{226}Ra (Fig. 3.2 B) are remarkably similar to that derived from formation waters produced by offshore oil and gas rigs in the OCS Gulf of Mexico (Rabalais et al., 1991). We therefore propose that these highly anomalous Ba, ^{226}Ra and ^{228}Ra values in the fluids from barite-bearing seeps are derived from deep-seated and highly saline formation waters advecting to the seafloor and mixing with modern seawater at the points of exit.

The data points in Figures 3.3 A and 3.3 B form two distinct mixing arrays between subsurface fluid sources and the ambient Gulf of Mexico bottom waters. One mixing line is characterized by a Ra/Ba ratio of 2.86 dpm/mg and a ^{228}Ra/^{226}Ra ratio of 0.84. The other mixing line is formed by points having a higher excess of Ra over Ba (Ra/Ba=4.82 dpm/mg) and a higher ^{226}Ra excess over ^{228}Ra (^{228}Ra/^{226}Ra=0.31). The separation between the two types of fluids are likely to be related to segregated sources in the subsurface having different Ra activities and Ba concentrations and distinct ^{232}Th/^{238}U parent ratios.

The Ra/Ba ratios of both fluid groups are anomalously low compared with seawater. For example, the Ra/Ba ratios of the seep fluids are about 0.4 to 0.21 times the ratio in surface ocean water (Ra/Ba=6.6 dpm/mg). The ^{228}Ra/^{226}Ra ratios of the fluids are 0.84 and 0.31 (derived from the slopes in Fig. 3.3 B) which are substantially higher than the ratio in the ambient Gulf of Mexico deepwater by a factor of 25 and 9, respectively (^{228}Ra/^{226}Ra=0.034, Orr, 1988).

3.1.2 Chemical and Isotope Compositions

Chemical and isotope compositions of pore fluids representative of seeps (n=47) and from the Gulf of Mexico bottom waters at bathyal and abyssal depths (n=2) are listed in Table 3.1. In order to ascertain the origin of the solutes in the pore fluids, we calculated enrichment factors by using the relation $Ef = (C_i/C_w)_f/(C_i/(C_w)_{sw}$ (Aharon et al., 1992), where C_i and C_w are the concentrations of constituent "i" and of water "w" and the the subscripts "f" and "sw" refer to fluids and the Gulf of Mexico appropriate deepwater, respectively. An Ef value of >1 indicates a net addition of the constituent to the source water, whereas an Ef value of <1 indicates removal of the constituent from the original seawater.

28

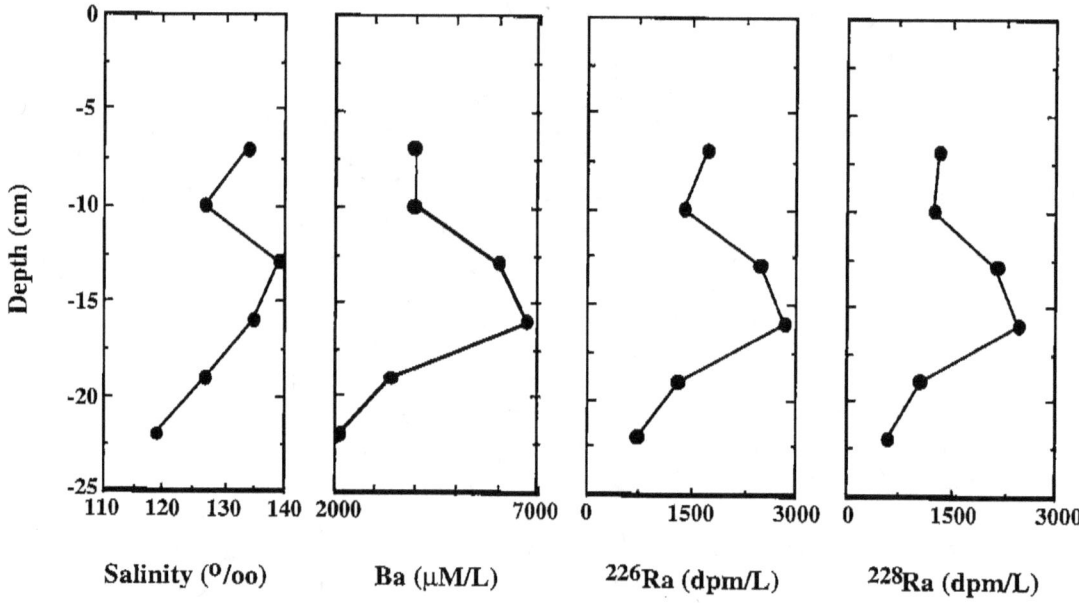

Figure 3.1. Depth profiles of salinity, Ba, and ^{226}Ra and ^{228}Ra activities in the pore fluids from core 3566-1 taken at Garden Banks block 382.

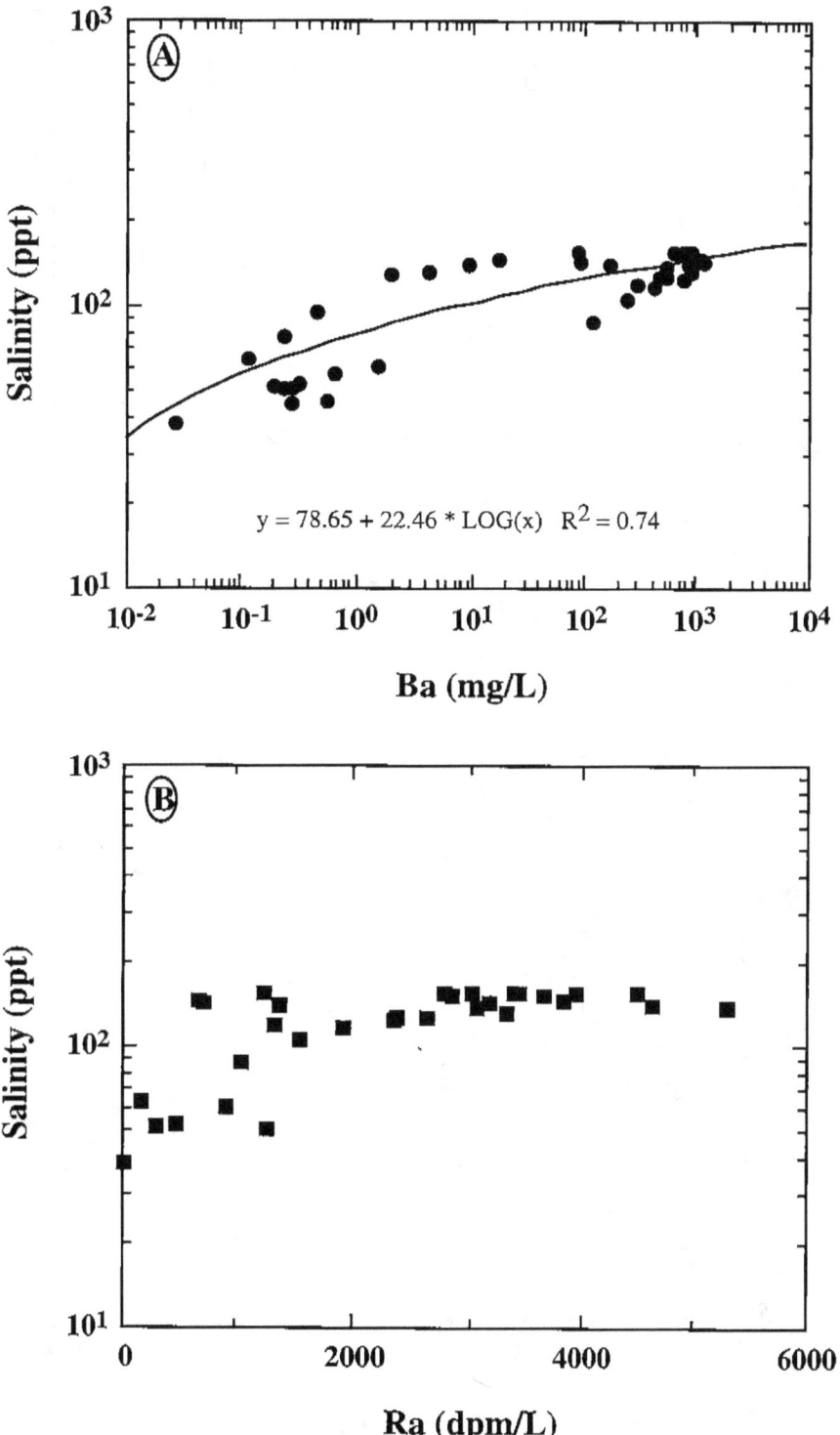

Figure 3.2. Salinity, Ba and Ra relationships in pore fluids from barite-bearing seeps.

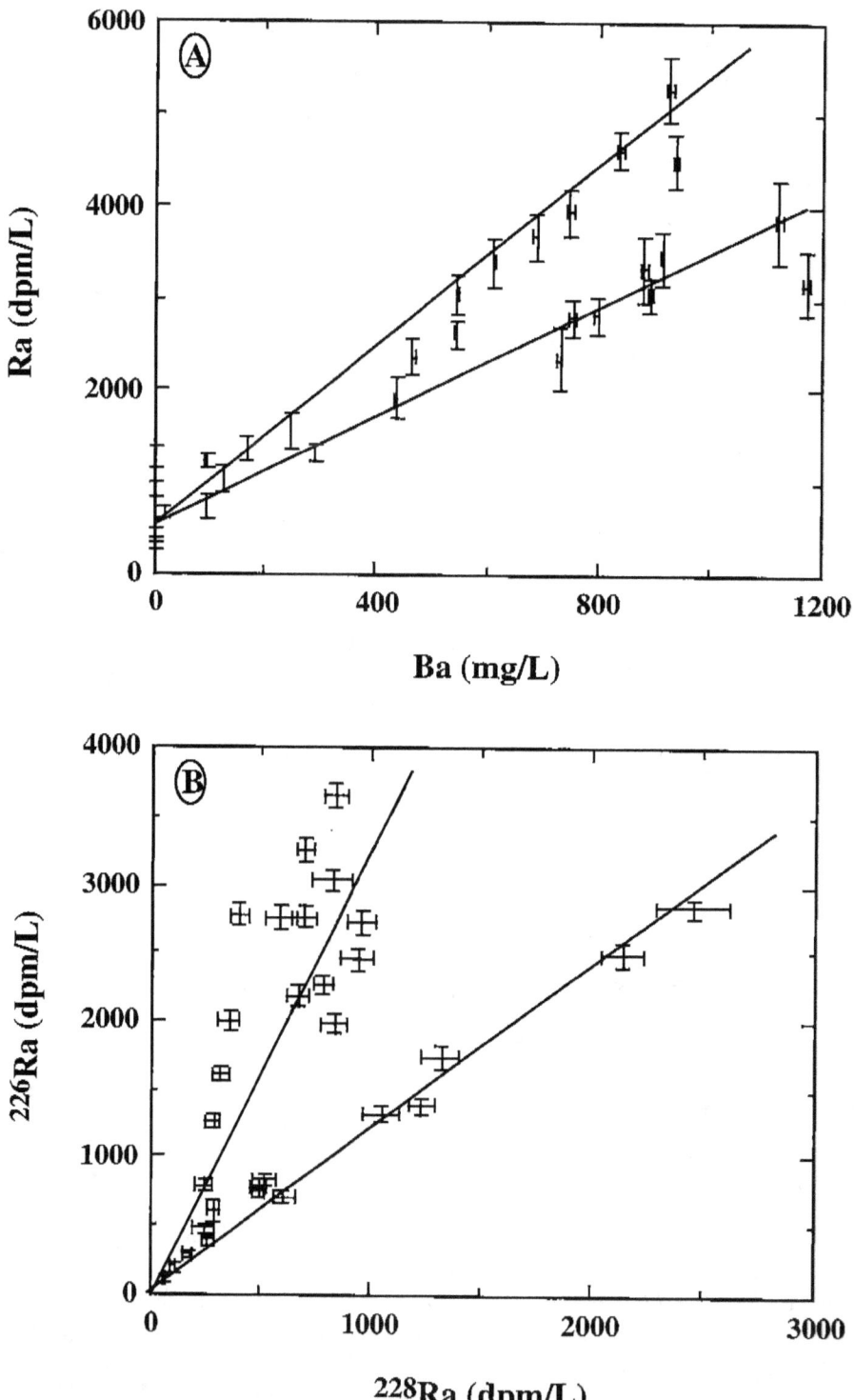

Figure 3.3. Ra-Ba and ^{226}Ra-^{228}Ra relationships in pore fluids from barite-bearing seeps.

Enrichment factors for the various chemical constituents are listed in Table 3.1. Three types of pore fluids (Fig. 3.4) can be discerned on the basis of molar Ca/Cl, Sr/Cl, Ba/Cl and SO_4/Cl ratios as indicated below.

Pore fluids pertaining to type I have the conservative elements (e.g., Na and Cl) at concentrations similar to the overlying seawater (Ef = 1, Table 3.1) but their Ca, Sr and SO_4 concentrations are depleted relative to seawater (Ef < 1, Table 3.1 and Figs. 3.4 A-C). These observations suggest that type I pore fluids are essentially derived from a contemporaneous seawater whose non-conservative elements, such as Ca, Sr and SO_4, were partly removed by processes occurring within the seep sediments. The Ba concentrations of these pore fluids are consistently higher than bottom water (Ef >1, Table 3.1 and Fig. 3.4 D) and therefore are analogous to pore fluids in normal marine sediments (Boulegue et al., 1990). The $^{87}Sr/^{86}Sr$ ratios (0.70916 $\pm 1 \times 10^{-5}$, n=3) are identical to the overlying seawater ratio (0.70917) thus supporting a seawater origin. In contrast, the $\delta^{18}O$ values that range from 0.3 to 1.3^o/oo (SMOW) are generally higher than the ambient deepwater at comparable depth (0.3^o/oo, SMOW, Table 3.1 and Fig. 3.5 A) and their inverse relation with Cl concentrations (Fig. 3.5 B) is attributed to *in situ* dissociation of gas hydrates. Pore fluids of type I occur at bathyal depths in hemipelagic sediments blanketed by clusters of chemosynthetic mussels (Bathymodiolus spp.) and patchy Beggiatoa mats and are often associated with gas hydrates. These fluids represent normal seawater whose chemical composition was modified by bacterial processes and mineral deposition.

Pore fluids type II are from brine-issuing sites on Green Knoll at 1920 m depth (Fig. 1.1). These fluids are highly saline (salinity range from 116°/oo to 182°/oo, Table 3.1) and show substantial enrichments in Na and Cl relative to the ambient abyssal seawater. The Ca contents are higher than both seawater and pore fluids type I but lower in comparison with pore fluids type III (Fig. 3.4 A). The Sr and Ba contents are similar to the pore fluids type I but are much lower than those of pore fluids type III (Figs. 3.4 B & C). An outstanding feature is the marked enrichment in SO_4 relative to seawater (Ef = 1.4 to 1.5, Table 3.1 and Fig. 3.4 C). The $^{87}Sr/^{86}Sr$, ranging from 0.70797 to 0.70897 (n=3), are significantly lower than the seawater (0.70917) whereas the $\delta^{18}O$ values (-1.4 to 0.1^o/oo SMOW) are similar to the ambient bottom water (-0.2^o/oo SMOW, Table 3.1 and Fig. 3.5 A).

Pore fluids Type III are clearly distinguished from the other two types of pore fluids by their high salinity (45°/oo to 155°/oo) coupled with anomalously high enrichments in Ca, Sr and Ba (Ef=8.2, 37.2, and 3.4×10^4, respectively, Table 3.1 and Figs. 3.4 A, B, D) and strong SO_4 depletions (Ef=0.02, Table 3.1, Fig. 3.4 C). The $\delta^{18}O$ values (maximum value up to 1.7^o/oo SMOW), are generally higher than the ambient seawater (Fig. 3.5 A) but their $^{87}Sr/^{86}Sr$ ratios (0.70843 to 0.70862 for n=8) are below the seawater value (0.70917). Pore fluids type III are unique to seeps associated with extensive barite deposits and are derived from deep-seated formation waters (Fu et al., 1994; Fu and Aharon, 1997).

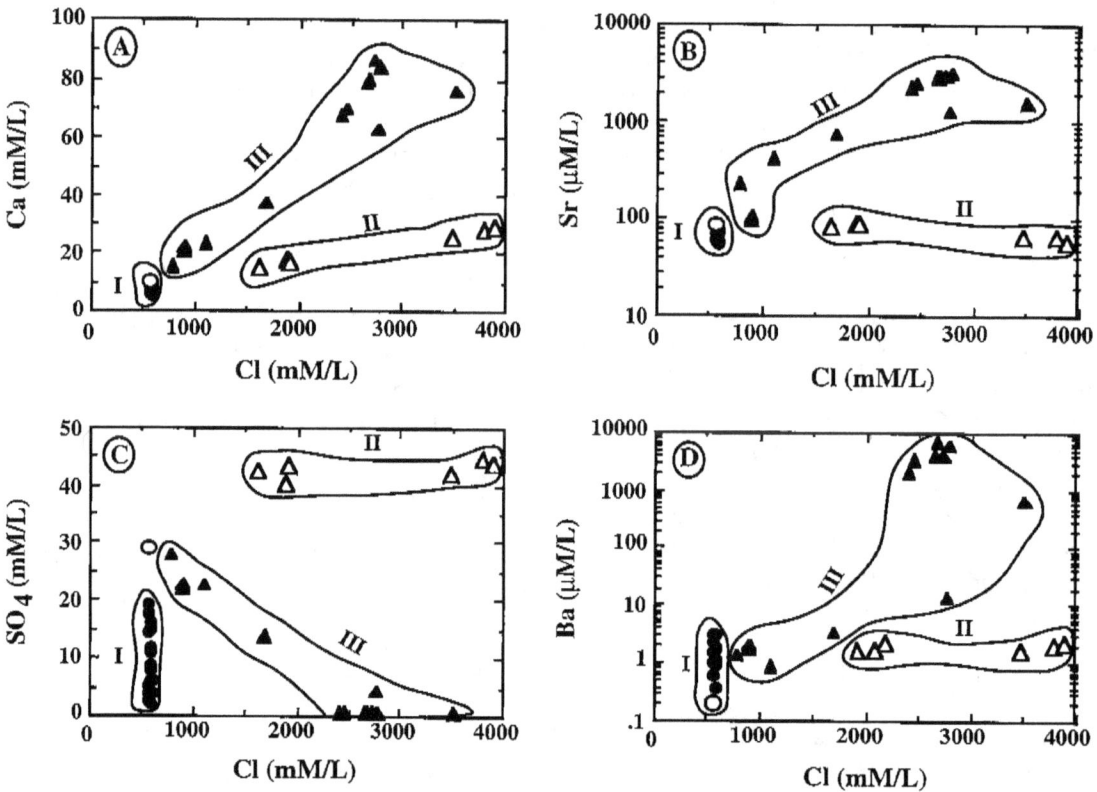

Figure 3.4. Plots of Cl against Ca, Sr, Ba and SO4 in pore fluids. Note that three types of pore fluids can be discerned on the basis of Ca/Cl, Sr/Cl, Ba/Cl and SO4/Cl molar ratios. The empty circle represents deepwater Gulf of Mexico, the solid circle, empty triangles, and solid triangles represent the pore fluids type I, II and III, respectively.

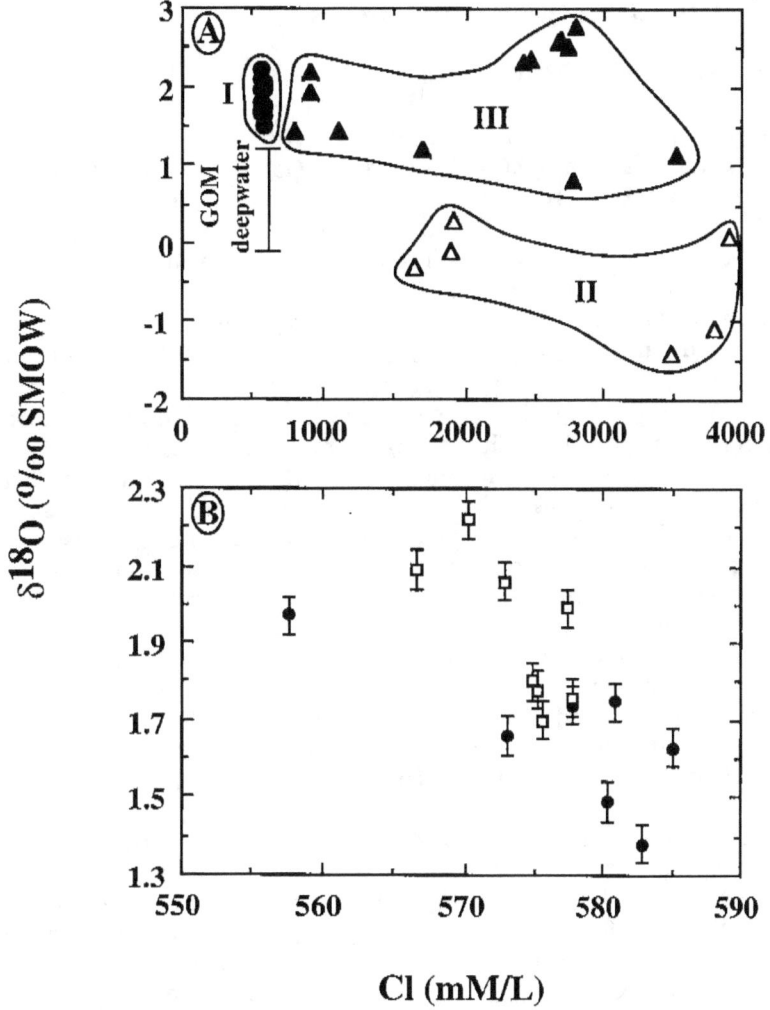

Figure 3.5. Cl-δ^{18}O relationships in pore fluids from seeps. A: pore fluids type I, II and III. The measured δ^{18}O values of the bathyal and abyssal Gulf of Mexico waters are 1.4°/$_{oo}$ and -0.15°/$_{oo}$ (SMOW), respectively. B: The inverse

relationship observed between Cl and δ^{18}O in pore fluids type I is attributed to sublimation of gas hydrates (see text). Empty squares are pore fluids from core 2639-2 (GC-232) and solid circles are pore fluids from core 2647-2 (GC-184/185, Bush Hill).

3.2 Barite Deposits Associated with Seeps

3.2.1. Morphology and Petrography

Barite chimneys and crusts were collected with the submersible Johnson-Sea-Link in Mississippi Canyon (MC-929) and in Garden Banks (GB-382; GB-338)(Fig. 1.1). The chimneys are 5 to 8 cm in diameter and generally exhibit porous and friable upright columnar structures rising 10 to 30 cm above the seabed (Figs. 1.2 C and 3.6 A). Most chimneys have central orifices up to several centimeters in diameter through which gas and fluid brines escape into the water column. Some chimneys have one to several small nodules which protrude laterally. Juvenile <u>Bathymodiolus</u> sp. methanotrophic mussels were found attached to the base and side of some chimneys. When sliced, the interiors of the chimneys exhibit growth layers which alternate between dark-gray and light (Fig. 3.6 B). The orange-white barite crusts of 2-10 cm thick are typically draping dormant mud volcanoes containing a brine-filled caldera (Fig. 1.2 A) or occur as thin pavements covering the seafloor.

Microscopic and SEM analyses reveal that the chimneys consist principally of high reflectance barite and contain minor amounts of pyrite-like iron sulfide (hereafter named pyrite), Mg-calcite, kerogen, and iron oxides. Detritalminerals such as quartz, feldspar, rutile and ilmenite are also present in trace amounts in the fine mud matrix.

The chimneys display two distinct morphologies that are rarely intermixed: (i) string-like (Fig. 3.7 A), and (ii) dendritic-like (Fig. 3.7 B). The string-like barite, up to 1.2 mm in length, forms, in association with pyrite, the gray-dark (growth) layers whereas dendritic-like barite, ranging in length from 0.2 to 5 mm, forms the light-yellow (growth) layers which contain little or no pyrite. Growth directions of both morphological types are often oriented perpendicular to the growth layers.

Interlocking, spherical to ellipsoidal-shaped rosette barite constitutes the basic building block of both morphological types. These rosette barites, ranging in size from 20 to 40 μm in diameter, are composed of euhedral to subhedral tabular crystals which radiate from a central core (Fig. 3.8 A). The core, occupying a space equal to between 1/4 to 1/2 of the rosette diameter, is brown to yellow in transmitted light suggesting the presence of iron oxides and/or organic matter in trace amounts. In cross polarized light, most rosette barites display pseudo-uniaxial extinction crosses.

SEM examination of polished thin sections reveal that the cores of rosette barites exhibit a high degree of structural variability. Most rosette barites possess porous cores which are possibly of a biogenic origin. When these core structures are well-preserved they have been identified as the relics of coccolith tests replaced by barites. Less commonly the cores are either empty or are filled by cryptocrystalline barite, Mg-calcite, quartz, and feldspar.

A three-dimensional view of the rosette-barite morphology has been obtained from examination of chimney fragments under SEM (Fig. 3.8 B). In this view, the individual rosettes display spherical shapes that show a single axial symmetry and multiple tabular crystals oriented around the central axis. The rosettes are often in contact with each other and coalesce to form string-like or dendritic-like barites.

Although the overall concentration of pyrite is low (generally 1 to 2% by volume), it is the next most abundant mineral in the chimneys after the barite. Pyrite grains of various sizes and shapes often occur in association with string-like barite or in the mud matrix. It can occur as (i) ovoids of sizes

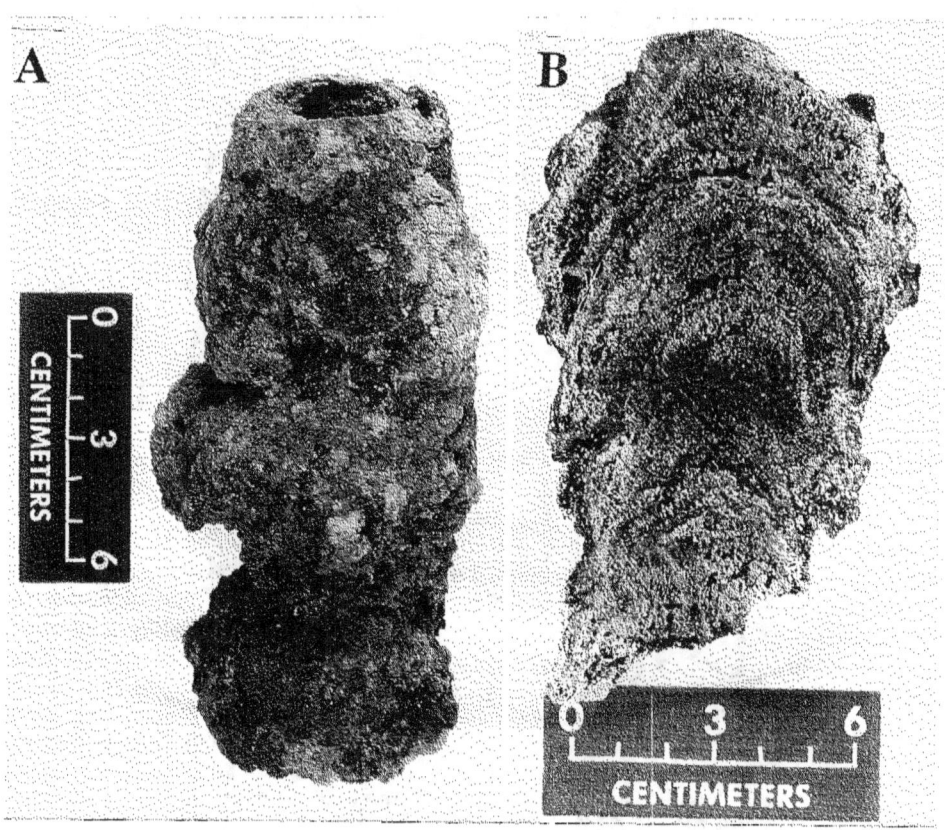

Figure 3.6. Barite chimney #2 from the Gulf of Mexico slope. A: Side view of the brown-reddish stained chimney. Note the protruding nodule on the middle left and the top orifice of the chimney; B: Transverse section through a chimney showing the alternating dark-gray and light-yellow growth layers.

36

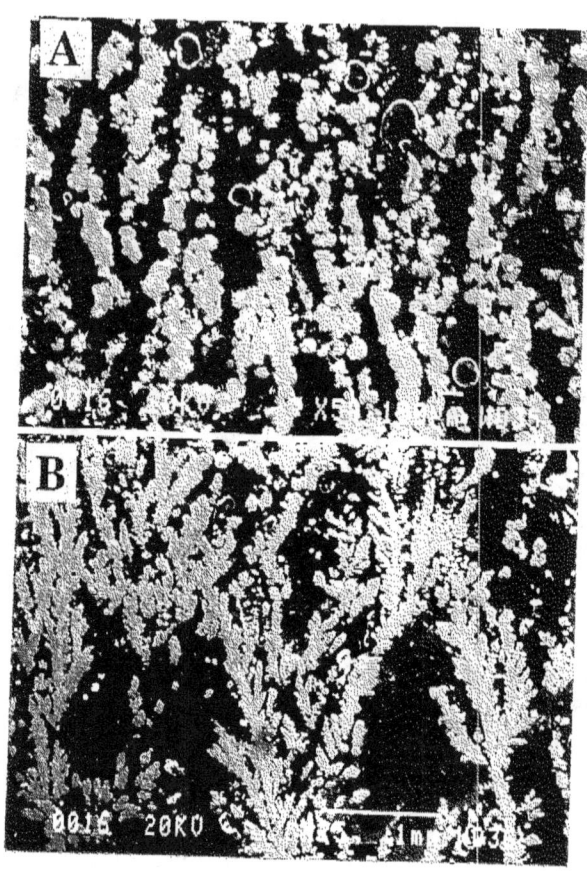

Figure 3.7. Distinct morphologies of the barite chimneys displayed in SEM photomicrographs from thin section. A: String-like morphology typical of the dark-gray growth layers. B: Dendritic-like morphology typical of the light-yellow growth layers.

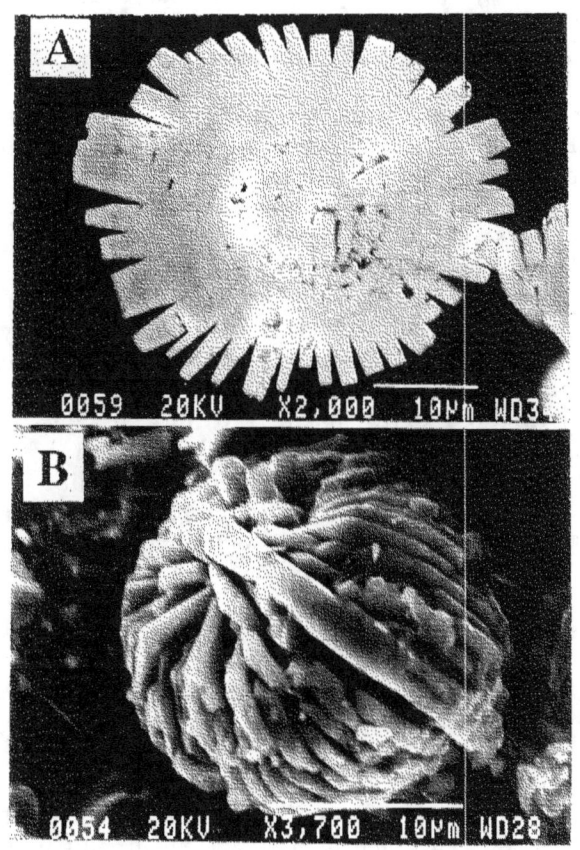

Figure 3.8. Principal building block of the barite in SEM views. A: Rosette-shaped barite from thin section. Note the pitted nature of the core. B: Three dimensional view of the rosette from a chimney fragment.

varying from 1 μm to 10 μm (Fig. 3.9 A); (ii) euhedral cubic grains; (iii) anhedral to subhedral grains of up to 20 μm across, and (iv) framboids varying in diameter up to 15 μm and containing microcrystallites of about 1 μm in diameter (Fig. 3.9 B). Some of the framboids exhibit coccolith structures suggesting that, in addition to barite, coccolith tests may have also been replaced by pyrite. Very small (generally < 1% in volume) amounts of accessory minerals such as Mg-calcite, quartz, feldspar, rutile and ilmenite have also been identified by the SEM analysis in the barites. These minerals often occur in the mud matrix as anhedral grains ranging in size from 0.5 to 10 μm.

The crusts are porous, friable and loosely cemented. Most crusts display two layers with the upper part exhibiting a orange to white color. This surface was partly covered by sediments (fine sand) before it was retrieved from the seafloor. In contrast, the lower part shows deep-gray to black and was buried in the black-colored anoxic sediments before sampling.

Microscopic and SEM analyses reveal that the crusts are dominated by barite and calcite with minor amounts of pyrite and kerogen. The calcite, up to 75% by weight, exhibits subhedral to euhedral crystals. Generally, the lower deep-gray parts of the crusts contain more calcite than the orange-colored upper parts. Barites in the crusts exhibit fine-grained massive morphology, euhedral crystals, or individual rosette barite. String-like and dendritic-like barites which are common in the chimneys are rarely found in the crusts. The barite and calcite in the crust are often interlocked and exhibit a mosaic texture, which indicates that calcite and barite precipitated simultaneously. Pyrite, up to 8% by volume, often occurs in association with calcite as ovoids, anhedral to euhedral cubic grains and framboids (Fig. 3.9).

3.2.2. Elemental Chemistry

Representative electron microprobe analyses of Ba, Sr, Ca, Na, and Fe in the barite chimneys and crusts are listed in Table 3.4. The Sr concentration ranges from 4.0 to 29.6 mol% (mean of 15.5 mol% ± 6.5 for n= 10) and 3.9 to 17.6 mol% (mean of 10.7 mol% ± 5.1 for n= 10) for chimneys and crusts, respectively, making Sr the most abundant minor element. The observed relative high abundance of Sr replacing Ba in the barite lattice can be attributed to their nearly matching ionic radii (1.18 Å for Sr^{2+} and 1.34 Å for Ba^{2+}). The Ca content ranges from 1.3 to 4.6 mol% (mean of 2.8 mol% ± 1.3 for n= 10) for the chimneys and from 1.2 to 5.3 mol% (mean of 3.0 mol% ± 1.2 for n= 10) for the crusts. The positive correlation observed between Ca and Sr contents (Fig. 3.10 A) and the inverse linear relationship observed between Sr and Ba (Fig. 3.10 B) in the barites support the inference that Sr and Ca are isomorphically replacing Ba in the lattice and do not form separate mineral phases.

The Na content in the barite is also relatively high, ranging from 1.1 to 3.2 mol% (mean of 1.9 mol% ± 0.6 for n= 10, Table 3.4) for the chimneys and from 1.1 to 6.9 mol% (mean of 3.65 mol% ± 2.4 for n= 10, Table 3.4) for the crusts. However, it is uncertain whether Na replaces Ba in the barite lattice or forms a separate authigenic mineral phase. In contrast to the other chemical elements reported here, the Fe content in the barites is relatively low, ranging from 0 to 0.7 mol% (mean of 0.3 mol% ± 0.22 for n=10, Table 3.4) for the chimneys and 0 to 0.3 mol% (mean of 0.2 mol% ± 0.1 for n=10, Table 3.4) for the crusts. High Fe contents, of up to 22 mol%, were generally found in the center of rosette cores in the chimneys. However, the poor stoichiometry of the analyses with higher Fe contents suggest that the anomalously high Fe may have been caused by the

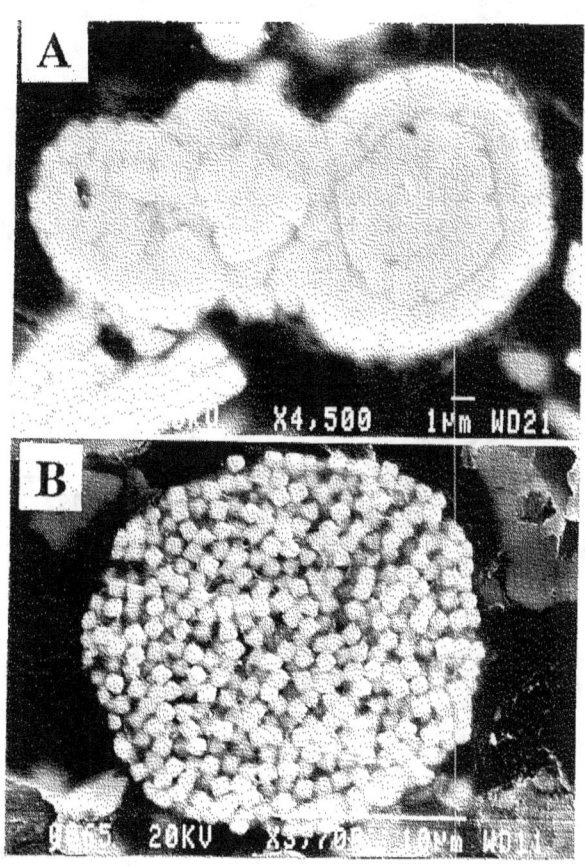

Figure 3.9. SEM view of the accessory pyrite associated with the barite chimneys. A: Core and rim of euhedral pyrite. B: pyrite framboid containing microcrystallites.

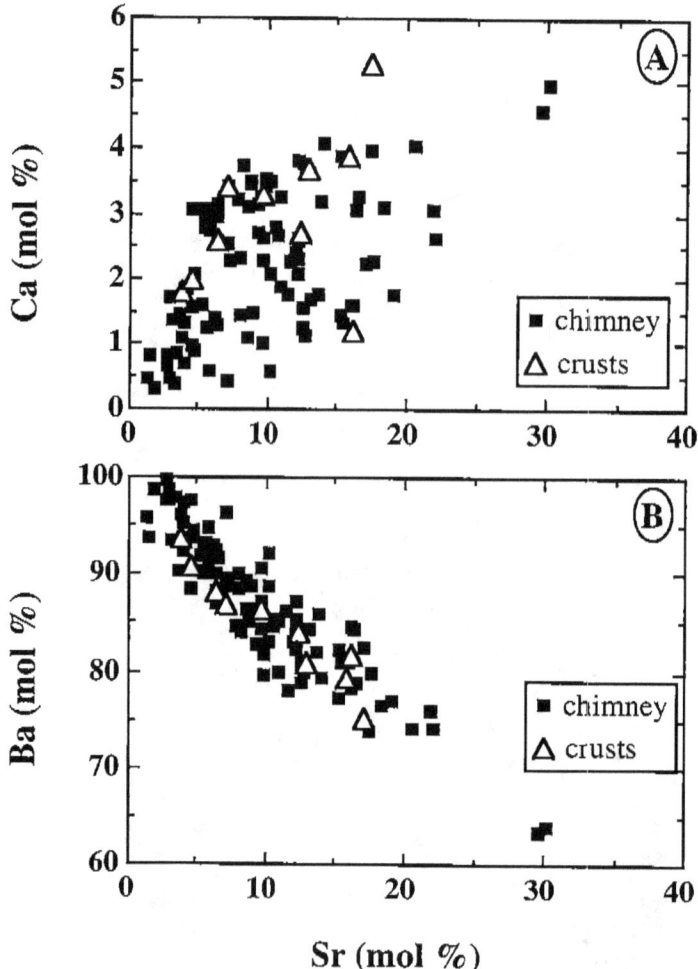

Figure 3.10. Microprobe analyses from barite chimneys and crusts. A: Positive linear relation between Sr and Ca compositions. B: Inverse linear relation between Ba and Sr compositions, suggesting that Sr replaces Ba in the barite lattice.

Table 3.4. Elemental chemistry of barite chimneys and crusts from the Gulf of Mexico slope.

Barite chimneys

	1	2	3	4	5	6	7	8	9	10
(Wt%)										
BaO	45.61	56.55	54.91	61.56	55.34	59.67	51.44	53.14	53.42	54.45
SrO	14.42	4.77	6.97	1.82	7.17	4.06	9.66	7.11	8.70	8.20
CaO	1.21	0.68	0.36	0.33	0.33	0.37	1.02	1.29	0.79	0.57
Na$_2$O	0.67	0.61	0.37	0.53	0.47	0.30	0.76	0.89	0.35	0.42
FeO	0.14	0.16	0.13	0.04	0.23	0.00	0.02	0.08	0.06	0.02
SO$_3$	37.57	34.83	34.82	34.83	35.65	35.12	36.05	35.97	36.53	35.47
Total	99.62	97.59	97.56	99.12	99.20	99.51	98.97	98.47	99.86	99.13
Atoms (based on 4 oxygens)										
Ba	0.633	0.846	0.821	0.923	0.810	0.89	0.741	0.770	0.765	0.798
Sr	0.296	0.106	0.154	0.040	0.155	0.09	0.206	0.152	0.184	0.178
Ca	0.046	0.028	0.015	0.014	0.013	0.015	0.040	0.051	0.031	0.023
2Na	0.023	0.023	0.014	0.020	0.017	0.011	0.027	0.032	0.012	0.015
Fe	0.004	0.005	0.004	0.001	0.007	0.000	0.001	0.003	0.002	0.001
Total	1.003	1.007	1.008	0.998	1.003	1.002	1.015	1.007	0.995	1.014
S	0.999	0.998	0.997	1.001	0.999	0.999	0.995	0.998	1.002	0.995

Barite crusts

	1	2	3	4	5	6	7	8	9	10
BaO	56.78	57.23	62.33	53.76	62.04	59.17	55.20	49.99	58.99	54.56
SrO	4.26	5.77	1.75	7.25	2.08	2.91	6.00	8.04	3.25	7.34
CaO	0.79	0.67	0.43	0.28	0.50	0.64	0.92	1.31	0.85	0.97
Na$_2$O	0.17	0.18	0.18	0.20	0.84	0.77	0.67	0.94	0.76	0.30
FeO	0.01	0.02	0.02	0.05	0.02	0.10	0.10	0.06	0.04	0.02
SO$_3$	34.55	35.71	34.59	34.03	33.78	35.72	35.98	37.52	35.71	36.01
Total	96.56	99.58	99.30	95.57	99.26	99.31	98.87	97.86	99.60	99.20
Ba	0.865	0.841	0.937	0.817	0.908	0.882	0.809	0.739	0.869	0.793
Sr	0.096	0.125	0.039	0.163	0.045	0.064	0.130	0.176	0.071	0.158
Ca	0.033	0.027	0.018	0.012	0.020	0.026	0.037	0.053	0.034	0.039
2Na	0.011	0.013	0.013	0.015	0.061	0.057	0.049	0.069	0.055	0.022
Fe	0.000	0.001	0.001	0.002	0.001	0.003	0.003	0.002	0.001	0.001
Total	1.005	1.007	1.008	1.008	1.034	1.032	1.027	1.039	1.031	1.012
S	1.008	1.005	0.996	0.990	0.947	1.019	1.009	1.063	1.008	1.003

Notes: The data are based on the analyses of chimney #2 and crust Cr-93-1-3/1. The overall error (±1σ) of the chemical analyses reported here are estimated, on the basis of standard analyses, to be (in weight % units): 0.39 for SO$_3$; 0.32 for BaO; 0.09 for SrO; 0.06 for CaO; 0.09 for Na$_2$O; 0.06 for FeO.

presence of iron oxides. This inference is consistent with the observation that most rosette cores show a brownish color under optical microscope. The above results indicate that the geochemistry of chimneys is similar to the crusts. in the barites support the inference that Sr and Ca are isomorphically replacing Ba in the lattice and do not form separate mineral phases.

The Na content in the barite is also relatively high, ranging from 1.1 to 3.2 mol% (mean of 1.9 mol% ± 0.6 for n= 10, Table 3.4) for the chimneys and from 1.1 to 6.9 mol% (mean of 3.65 mol% ± 2.4 for n= 10, Table 3.4) for the crusts. However, it is uncertain whether Na replaces Ba in the barite lattice or forms a separate authigenic mineral phase. In contrast to the other chemical elements reported here, the Fe content in the barites is relatively low, ranging from 0 to 0.7 mol% (mean of 0.3 mol% ± 0.22 for n=10, Table 3.4) for the chimneys and 0 to 0.3 mol% (mean of 0.2 mol% ± 0.1 for n=10, Table 3.4) for the crusts. High Fe contents, of up to 22 mol%, were generally found in the center of rosette cores in the chimneys. However, the poor stoichiometry of the analyses with higher Fe contents suggest that the anomalously high Fe may have been caused by the presence of iron oxides. This inference is consistent with the observation that most rosette cores show a brownish color under optical microscope. The above results indicate that the geochemistry of chimneys is similar to the crusts.

3.2.3. Sulfur, Oxygen and Strontium Isotope Assays

Sulfur, oxygen and strontium isotopes are commonly used to decipher the origin of barites (Sakai, 1971; Claypool et al., 1980; Cecile et al., 1983; Kesler et al., 1988; Fu and Aharon, 1995). This is because sulfur and oxygen isotopes are reliable fingerprints of the source of sulfate whereas the strontium isotopes are excellent tracers of fluid sources and transport history. The purpose of measuring these isotopes in the barites from the Gulf of Mexico is to use them as tracers in order to elucidate the origin of the barites and outline a depositional model for these highly unusual occurrences based on the data in hand.

Sulfur, oxygen and strontium isotope compositions of barite, along with the carbon isotope compositions of carbonates in the crusts are listed in Table 3.5. As previously indicated, these barites were recovered from two areas, Garden Banks block 382 and Mississippi Canyon block 929. Barite chimneys from MC-929 and GB-382 have similar $\delta^{34}S$ and $\delta^{18}O$ compositions which range from 20.3 to 21.6⁰/oo (CDT) and from 9.6 to 11.7⁰/oo (SMOW), respectively (Table 3.5 and Fig. 3.11). These values are similar to, or slightly higher than, those of modern seawater sulfate ($\delta^{34}S$ = 20.3⁰/oo CDT and $\delta^{18}O$ = 9.7⁰/oo SMOW, Cecile et al., 1983; Faure, 1986). Generally, samples from the inner side of chimneys tend to yield relatively higher $\delta^{34}S$ and $\delta^{18}O$ values than samples from the outer part of chimneys (Table 3.5 and Figure 3.12). In contrast, $\delta^{34}S$ and $\delta^{18}O$ values of barite crusts range from 26.1 to 62.3⁰/oo CDT and 12.4 to 21.9⁰/oo SMOW, respectively, which are anomalously enriched in both ^{34}S and ^{18}O relative to the modern seawater sulfate (Table 3.5 and Fig. 3.11). Most barite crusts exhibit two sublayers: the upper layer is light gray and the lower layer exhibits a black or deep gray color. $\delta^{34}S$ and $\delta^{18}O$ values of the lower layers are generally higher than those of the upper layers (Table 3.5). chimneys (Table 3.5 and Figure 3.12). In contrast, $\delta^{34}S$ and $\delta^{18}O$ values of barite crusts range from 26.1 to 62.3⁰/oo CDT and 12.4 to 21.9⁰/oo SMOW, respectively, which are anomalously enriched in both ^{34}S and ^{18}O relative to the modern seawater sulfate (Table 3.5 and Fig. 3.11). Most barite crusts exhibit two sublayers: the

Table 3.5. S, O and Sr isotope compositions of the barites and C and O isotope compositions of the coexisting carbonates.

Type of sample	Sample	Description of sample	δ¹⁸O (SO₄) (‰ SMOW)	δ³⁴S (SO₄) (‰ CDT)	CaCO₃ (%)	δ¹³C (CaCO₃) (‰ PDB)	δ¹⁸O (CaCO₃) (‰ PDB)	⁸⁷Sr/⁸⁶7Sr
		Barite chimneys from Garden Banks block 382						
	Ch#2-a	inner part, deep gray	9.9	20.5	-	-	-	-
	Ch#2-b	outer part, light gray	10.0	20.5	-	-	-	-
	Ch#4-a	inner part, deep gray	10.8	21.5	-	-	-	-
	Ch#4-b	middle part, gray	9.6	20.6	-	-	-	-
	Ch#4-c	outer part, redish	9.7	20.4	-	-	-	-
	Ch#5-a	inner part, gray	10.2	20.7	-	-	-	-
	Ch#5-b	outer part, redish	9.6	20.3	-	-	-	-
	Ch#9-T/a	top, inner part, gray	10.9	21.6	-	-	-	-
	Ch#9-T/b	top, center part, yellow	10.2	21.1	-	-	-	0.70858
Barite	Ch#9-T/c	top,outer part, orange	9.7	20.3	-	-	-	0.70861
	Ch#9-M/a	middle, inner part, yellow	11.7	21.3	-	-	-	-
	Ch#9-M/b	middle, inner part, gray	10.9	20.4	-	-	-	-
	Ch#9-M/c	middle, center part, yellow	9.8	20.5	-	-	-	-
chimneys	Ch#9-M/d	middle, outer part, red	9.8	20.1	-	-	-	-
	Ch#9-B/a	bottom, inner part, gray	10.7	21.3	-	-	-	0.70859
	Ch#9-B/b	bottom, center part, yellow	9.8	20.9	-	-	-	0.70858
	Ch#9-B/c	bottom, outer part, red	9.5	20.2	-	-	-	-
	Ch#10-T/a	top, inner part, gray	10.0	20.3	-	-	-	-
	Ch#10-T/b	top, outer aprt, red	9.9	20.3	-	-	-	-
	Ch#10-M/a	middle, inner part, gray	9.9	20.4	-	-	-	-
	Ch#10-M/b	middle, outer part, red	9.8	20.3	-	-	-	-
	Ch#10-B/a	bottom, inner part, gray	10.3	20.5	-	-	-	-
	Ch#10-B/b	bottom, outer part, red	9.9	20.3	-	-	-	-
		Barite chimneys from Mississippi Canyon						
	Ch#11-a	inner part, gray	10.7	20.3	-	-	-	0.70848
	Ch#11-b	outer part, orange	9.8	20.1	-	-	-	0.70849
		Barite crusts from Garden Banks block 382						
	Cr-93-7-7/1	light gray	12.9	28.1	-	-	-	-
	Cr-93-8-5/3/l	lower part, deep gray	13.5	28.9	-	-	-	-
	Cr-93-8-5/3/u	upper part, gray	12.7	26.5	8.0	-27.3	4.4	0.70857
Barite	Cr-93-8-7/2/l	lower part, black	15.5	33.6	52.2	-21.0	4.2	-
	Cr-93-8-7/2/u	upper part, gray	12.4	26.1	16.3	-24.1	2.6	-
crusts		Barite crusts from Mississippi Canyon block 929						
	Cr-93-1-3/1/l	lower part, black	21.9	62.3	-	-	-	-
	Cr-93-1-3/1/u	upper part, deep gray	21.5	61.5	63.6	-36.2	2.8	0.70845
	Cr-93-4-4/1/l	lower part, dark	14.3	33.0	56.8	-29.5	2.9	-
	93-93-4-4/1/u	upper part, gray	12.6	28.7	26.3	-31.2	3.1	-

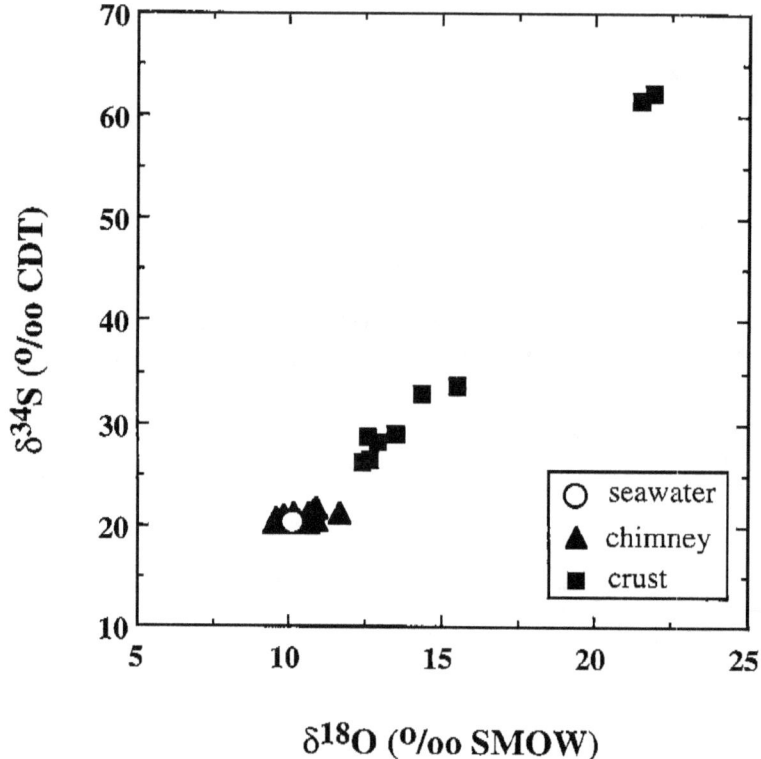

Figure 3.11. Sulfur and oxygen isotope compositions of GOM barites (n = 34). Sulfur and oxygen isotope compositions of the chimneys are similar to those of modern seawater sulfate. In contrast, the crusts are enriched in both 34S and 18O relative to seawater sulfate.

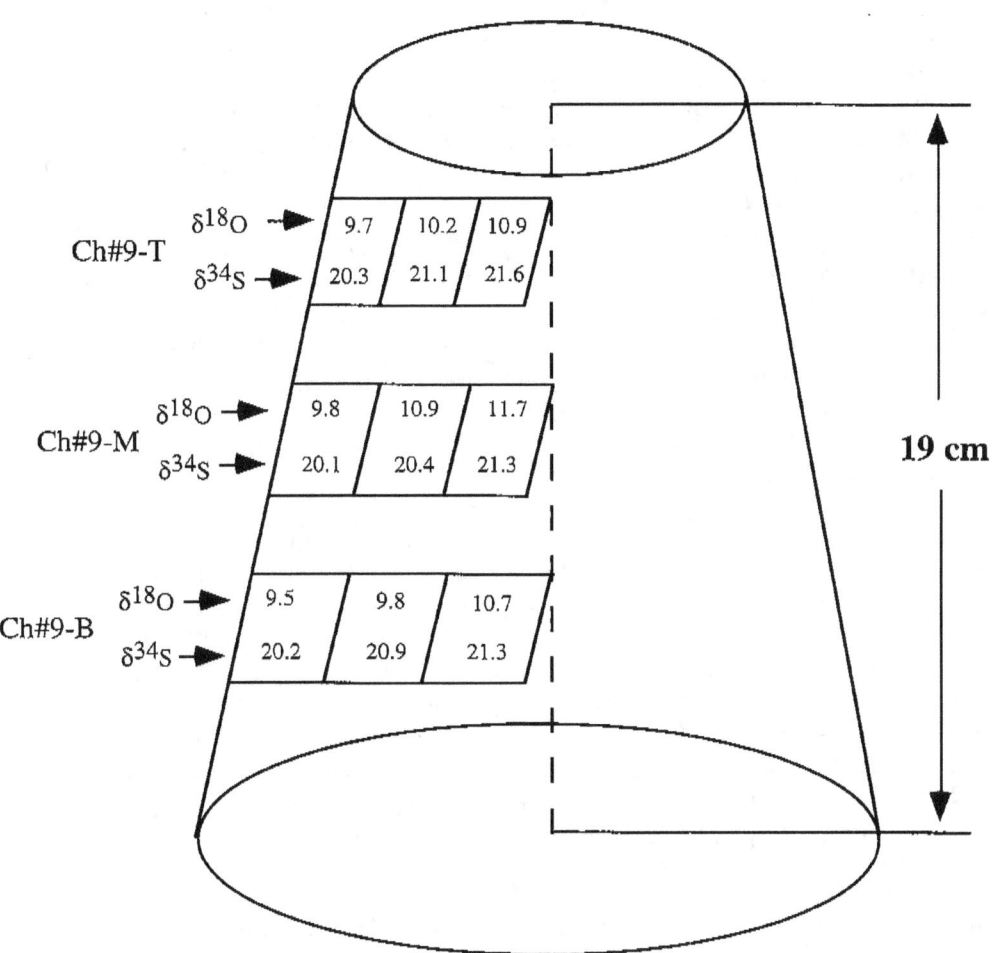

Figure 3.12. Sulfur and oxygen isotope compositions profile of chimney #9. Note: sulfur and oxygen isotope compositions of the barite increase laterally from the outer part to the inner part of the chimney.

upper layer is light gray and the lower layer exhibits a black or deep gray color. $\delta^{34}S$ and $\delta^{18}O$ values of the lower layers are generally higher than those of the upper layers (Table 3.5).

The $^{87}Sr/^{86}Sr$ ratios of barite chimneys and crusts range from 0.70845 to 0.70861 which are significantly lower than the ambient Gulf of Mexico deepwater (0.70917, Table 3.1); small regional variations in $^{87}Sr/^{86}Sr$ ratios exist between MC and GB sites. In general, barite chimneys and crusts from Garden Banks have higher $^{87}Sr/^{86}Sr$ ratios (0.70857 - 0.70861, n = 5) than chimneys and crusts from Mississippi Canyon (0.70845 - 0.70849, n = 3) Table 3.5 and Fig. 3.13).

The $\delta^{13}C$ compositions of carbonates occurring in the barite crusts range from -21.0 to -36.2^o/oo PDB (Table 3.5), which are substantially depleted in ^{13}C relative to the ambient seawater (0.6^o/oo).

3.2.4. Radioisotope Assays

Barite deposits including chimneys and crusts associated with hydrocarbon seeps in the Gulf of Mexico (Fig. 1.1) were examined with a portable gamma-ray detector (μR meter) which showed that they were unusually radioactive. These initial radioactivity measurements led to a more detailed gamma-ray spectrometric investigation which revealed that ^{226}Ra and ^{228}Ra were unsupported by their parents ^{238}U and ^{232}Th, respectively, and therefore can be considered orphans. The apparent ages of the barite samples, therefore, can be determined using the Ra decay series isotopes. Here we report the results of the $^{228}Th/^{228}Ra$ and $^{210}Pb/^{226}Ra$ daughter/parent assays which led to estimation of the chronology of these barite deposits and their growth rates. Some of the preliminary results shown here have already been published (Van Gent et al., 1995).

The isotope activities and ages obtained from soft and hardened barite chimneys are listed in Tables 3.6 and 3.7 and the ones from the barite crusts are reported in Table 3.8. All errors reported here are at the 95% confidence level (2 σ). The radioactivity unit used here is dpm/g (disintegration per minute/gram of material).

Two age nomenclatures are used here and in the following sections; measured age and sampling age. The measured age is based on the direct measurement data which represents the age from the formation of barite to the time of dating. Because samples were measured several years after collection, the sampling age which is corrected to the time of collection (July, 1993) is reported here in addition to the measured age. It must also be stated that an additional time-lag error was introduced during the calculation of the sampling age. This time-lag error depends on the amount of time that has elapsed between the time of collection and the time of measurement. Consequently the age error reported here for the sampling age is the maximum. Except when specified, ages reported below represent sampling ages.

Representative gamma spectra of barite chimneys and crusts, along with the gamma-ray spectra of uranium and thorium standards for the energy range from 750 keV to 1050 keV are shown in Figure 3.14. It follows that all the gamma-ray peaks of ^{226}Ra daughter nuclides occurring in the uranium standard also show up in both the barite chimneys and crusts. These gamma-ray peaks are primarily caused by ^{214}Pb (half life 26.8 min), ^{214}Bi (half life

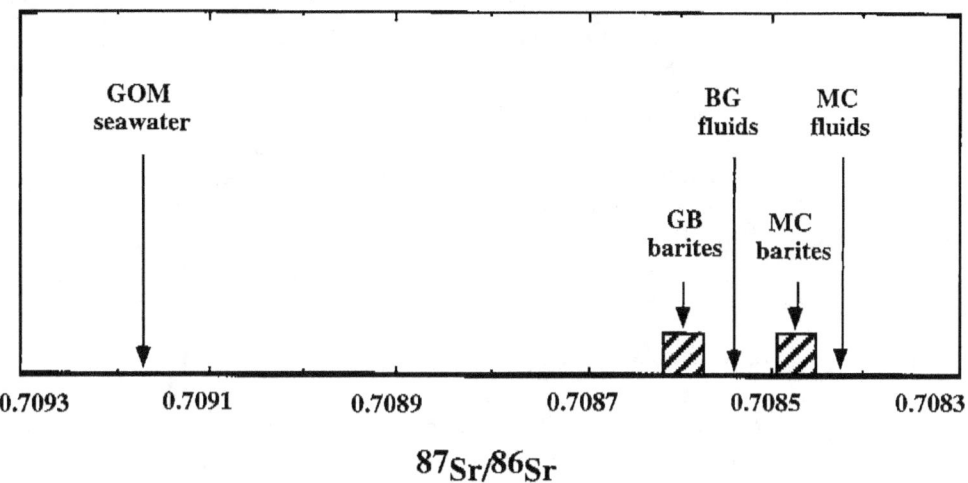

Figure 3.13. 87Sr/86Sr ratios of Gulf of Mexico barites and seawater. Notes: MC and GB represent Mississippi Canyon and Garden Banks, respectively. The 87Sr/86Sr ratios of MC and GB end member fluids are from Table 3.1.

19.7 min) and ^{210}Pb (half life 22.3 yr). The presence of ^{214}Pb with its short half life attests to the presence of ^{226}Ra in the barite chimneys and crusts.

Except for ^{232}Th at 59 keV, all the gamma-ray peaks occurring in the thorium standard spectrum are also observed in the barite chimneys (Fig. 3.14). These gamma rays are mainly caused by ^{228}Ac (half life 6.13 hr), ^{212}Pb (half life 10.6 hr), ^{212}Bi (half life 60.6 min) and ^{208}Tl (half life 3.05 min). The presence of the short lived ^{228}Ac daughter isotope is indicative of the presence of ^{228}Ra parent isotope in the barite chimneys.

In contrast to the chimneys, all the peaks in the thorium decay series observed in the thorium standard are absent in the typical barite crusts (Fig. 3.14). The absence of all the daughter nuclides of the Th decay series in the barite crusts is attributed to their older ages. As shown later, most barite crusts yield measured ages >15 years. Within this time frame, 95% of ^{228}Ra in the barites would have been decayed due to its relatively short half life (5.75 yr).

3.2.4.1. Soft and Fragmented Chimneys

Sixteen fragments from four barite chimneys (three from GB-382 and one from MC-929) were chosen for dating. A raw sample and a purified barite was prepared and analyzed for each of the 16 chimney fragments as indicated in Table 3.6. Since these samples represent chimneys which disintegrated during sampling, and the exact position of each fragment is uncertain, the ages yielded by the fragments do not represent the time when the chimneys started forming, but only reflect the age of the particular part of the chimney. Description of the chimneys and results follow.

Chimney #2, recovered from GB-382 (Fig. 1.1), was broken during sampling on the seafloor. The fragment used for dating of about 2 cm long, 4 cm wide and 3 cm thick, exhibited two sublayers: an inner dark-gray layer and an outer light-gray layer (Table 3.6). Microscope and SEM analyses indicate that both sublayers are dominated by barite but the inner layer (Ch#2-a) contains relatively more sulfide than the outer layer (Ch#2-b). The raw samples yield ^{228}Th/^{228}Ra ages of 1.26 ±0.06 years and 2.11 ±0.07 years for for Ch# 2-a and Ch#2-b, respectively. After barite purification, the ages were shifted to 0.93 ±0.06 and 1.94 ±0.08 years, respectively. Raw samples Ch#2-a and Ch#2-b yield ^{210}Pb/^{226}Ra ages of 2.52 ±2.39 and 0.55 ±2.23 years (see section 3.2.5 for a discussion of the reasons for large errors when dating chimneys using the ^{210}Pb/^{226}Ra method), respectively, and substantially younger ages for the purified barites (Table 3.6).

Chimney #9 and #10, recovered from GB-382, were well preserved during sampling at the seafloor but began to fall apart when unwrapped in the laboratory. The paired conical-shaped chimneys are of similar size; 18 to 19 cm in height and 7 to 10 cm in bottom diameter. Six subsamples from different sections of each chimney were used for dating and the results are listed in Table 3.6 and graphed in Figures 3.15 and 3.16. The ^{228}Th/^{228}Ra ages of the purified barites show a consistent trend in the vertical profiles with the ages becoming progressively younger from bottom (2.1 to 2.2 years old) to top of chimneys (1.3 to 1.2 years old). Generally the exterior samples yield older ages relative to the inner samples by amounts varying from 20 to 137% (Figs. 3.15 and 3.16) suggesting that the chimneys buildup started with the outer frame and then progressively infilled the inner conduits.

Table 3.6. Activities and ages of barite chimneys.

Sample name	Sample type	210Pb dpm/g	226Ra dpm/g	228Th dpm/g	228Ra dpm/g	210Pb/226Ra	228Th/228Ra	228Ra/226Ra	Measured 210Pb/226Ra age (yr)	Sampling 210Pb/226Ra age (yr)	Measured 228Th/228Ra age (yr)	Sampling 228Th/228Ra age (yr)	Initial 228Ra/226Ra ratio
Chimneys from Garden Banks block 382													
Ch#2-a	R	144	1088	643	774	0.133±0.032	0.831±0.004	0.718±0.001	4.601±2.388	2.518±2.388	3.341±0.056	1.258±0.056	1.074±0.017
Ch#2-a	P	113	1452	819	1135	0.079±0.058	0.722±0.006	0.789±0.001	2.636±4.066	0.553±4.066	2.716±0.064	0.933±0.064	1.094±0.020
Ch#2-b	R	102	1310	726	760	0.079±0.032	0.956±0.004	0.586±0.001	2.630±2.254	0.547±2.254	4.196±0.066	2.113±0.066	0.971±0.019
Ch#2-b	P	71	1184	624	690	0.061±0.040	0.904±0.006	0.588±0.001	2.013±2.292	-0.070±2.292	3.821±0.076	1.938±0.076	0.933±0.020
Ch#9-T/a	R	191	1305	848	906	0.146±0.041	0.936±0.005	0.694±0.002	5.075±3.084	1.965±3.084	4.052±0.080	0.942±0.080	1.131±0.028
Ch#9-T/a	P	170	1279	778	842	0.133±0.032	0.924±0.005	0.658±0.001	4.582±2.376	1.472±2.376	3.963±0.070	0.853±0.070	1.061±0.021
Ch#9-M/a	R	141	1178	739	791	0.120±0.029	0.935±0.006	0.672±0.002	4.124±2.116	1.014±2.116	4.041±0.091	0.931±0.091	1.093±0.031
Ch#9-M/a	P	153	1246	769	820	0.123±0.038	0.937±0.004	0.658±0.001	4.217±2.786	1.107±2.786	4.054±0.062	0.944±0.062	1.073±0.019
Ch#9-B/a	R	175	1401	876	838	0.125±0.027	1.045±0.005	0.598±0.002	4.294±1.980	0.994±1.980	4.942±0.094	1.642±0.094	1.085±0.032
Ch#9-B/a	P	115	1339	789	765	0.086±0.041	1.032±0.005	0.571±0.001	2.875±2.878	-0.425±2.878	4.825±0.091	1.525±0.091	1.021±0.026
Ch#9-T/b	R	151	1208	749	755	0.125±0.032	0.993±0.004	0.624±0.001	4.285±2.350	0.985±2.350	4.493±0.066	1.193±0.066	1.073±0.020
Ch#9-T/b	P	141	1229	707	708	0.115±0.031	0.998±0.004	0.576±0.002	3.921±2.258	0.621±2.258	4.534±0.072	1.234±0.072	0.995±0.024
Ch#9-M/b	R	153	1275	818	847	0.120±0.028	0.966±0.006	0.664±0.001	4.114±2.040	1.034±2.040	4.280±0.084	1.200±0.084	1.112±0.026
Ch#9-M/b	P	118	1346	788	822	0.088±0.037	0.958±0.006	0.611±0.001	2.979±2.604	-0.101±2.604	4.212±0.094	1.132±0.094	1.015±0.026
Ch#9-B/b	R	122	1170	756	772	0.105±0.039	0.979±0.005	0.666±0.001	3.568±1.398	1.485±1.398	4.376±0.074	2.293±0.074	1.129±0.025
Ch#9-B/b	P	116	1174	708	739	0.099±0.042	0.958±0.005	0.635±0.001	3.370±1.500	1.287±1.500	4.217±0.081	2.134±0.081	1.056±0.024
Ch#10-T/a	R	52	1236	784	1044	0.042±0.039	0.750±0.003	0.853±0.001	1.387±1.335	-0.696±1.335	2.871±0.032	0.718±0.032	1.205±0.012
Ch#10-T/a	P	44	1125	649	876	0.040±0.045	0.741±0.004	0.785±0.002	1.310±1.186	-0.773±1.186	2.819±0.042	0.666±0.042	1.103±0.017
Ch#10-M/a	R	136	1410	856	1168	0.097±0.036	0.733±0.002	0.836±0.001	3.102±1.281	1.209±1.281	2.777±0.026	0.694±0.026	1.169±0.010
Ch#10-M/a	P	121	1332	754	1041	0.092±0.036	0.724±0.003	0.788±0.001	3.232±1.273	1.019±1.273	2.729±0.034	0.646±0.034	1.095±0.012
Ch#10-B/a	R	104	1086	687	832	0.097±0.045	0.826±0.001	0.774±0.002	3.271±1.599	1.188±1.599	3.309±0.018	1.226±0.018	1.123±0.011
Ch#10-B/a	P	73	1250	709	967	0.059±0.039	0.733±0.001	0.781±0.001	1.956±1.354	-0.127±1.354	2.776±0.012	0.996±0.012	1.091±0.006
Ch#10-T/b	R	159	1307	854	873	0.122±0.038	0.978±0.002	0.668±0.001	4.192±2.810	0.972±2.810	4.372±0.036	1.152±0.036	1.132±0.013
Ch#10-T/b	P	156	1345	784	793	0.116±0.032	0.988±0.001	0.590±0.001	3.953±2.328	0.733±2.328	4.451±0.018	1.250±0.018	1.011±0.008
Ch#10-M/b	R	150	1171	752	728	0.128±0.042	1.034±0.001	0.621±0.003	4.385±3.106	1.165±3.106	4.843±0.018	1.623±0.018	1.114±0.016
Ch#10-M/b	P	147	1211	680	669	0.121±0.039	1.017±0.002	0.552±0.002	4.128±2.850	0.978±2.850	4.691±0.036	1.541±0.036	0.972±0.015
Ch#10-B/b	R	167	1297	980	908	0.129±0.041	1.079±0.001	0.700±0.001	4.424±3.038	1.274±3.038	5.265±0.021	2.115±0.021	1.321±0.027
Ch#10-B/b	P	160	1302	819	755	0.123±0.045	1.086±0.003	0.580±0.003	4.206±3.302	1.056±3.302	5.330±0.062	2.180±0.062	1.102±0.028
Chimneys from Mississippi Canyon block 929													
Ch#11-F/1	R	229	2464	1134	1112	0.094±0.031	1.020±0.002	0.456±0.001	3.167±1.101	1.084±1.101	4.716±0.028	2.633±0.028	0.804±0.028
Ch#11-F/1	P	348	3945	1670	1680	0.089±0.032	0.994±0.003	0.430±0.001	3.000±1.131	0.917±1.131	4.501±0.044	2.418±0.044	0.729±0.009
Ch#11-F/2	R	451	2769	1049	819	0.163±0.036	1.281±0.002	0.296±0.002	5.704±2.764	2.454±2.764	7.991±0.084	4.741±0.084	0.775±0.026
Ch#11-F/2	P	562	3697	1286	1011	0.152±0.032	1.273±0.002	0.273±0.001	5.311±2.400	2.061±2.400	7.841±0.074	4.564±0.074	0.701±0.018

Note: R = raw samples.

P = pure barite.

Measured age is obtained by the measured isotope ratio.

Sampling age = ages corrected to the time of sample collection.

Error = 2σ.

Table 3.7. Ages of hardened chimneys.

Sample	$^{228}Th/^{228}Ra$	$^{228}Ra/^{226}Ra$	Measured $^{228}Th/^{228}Ra$ age (yr)	Sampling $^{228}Th/^{228}Ra$ age (yr)	Initial $^{228}Ra/^{226}Ra$
Chimneys from Garden Banks block 382					
Ch#6-1	1.011±0.002	0.584±0.001	4.644±0.035	2.477±0.035	1.022±0.012
Ch#6-2	0.972±0.001	0.681±0.001	4.322±0.008	2.154±0.008	1.127±0.006
Ch#6-3	0.943±0.001	0.676±0.001	4.103±0.018	1.936±0.018	1.108±0.008
Ch#6-4	0.928±0.002	0.705±0.001	3.992±0.006	1.778±0.006	1.141±0.005
Ch#6-5	0.908±0.001	0.684±0.001	3.848±0.008	1.623±0.008	1.087±0.005
Ch#8-1	0.997±0.001	0.578±0.001	4.523±0.016	2.106±0.016	0.997±0.007
Ch#8-2	0.944±0.001	0.577±0.002	4.110±0.010	1.693±0.010	0.947±0.020
Ch#8-3	0.829±0.002	0.611±0.001	3.741±0.011	1.324±0.011	0.959±0.008
Ch#8-4	0.828±0.001	0.731±0.001	3.323±0.012	0.906±0.012	1.091±0.006
Ch#8-5	0.822±0.001	0.790±0.001	3.287±0.010	0.770±0.010	1.173±0.006
Ch#8-6	0.786±0.001	0.803±0.002	3.073±0.008	0.656±0.008	1.163±0.007
Ch#8-7	0.743±0.001	0.826±0.001	2.832±0.016	0.415±0.016	1.162±0.007
Chimney from Mississippi Canyon block 929					
Ch#11-1	1.357±0.004	0.186±0.001	9.775±0.232	6.442±0.232	0.605±0.040
Ch#11-2	1.312±0.001	0.241±0.001	8.619±0.018	5.286±0.018	0.681±0.009
Ch#11-3	1.281±0.002	0.236±0.001	7.983±0.018	4.650±0.018	0.617±0.008
Ch#11-4	1.257±0.002	0.312±0.002	7.547±0.010	4.214±0.010	0.775±0.012
Ch#11-5	1.244±0.001	0.322±0.001	7.330±0.004	3.997±0.004	0.779±0.006

Notes: Measured age is based on the direct measurement data which represents the age from the formation of barite to the time of dating. Sampling age is corrected to the time of sample collection (July, 1993).

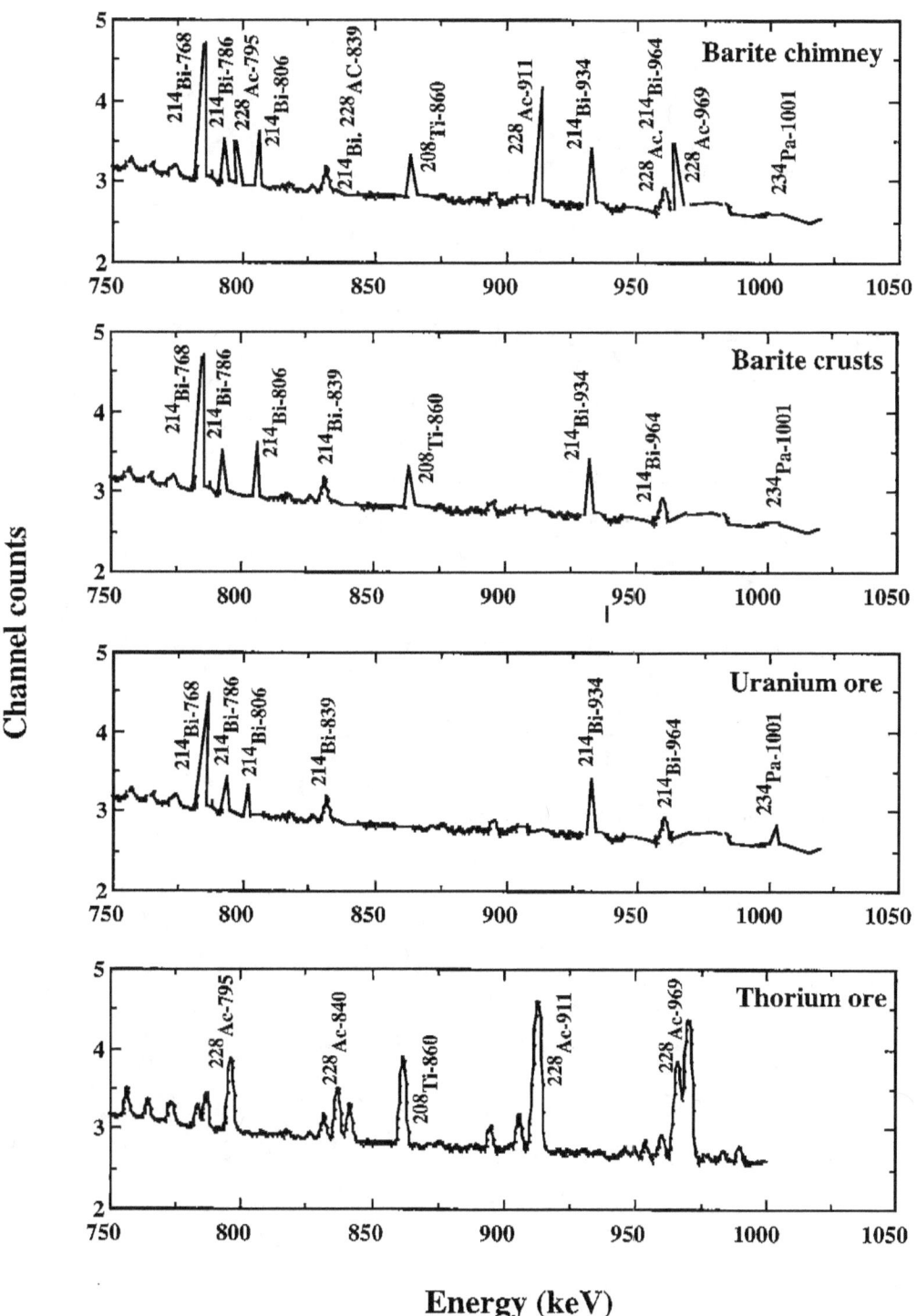

Figure 3.14. Gamma-ray spectra of uranium, thorium ore standards and GOM barite chimneys and crusts.

52

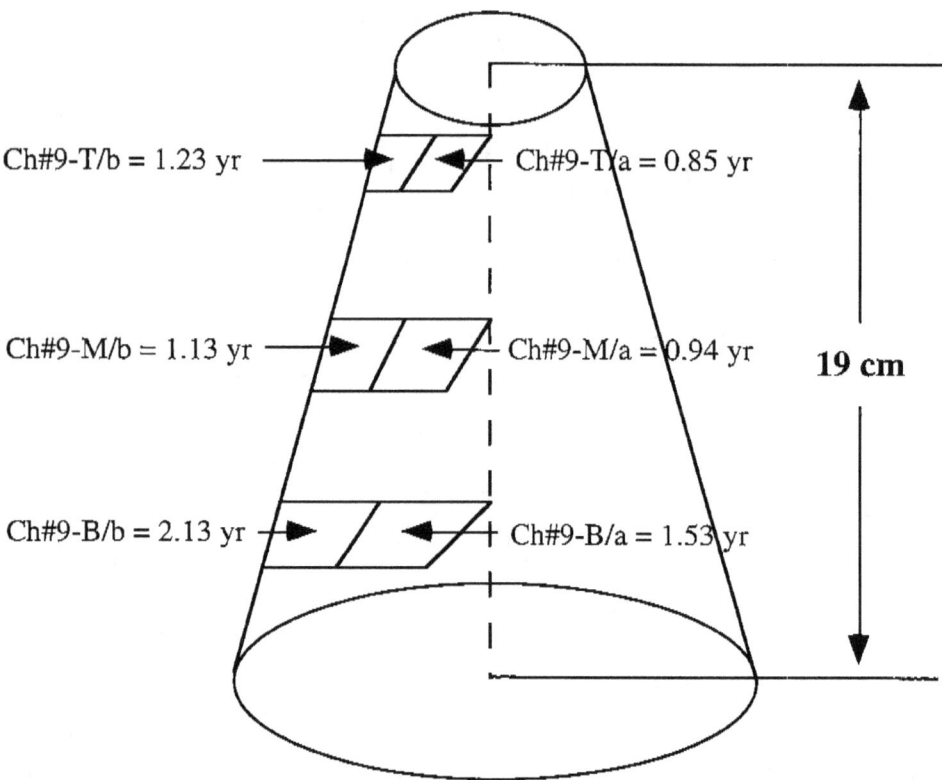

Ch#9-T/b = 1.23 yr

Ch#9-T/a = 0.85 yr

Ch#9-M/b = 1.13 yr

Ch#9-M/a = 0.94 yr

Ch#9-B/b = 2.13 yr

Ch#9-B/a = 1.53 yr

19 cm

Figure 3.15. Chimney #9 from Garden Banks block 382. The ages shown here are based on the ^{228}Th/^{228}Ra assays.

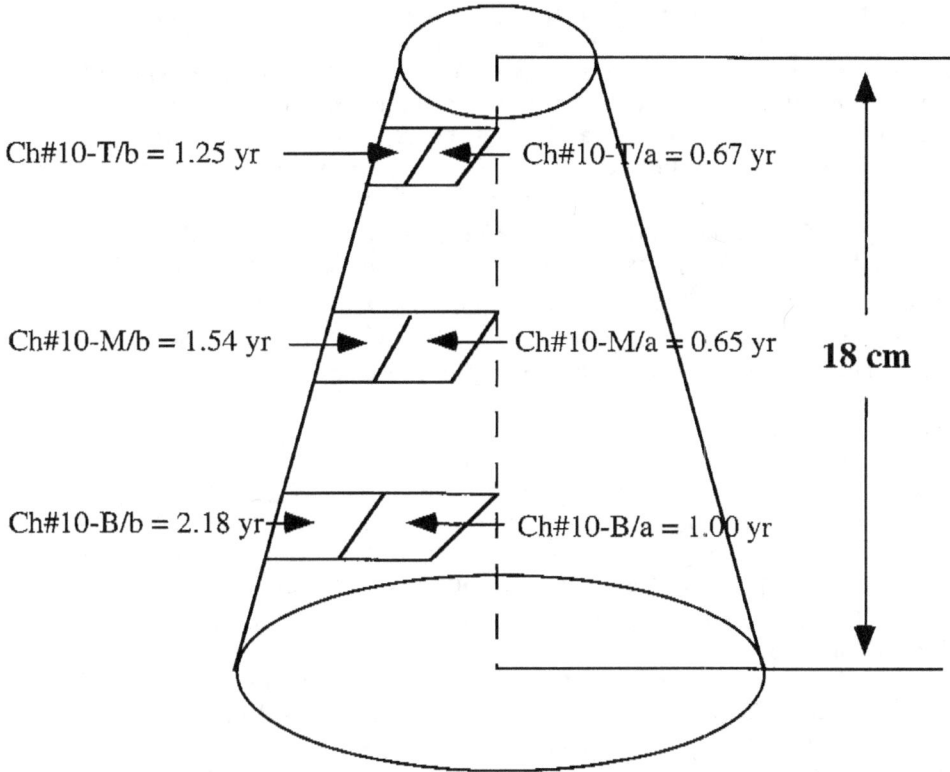

Ch#10-T/b = 1.25 yr — Ch#10-T/a = 0.67 yr

Ch#10-M/b = 1.54 yr — Ch#10-M/a = 0.65 yr

Ch#10-B/b = 2.18 yr — Ch#10-B/a = 1.00 yr

18 cm

Figure 3.16. Chimney #10 from Garden Banks block 382. The ages shown here are based on the ^{228}Th/^{228}Ra assays.

In general, purified barites yield $^{210}Pb/^{226}Ra$ ages comparable to the $^{228}Th/^{228}Ra$ ages in chimney #9 but yield discordant ages in chimney #10, including some "negative" ages. The negative values in conjunction with the large errors clearly indicate that the $^{210}Pb/^{226}Ra$ ages of chimneys are unreliable.

Chimney #11 is the only one recovered from MC-929. The conical-shaped chimney is 11 cm in height and its base and top diameters are 10 cm and 3 cm, respectively. Two fragments (Ch#11-F/1 and Ch#11-F/2) from the outside of the chimney (sampled before hardening) were dated. The whole chimney was later hardened with resin and the dating profile based on the hardened samples was also obtained (see below). The purified barites yield $^{228}Th/^{228}Ra$ ages of 4.56 ±0.07 and 2.42 ±0.04 years for base and top of chimney (Table 3.6) while the corresponding $^{210}Pb/^{226}Ra$ ages are 2.06 ±2.40 and 0.92 ±1.13 years, respectively. The effects of barite purification on the $^{210}Pb/^{226}Ra$ age determinations can also be gauged for these samples (Table 3.6).

3.2.4.2 Hardened Chimneys

Three barite chimneys (chimneys# 6 and #8 from GB-382 and chimney #11 from MC-929) were resin-hardened and sliced vertically. Subsamples at 2 to 3 cm intervals were sectioned along the growth bands from each chimney and were subjected to radioisotope analyses for the purpose of obtaining $^{228}Th/^{228}Ra$ ages. The analytical data for these chimneys are listed in Table 3.7 and graphed in Figures 3.17, 3.18, and 3.19.

Chimneys #6 and #8, recovered in pair from GB-382, are 15 and 20 cm tall and the base and top diameters of the cones are 7 to 8 cm and 4 cm, respectively. The $^{228}Th/^{228}Ra$ ages of five distinct growth bands from chimney #6 and eight from chimney #8 decrease systematically from the base to the top as follows: 2.48 ±0.04 and 2.11±0.02 years at the bases to 1.62 ±0.01 and 0.42 ±0.02 years at the top, respectively (Figs. 3.17 & 3.18).

Chimney #11, the only specimen recovered from MC-929, is a cone-shaped, 18 cm tall chimney with 14 cm and 5 cm diameters at the base and top, respectively. The $^{228}Th/^{228}Ra$ ages of five growth bands decrease systematically from 6.44 ±0.23 years at the base to 4.00 ± 0.01 years at the top (Fig. 3.19).

3.2.4.3 Barite Crusts

Barite crusts occur either on the flanks of mud volcanoes or as tee-pees covering the seafloor. Unlike the chimneys which are predominantly barite (>95% by volume), the crusts also contain variable amounts of carbonates and sulfides. Six crust samples, four from GB-382 and two from MC-929, were recovered for radioisotope assays and both raw and purified barites were analyzed. With the exception of Cr-93-1-3/1, all other crusts contain ^{228}Ra and ^{228}Th activity levels below our detection limit and therefore only the $^{210}Pb/^{226}Ra$ ages were determined (Table 3.8).

The light-gray Cr-93-7-7/1 crust was recovered from the flank of an active mud volcano in GB-382. An age of 29.67±2.40 years was obtained for the raw sample and a younger age of 12.17±1.39 years for the purified barite.

The Cr-93-8-5/3 crust, occurring as a teepee draping the seafloor, was recovered from GB-382. The crust is about 7 cm thick and displays two distinct

Sample name	Age (yrs)	Initial $^{228}Ra/^{226}Ra$
Ch#6-5	1.62±0.01	1.09±0.01
Ch#6-4	1.78±0.01	1.14±0.01
Ch#6-3	1.94±0.02	1.11±0.01
Ch#6-2	2.15±0.01	1.13±0.01
Ch#6-1	2.48±0.04	1.02±0.01

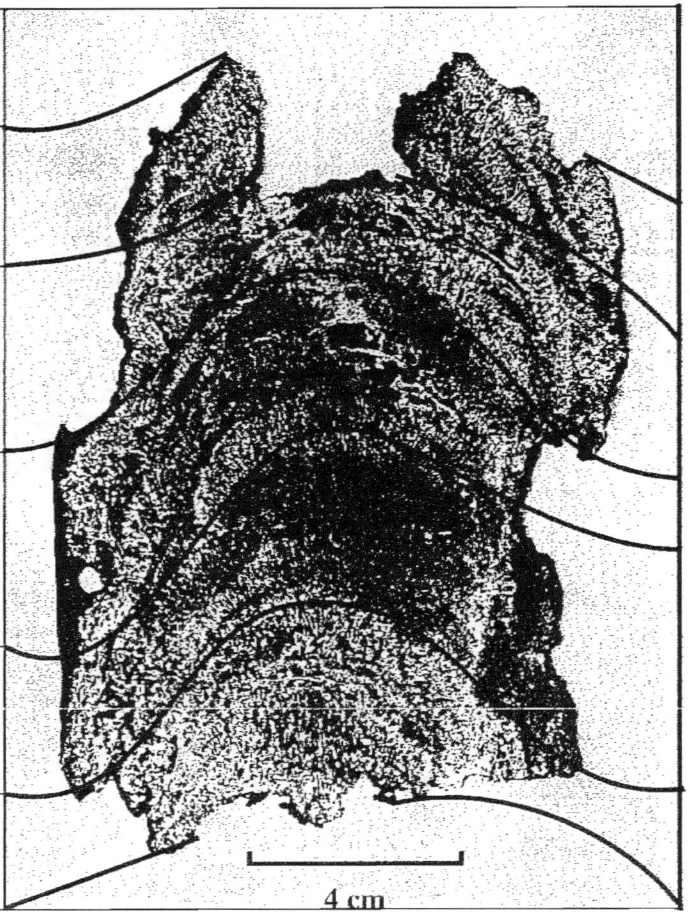

Figure 3.17. Dating profile of growth increments in barite chimney# 6 from Garden Banks Block 382 using the $^{228}Th/^{228}Ra$ method. Ages were corrected to July 20, 1993 when the chimney was sampled.

56

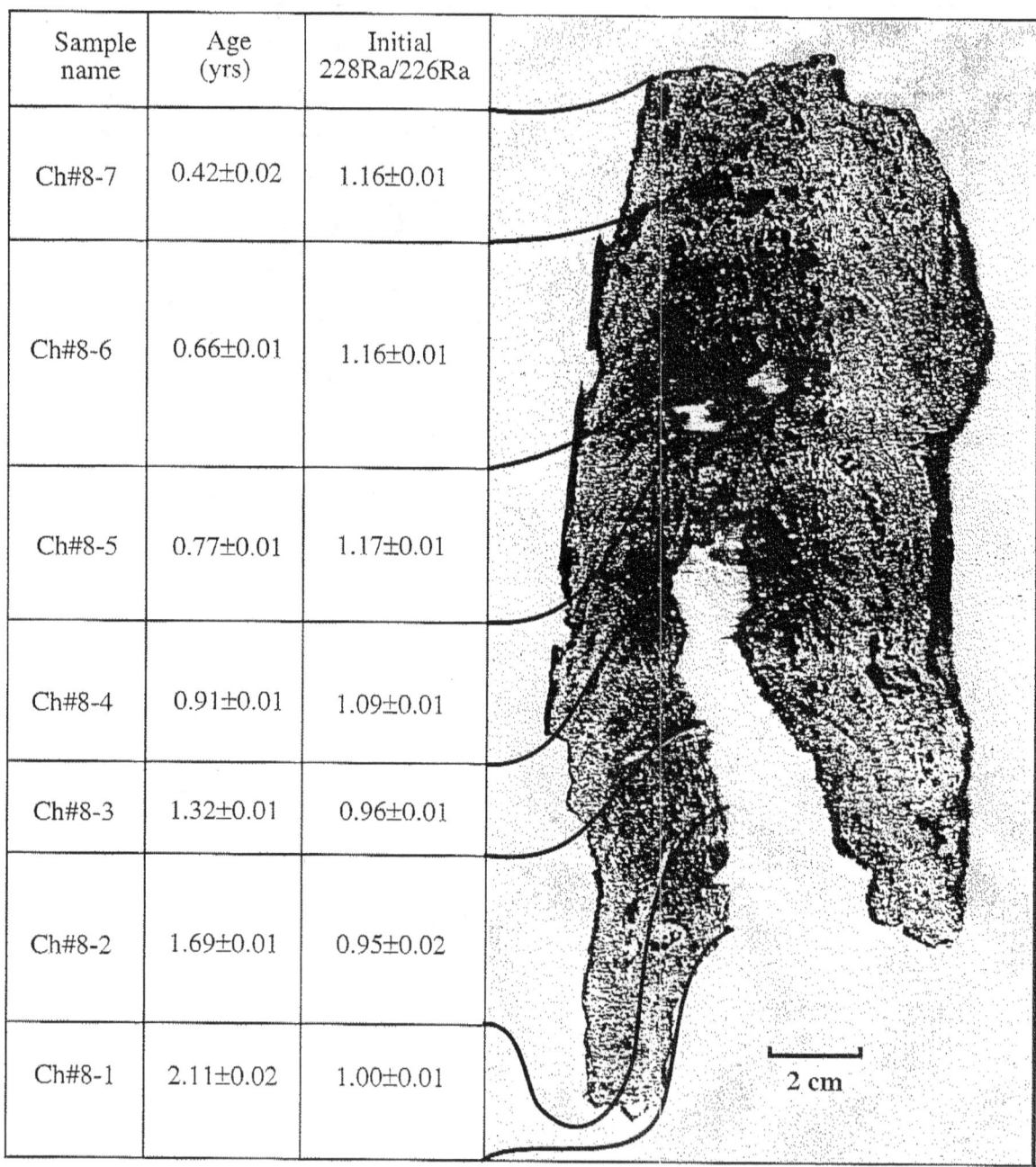

Sample name	Age (yrs)	Initial 228Ra/226Ra
Ch#8-7	0.42±0.02	1.16±0.01
Ch#8-6	0.66±0.01	1.16±0.01
Ch#8-5	0.77±0.01	1.17±0.01
Ch#8-4	0.91±0.01	1.09±0.01
Ch#8-3	1.32±0.01	0.96±0.01
Ch#8-2	1.69±0.01	0.95±0.02
Ch#8-1	2.11±0.02	1.00±0.01

Figure 3.18. Dating profile of growth increments in barite chimney# 8 from Garden Banks block 382 using ^{228}Th/^{228}Ra method. Ages were corrected to July 20, 1993 when the chimney was sampled.

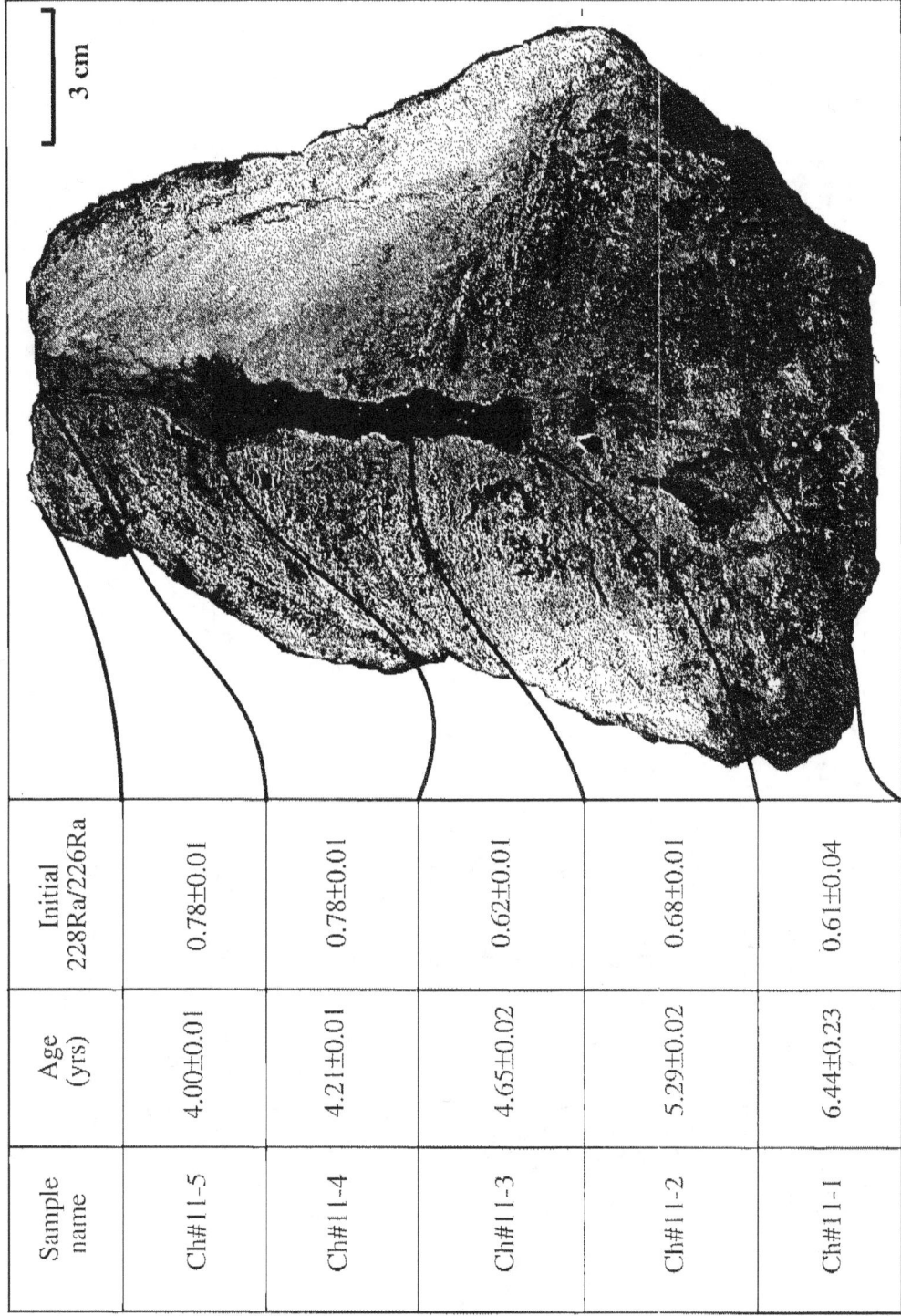

Sample name	Age (yrs)	Initial 228Ra/226Ra
Ch#11-5	4.00±0.01	0.78±0.01
Ch#11-4	4.21±0.01	0.78±0.01
Ch#11-3	4.65±0.02	0.62±0.01
Ch#11-2	5.29±0.02	0.68±0.01
Ch#11-1	6.44±0.23	0.61±0.04

Figure 3.19. Dating profile of growth increments in barite chimney #11 from Mississippi Canyon block 929 using 228Th/228Ra method. Ages were corrected to July 20, 1993 when the chimney was sampled.

Table 3.8. Activities and ages of barite crusts.

Sample name	Sample type	^{210}Pb dpm/g	^{226}Ra dpm/g	^{228}Th dpm/g	^{228}Ra dpm/g	^{210}Pb/^{226}Ra	Measured ^{228}Ra/^{226}Ra	Measured ^{210}Pb/^{226}Ra age (yr)	Sampling ^{210}Pb/^{226}Ra age (yr)
Barite crusts from Garden Banks block 382									
Cr-93-7-7/1	R	553	887	-	-	0.629±0.014	-	31.6±2.4	29.7±2.4
Cr-93-7-7/1	P	476	1352	-	-	0.356±0.014	-	14.1±1.4	12.2±1.4
Cr-93-8-5/3/u	R	1165	1475	-	-	0.797±0.004	-	50.3±1.2	48.4±1.2
Cr-93-8-5/3/u	P	816	1545	-	-	0.533±0.002	-	24.3±0.3	22.4±0.3
Cr-93-8-5/3/l	R	862	1381	-	-	0.629±0.006	-	31.6±1.0	29.7±1.0
Cr-93-8-5/3/l	P	761	1502	-	-	0.511±0.005	-	22.9±0.7	21.0±0.7
Cr-93-8-7/2/u	R	511	672	-	-	0.768±0.011	-	46.2±2.9	44.2±2.9
Cr-93-8-7/2/u	P	449	1203	-	-	0.376±0.013	-	15.1±1.3	13.2±1.3
Cr-93-8-7/2/l	R	382	269	-	-	1.431±0.048	-	-	-
Cr-93-8-7/2/l	P	640	1725	-	-	0.374±0.021	-	15.0±2.1	13.1±2.1
Cr-93-8-7/3	R	292	145	-	-	2.038±0.070	-	-	-
Cr-93-8-7/3	P	654	1271	-	-	0.519±0.015	-	23.4±1.9	21.5±1.9
Barite crusts from Mississippi Canyon block 929									
Cr-93-1-3/l	R	705	1934	-	262	0.368±0.006	0.135±0.010	14.7±0.6	12.8±0.6
Cr-93-1-3/l	P	1085	3797	-	180	0.288±0.005	0.047±0.009	10.9±0.5	9.0±0.5
Cr-93-4-4/1/u	R	2443	2434	-	-	1.013±0.005	-	-	-
Cr-93-4-4/1/u	P	1451	2701	-	-	0.542±0.002	-	24.9±0.2	23.1±0.3
Cr-93-4-4/1/l	R	1374	689	-	-	2.013±0.005	-	-	-
Cr-93-4-4/1/l	P	2002	3940	-	-	0.513±0.001	-	23.0±0.1	21.1±0.1

Notes: R= raw sample.

P = pure barite

- = below detection limit.

Measured age is obtained by the measured isotope ratio.

Sampling age = age corrected to the time of sample collection.

sublayers; an upper light-gray (Cr-93-8-5/3/u) overlying a black-colored (Cr-93-8-5/3/l) layer buried within the sediment at the time of sampling. Raw samples Cr-93-8-5/3/u and Cr-93-8-5/3/l yield ages of 29.72 ±1.02 and 48.39 ±1.20 years, respectively. Purification of samples caused a significant reduction of the $^{210}Pb/^{226}Ra$ ages to 22.42 ±0.27 years and 20.99 ±0.66 years for Cr-93-8-5/3/u and Cr-93-8-5/3/l, respectively.

Crust Cr-93-8-7/2 was collected from the wall of a small depression in the GB-382. The crust is about 8 cm thick and exhibits an upper light-gray colored layer (Cr 93-8-7/2/u) overlying a black-colored lower layer (Cr-93-8-7/2/l). The raw sample Cr-93-8-7/2/u yields an age of 44.23 ±2.92 years which is about 30 years older than the purified barite age of 13.22 ±1.33 years. The measured $^{210}Pb/^{226}Ra$ activity ratio of the Cr-93-8-7/2/l raw sample is 1.43 indicating the presence of excess ^{210}Pb unsupported by the decay of the measured ^{226}Ra. The measured $^{210}Pb/^{226}Ra$ activity ratio after purification was reduced to 0.37 which yields a corresponding age of 13.11±2.13 years. Crust Cr-93-8-7/3 was recovered from a different part of the same depression where Cr-93-8-7/2 was sampled. The measured $^{210}Pb/^{226}Ra$ of the raw sample is 2.04 which indicates an excess of unsupported ^{210}Pb. The measured $^{210}Pb/^{226}Ra$ after purification decreased to 0.52 and yields an age of 21.50 ±1.97 years.

Crusts Cr-93-1-3/1 and Cr-93-4-4/1 were sampled from the flank of a mud volcano in MC-929 and were serving as substrate for methanotrophic mussels. Microscope and SEM analyses indicate that Cr-93-1-3/1 contains a large proportion of carbonates (about 50% by volume) in addition to barite. This is the only crust measured in the study containing detectable ^{228}Ra but no $^{228}Th/^{228}Ra$ age was obtained due to low concentrations of ^{228}Th. The $^{210}Pb/^{226}Ra$ age of the raw Cr-93-1-3/1 sample is 12.79 ±0.61 years and 9.00 ±0.45 years for the purified barite.

Crust Cr-93-4-4/1 is about 10 cm thick and consists of an upper light gray layer (Cr-93-4-4/1/u) and a lower dark layer (Cr-93-4-4/1/l). No $^{210}Pb/^{226}Ra$ ages were obtained for the raw samples because their measured $^{210}Pb/^{226}Ra$ were >1 (Table 3.8). The measured $^{210}Pb/^{226}Ra$ after purification were reduced to 0.54 and 0.51 which gave corresponding ages of 23.05 ±0.25 and 21.07 ±0.13 years for Cr-93-4-4/1/u and Cr-93-4-4/1/l, respectively.

3.2.5. Validation of the Ra-Series Dating Methods

The accuracy of $^{228}Th/^{228}Ra$ and $^{210}Pb/^{226}Ra$ ages in barites depends upon the validity of the following assumptions: (i) ^{226}Ra and ^{228}Ra in the barites must be orphans; (ii) there must be no initial ^{228}Th and ^{210}Pb in the barites (i.e., they must be fully supported by their respective ^{228}Ra and ^{226}Ra parents), and (iii) the system must have remained closed with respect to the radioactive nuclides, ^{228}Ra, ^{228}Th, ^{226}Ra, and ^{210}Pb since the formation of the barites.

In order to check the validity of the first assumption above, gamma-ray spectra of uranium and thorium standards were compared with those of barite chimneys and crusts (Fig. 3.14). It is important to note that the gamma peak at 1001 keV from ^{234}Pa in the uranium standard spectrum is absent in both the chimney and crust spectra. As ^{234}Pa reaches equilibrium with ^{238}U within few months (the intermediate isotope ^{234}Th has a 24.1 day half life), this indicates that ^{238}U is absent or at a very low concentration in the barites. Furthermore, the gamma peak at 67.7 keV from ^{230}Th occurring in the uranium standard spectrum is also absent in the barite spectra. These features confirm that ^{226}Ra in the barites is unsupported (orphan).

The gamma peak of ^{232}Th at 59 keV is present in the thorium standard spectrum but it is absent in both the barite chimney and crust spectra (outside the energy range of Fig. 3.14). This observation indicates that ^{228}Ra in the barites is unsupported (orphan) as well.

In order to determine whether or not initial ^{228}Th was present in the barites, the dating of five barite chimney samples were repeated two years after the initial dating measurements. If significant initial ^{228}Th were present, the ^{228}Th/^{228}Ra ages measured at about 2 years interval should yield a large discrepancy because of the short half life of ^{228}Th (1.91 yr). The experimental data are summarized in Table 3.9 and are plotted in Figure 3.20. It is noted that the two sets of ages of the same samples agree within a 13% margin of error (error calculated on the basis of data in Table 3.9) and converge along a line with a slope of 1 (Fig. 3.20) thus confirming that the barites contain a negligible initial ^{228}Th. Therefore all the ^{228}Th in the barites can be considered to be supported by the decay of ^{228}Ra and the ^{228}Th/^{228}Ra ages are regarded as valid.

As shown later, some ^{210}Pb, unsupported by the decay of ^{226}Ra, do occur in the raw barite samples but most of the excess ^{210}Pb is hosted in the sulfide rather than in the barite phase. Therefore it is assumed that the initial ^{210}Pb in the sulfide-free purified barites is insignificant. This assumption is supported by the observation that all the young chimneys yield concordant ^{210}Pb/^{226}Ra and ^{228}Th/^{228}Ra ages (Table 3.6), although the ^{210}Pb/^{226}Ra ages of the chimneys have only qualitative values.

The third assumption above states that the ^{228}Th derived by decay of ^{228}Ra, and the ^{210}Pb derived by decay of ^{226}Ra do not migrate after the formation of the barites. In most cases the migration of daughter isotopes from minerals is attributed to alpha recoil (Kigoshi, 1971) but the decay of ^{228}Ra and ^{228}Ac (^{228}Ac is used to determine the ^{228}Ra activity) is by beta emission which causes the recoil energy associated with the ^{228}Th production to be insignificant (Stakes & Moore, 1991). In contrast, the decays of ^{226}Ra and ^{228}Th are by alpha emission and if the system is leaking because of alpha recoiling, the most probable leakage is likely by gaseous ^{222}Rn in the ^{226}Ra decay series and by gaseous ^{220}Rn in the ^{228}Ra decay series. Leakage of ^{222}Rn and ^{220}Rn could definitely affect both ^{228}Th/^{228}Ra and ^{210}Pb/^{226}Ra dating methods. This is because in the ^{210}Pb/^{226}Ra method, both ^{214}Pb which is used to calculate the ^{226}Ra activity and ^{210}Pb are the daughters of ^{222}Rn, whereas in the ^{228}Th/^{228}Ra method the activity of ^{228}Th is calculated from the activity of ^{212}Pb which is the daughter of ^{220}Rn.

A test of the potential loss of ^{220}Rn and ^{222}Rn in the barites was made by monitoring for 10 days the gamma-ray emission of a sealed barite sample. The results showed a leakage of less than 0.05% of Rn which indicates an

Table 3.9. Results of repeat dating of chimneys.

Sample name	Date of measurement	^{228}Th (dpm/g)	^{228}Ra (dpm/g)	^{228}Th/^{228}Ra	Measured ^{228}Th/^{228}Ra age (yr)	Sampling ^{228}Th/^{228}Ra age (yr)
First dating						
Ch#2-a	Apr-95	819	1135	0.772±0.006	2.72±0.06	0.93±0.06
Ch#2-b	May-95	624	690	0.904±0.006	3.82±0.08	1.94±0.08
Ch#9-B/b	Aug-95	708	739	0.958±0.005	4.22±0.08	2.13±0.08
Ch#10-T/b	Sep-96	784	793	0.988±0.001	4.45±0.02	1.25±0.02
Ch#10-B/b	Sep-96	819	755	1.086±0.003	5.33±0.06	2.18±0.06
Second dating						
Ch#2-a	Feb-98	955	860	1.110±0.005	5.58±0.11	1.08±0.11
Ch#2-b	Feb-98	684	570	1.200±0.003	6.67±0.08	2.10±0.08
Ch#9-B/b	Feb-98	647	535	1.210±0.006	6.81±0.09	2.31±0.09
Ch#10-T/b	Feb-98	620	559	1.110±0.004	5.59±0.09	1.09±0.09
Ch#10-B/b	Feb-98	727	599	1.214±0.003	6.87±0.09	2.00±0.08

See Table 3.7 for explanation of measured and sampling ages.

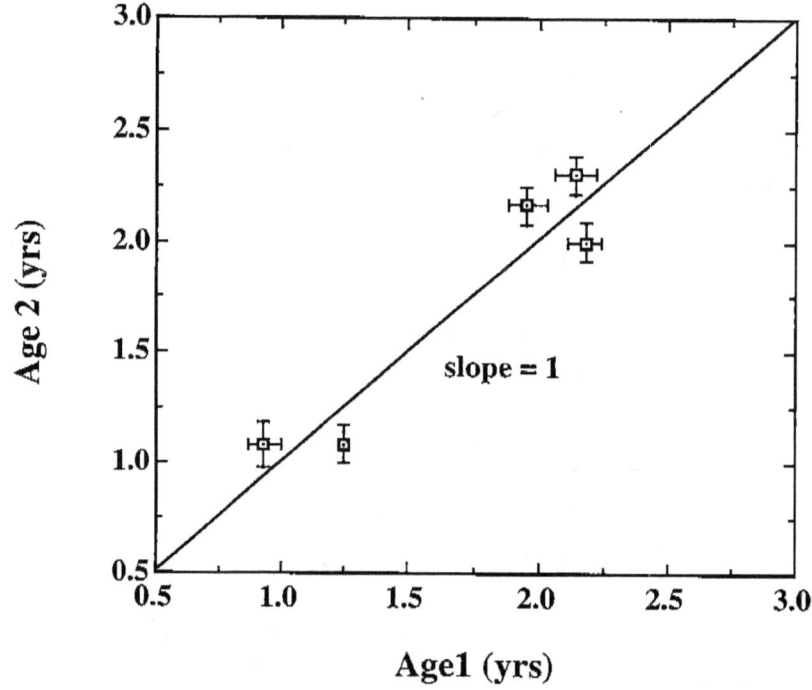

Figure 3.20. Relationship between the first and second $^{228}Th/^{228}Ra$ dating of pure barites. The second dating was performed two years after the first dating. The ages are sampling ages. Data converge along the line with a slope of 1:1 indicating that the initial ^{228}Th in the barites is negligible.

insignificant loss of radon decay products in the barites. Therefore, the barites can be considered a closed system for all practical purposes.

In summary, all three assumptions for both $^{228}Th/^{228}Ra$ and $^{210}Pb/^{226}Ra$ dating methods are satisfied and the barite ages reported here are considered reliable.

3.2.6. $^{210}Pb/^{226}Ra$ Ages

The $^{210}Pb/^{226}Ra$ method has been applied here to derive the ages of barite chimney fragments and barite crusts (Tables 3.6 and 3.8). The $^{210}Pb/^{226}Ra$ ages of purified barites, plotted in Figure 3.21, show that the ages of chimneys range from 0 (some chimneys yielding negative ages) to 2.5 years, whereas the age of the crusts range from 9.0 to 22.5 years old. Because the half life of ^{210}Pb is 22.3 years, serious questions arise as to the accuracy of this technique when applied to young barite chimneys (<5 yrs). As shown in Figure 3.21, large analytical errors (up to 77%) in age determinations occur when calculating the chimney ages. In addition, some chimneys yield negative ages (e.g. -0.13 yr for Ch# 10-B/a) which are impossible. All these features are attributed to the low activity of ^{210}Pb in the chimneys due to their young ages which makes it harder for the instrument to detect the nuclide and hence causes serious statistical errors. Additionally, the gamma peak at 46.52 keV measured for ^{210}Pb is significantly attenuated because of self absorption at low energy. Therefore, the $^{210}Pb/^{226}Ra$ pair is not an appropriate technique for quantitatively dating young chimneys. These disadvantages, however, do not preclude the method's qualitative value in estimating the approximate age of chimneys; all the chimneys that have low $^{210}Pb/^{226}Ra$ are also very young which is confirmed by the $^{228}Th/^{228}Ra$ dating method (Tables 3.6 and 3.8).

Whereas the $^{210}Pb/^{226}Ra$ method is inaccurate for determining the age of young chimneys, the following observations suggest that the $^{210}Pb/^{226}Ra$ ages of purified crust barites are reliable. First, all the crust samples exhibit strong ^{210}Pb peaks due to their relative older ages (measured ages >15 yr) which greatly reduce the analytical errors (<10%). Second, most barite crusts yield $^{210}Pb/^{226}Ra$ ages older than 15 years and this is consistent with the observation that most of the crusts are lacking ^{228}Th and ^{228}Ra (Table 3.8).

One interesting aspect of the $^{210}Pb/^{226}Ra$ dating method is that the barite purification procedure appears to affect its age determination. It is noted that the purified barite ages of both chimneys and crusts tend to be younger than those of their matching raw samples (Table 3.6 and 3.8). A comparison of $^{210}Pb/^{226}Ra$ data of raw and purified barites in Figure 3.22 indicates that all the chimney samples converge along the line with a slope of 1 whereas the crusts deviate significantly from the line. This observation indicates that the raw crust barites yield ages much older than those of the purified barites and hence produce anomalous and biased results. These discrepancies suggest that some ^{210}Pb in the raw samples are not supported by indigenous ^{226}Ra decay. The inference is confirmed by the fact that some raw barite crusts possess $^{210}Pb/^{226}Ra$ >1 (e.g. 2.01 for Cr-93-4-4/1-1; 2.04 for Cr-93-8-7/3; and 1.43 for Cr-93-8-7/2), which are impossible if the only source of ^{210}Pb is from the decay of the parent ^{226}Ra indigenous to the sample.

64

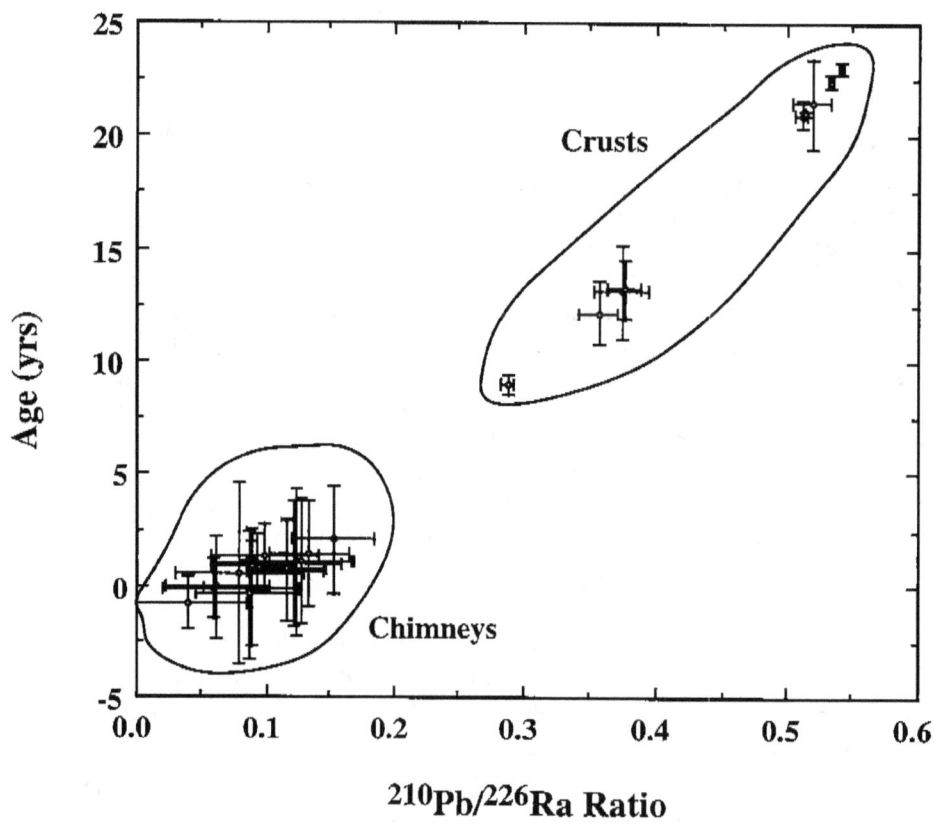

Figure 3.21. ^{210}Pb/^{226}Ra ages of pure barites. Bars represent 2σ errors.

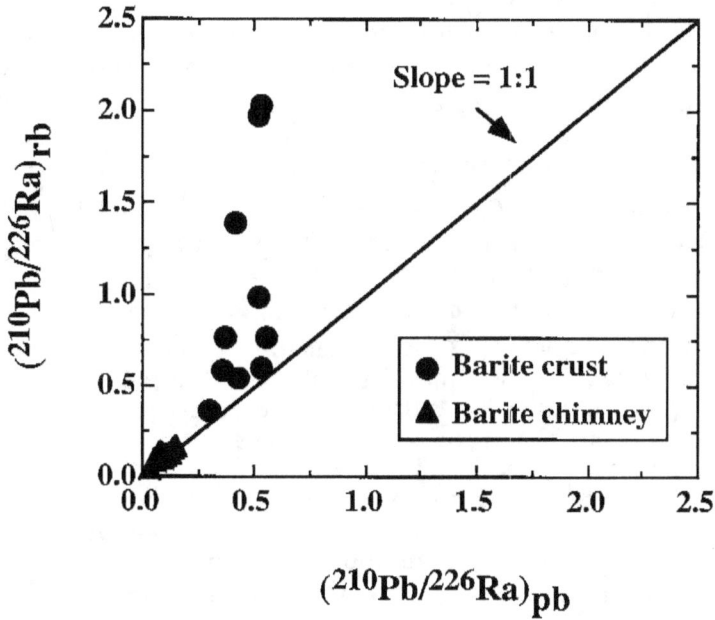

Figure 3.22. $^{210}Pb/^{226}Ra$ of barites before (rb) and after (pb) purification. Note that all the barite chimneys are on the 1:1 line whereas most crust data are above the 1:1 line. This indicates that raw crust samples tend to give spurious ages.

Another question that needs to be addressed is the exact source of excess ^{210}Pb in the raw barite crusts. Microscope and SEM analyses indicate that the most abundant minerals other than barite in the crusts are carbonates and sulfides. Since Pb has two oxidation states (+2 and +4) and could react with sulfide to form PbS, it is not unreasonable to assume that sulfide in the crusts may act as a Pb sink which accounts for the excess ^{210}Pb in the raw samples. This inference is confirmed by the observed relationship between the concentration of sulfides and the degree of discrepancy in ^{210}Pb/^{226}Ra data before and after barite purification (Table 3.10 and Fig. 3.23) indicating that the higher the sulfide concentration in the sample, the larger the discrepancy of ^{210}Pb/^{226}Ra before and after barite purification. This positive relationship strongly suggests that the excess of ^{210}Pb in the raw samples stems from the Pb association with sulfides in the crusts.

The excess ^{210}Pb added to the sulfide coexisting with the barite is likely to have originated from the decay of ^{222}Rn emanating from the venting fluids. This contention is supported by the study of LaRock et al., 1996) which indicates that Pb coprecipitates with sulfide if the hydrogen sulfide concentrations are high. As it will be discussed later, microbial sulfate reduction plays an important role in the formation of the barite crusts. Because hydrogen sulfide is one of the two main by-products of microbial sulfate reduction, the hydrogen sulfide concentration remains high during the formation of the barite crusts. In addition, the advecting fluids in the barite-bearing seeps are likely to be enriched in ^{222}Rn due to the high concentration of ^{226}Ra in the seeping fluids (Table 3.3, and Fu et al., 1996). Thus when radon gas diffuses through the crusts, ^{210}Pb will rapidly deposit because the half life of ^{222}Rn is 3.82 days and all the intermediate isotopes have half life are less than an hour. This ^{210}Pb will react with the hydrogen sulfide resulting from the microbial sulfate reduction and precipitate as pyrite. Because the ^{210}Pb in the sulfides had not originated from the decay of ^{226}Ra in barites, the exogenous or excess ^{210}Pb in the sulfide coexisiting with barite will make the ^{210}Pb/^{226}Ra of the raw sample larger than that of purified sample and hence yield a spurious age.

The purification of barites outlined previously removes carbonates, organic matter and fine sulfides from the raw sample and effectively removes exogenous ^{210}Pb. Thus the ^{210}Pb/^{226}Ra dating method can be accurately applied to the crust barites and yield true ages after emoval of the sulfides. Contrary to the systematics of the impure barite crusts, the similarity of ^{210}Pb/^{226}Ra between raw and purified barite chimneys is attributed to the lower concentration of sulfides in the chimneys (Fu et al, 1994).

3.2.7. ^{228}Th/^{228}Ra Ages

The ^{228}Th/^{228}Ra ages of purified barite chimneys range from 0.5 to about 5 years (Fig. 3.24) indicating that the chimneys are of young age and some formed just several months before they were recovered in July 1993. As previously reported, excess ^{210}Pb present in the sulfide-bearing crusts tend to yield spurious ^{210}Pb/^{226}Ra ages. Any sulfides in the chimneys could also affect the ^{228}Th/^{228}Ra age determinations because the activity of ^{228}Th used

Table 3.10. Sulfide concentrations of barites and their effect on $^{210}Pb/^{226}Ra$ dating.

Sample name	$^{210}Pb/^{226}Ra$ raw	$^{210}Pb/^{226}Ra$ pure	$\Delta(^{210}Pb/^{226}Ra)$	Pyrite (wt%)
Barite chimneys				
Ch#2-a	0.133	0.079	0.054	9.6
Ch#2-b	0.079	0.061	0.018	5.2
Ch#9-T/b	0.125	0.115	0.010	4.7
Ch#9-B/b	0.105	0.099	0.006	4.3
Ch#10-T/a	0.042	0.040	0.002	5.1
Ch#10-B/a	0.097	0.059	0.038	4.8
Barite crusts				
Cr-93-1-3/l	0.368	0.288	0.080	8.9
Cr-93-4-4/1/u	1.013	0.542	0.471	28.5
Cr-93-4-4/1/l	2.013	0.513	1.500	30.5
Cr-93-7-7/1	0.629	0.356	0.273	16.9
Cr-93-8-5/3/u	0.797	0.533	0.264	9.0
Cr-93-8-5/3/l	0.629	0.511	0.118	20.1
Cr-93-8-7/2/u	0.768	0.376	0.392	22.2
Cr-93-8-7/2/l	1.431	0.374	1.057	31.7

68

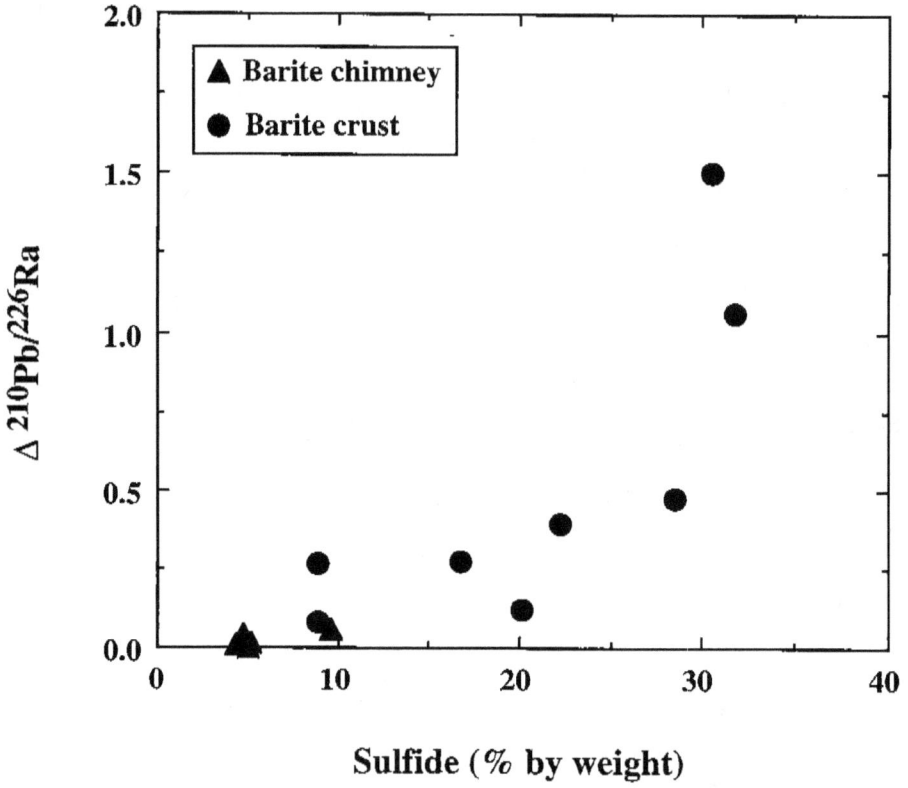

Figure 3.23. Sulfide effects on the $^{210}Pb/^{226}Ra$ dating. Note the positive relationship between the sulfide concentration and the difference in $^{210}Pb/^{226}Ra$ before and after barite purification.

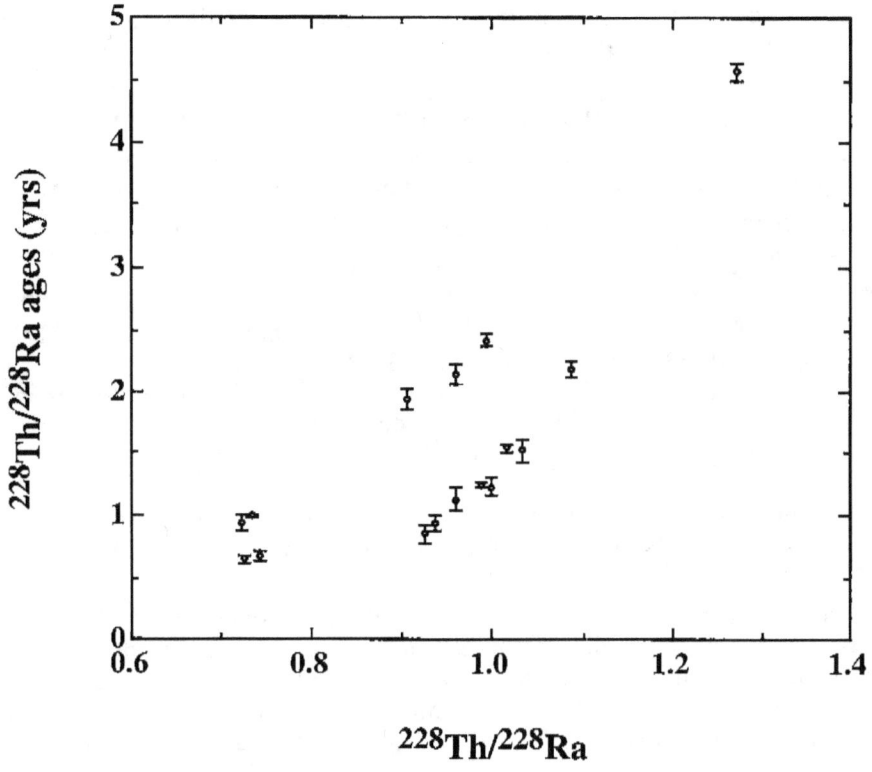

Figure 3.24. ^{228}Th/^{228}Ra ages plotted against their ^{228}Th/^{228}Ra ratios of chimneys based on pure barites.

in ^{228}Th/^{228}Ra dating method is obtained from the activity of ^{212}Pb which, if unsupported, could also be derived from the decay of ^{220}Rn in the advecting fluids. In order to test the possible sulfide effect on the ^{228}Th/^{228}Ra dating, ^{228}Th/^{228}Ra ages of the raw chimney barites are plotted in Figure 3.25 against those of their paired purified barites. Because the ages of the raw chimney barites and purified barites are concordant, it can be concluded that (i) raw (untreated) chimneys contain a very small amount sulfide (< 2% by volume) and therefore unsupported ^{212}Pb is insignificant, and (ii) barite purification scheme does not impair the ^{228}Th/^{228}Ra ages. On the basis of this observation, subsamples sectioned from the hardened chimneys were dated without purification and their ^{228}Th/^{228}Ra ages are likely to represent "true" chimney's ages (Table 3.7).

It can be concluded that the ^{228}Th/^{228}Ra ages obtained from the chimneys are (i) highly reliable; (i) the ^{228}Th/^{228}Ra age errors are small (<8%, Table 3.6 and 3.7), and (iii) the three age profiles (Figs. 3.17, 3.18, and 3.19) show a systematic decrease in the ages from the bottom to the top of the chimneys which is consistent with the expectation of older ages at the bottom and younger ages at the top.

3.3. Radium and Barium Systematics in Chemotrophic and Heterotrophic Benthic Fauna from Barite-Bearing Seeps

The data listed in Tables 3.11 and 3.12 show that the range of ^{226}Ra concentrations among seep fauna samples is large. Methanotrophic endosymbiont-bearing mussel samples (Bathymodiolus spp.) consist of body and calcareous shells separated from one another; galatheid crab samples are composed of soft tissues and chitin exoskeletons. In the case of polychaetes, only the chitinous exoskeleton parts were available for ^{226}Ra measurements. Starfish carbonate skeleton and soft tissue samples were analyzed as whole entities because of the inordinate difficulties associated with completely separating soft tissue from calcareous parts.

3.3.1. Mussels with Methanotrophic Endosymbionts

Radium-226 results for Bathymodiolus spp. paired soft tissues and calcareous shells are summarized in Table 3.11 and the results are depicted in Figures 3.26 and 3.27 for comparative purposes.

^{226}Ra of soft tissue mussels exhibit a broad range of radioactivity from the lower limit of detection (0.1 dpm/g) to 1.5 dpm/g. Mussel tissues from barite-bearing seeps averaged 0.6 ±0.4 dpm/g (n=7) ^{226}Ra and ranged from 0.1 to 1.3 dpm/g. Mussel tissues from carbonate-bearing seeps, serving as controls, averaged 0.8 ±0.5 dpm/g (n=9) ^{226}Ra and ranged from 0.0 to 1.5 dpm/g. An unpaired, two-tailed t-test reveals that there is no significant difference between mussel soft tissues from barite and carbonate-bearing seeps at 95% confidence level.

Not unlike the body tissues, the ^{226}Ra in mussel shells also spans a broad range of radioactivity, from below detection limit to 2.3 dpm/g. Mussel shells sampled from barite seeps average 0.6 ±0.7 dpm/g ^{226}Ra (n=7) and range from

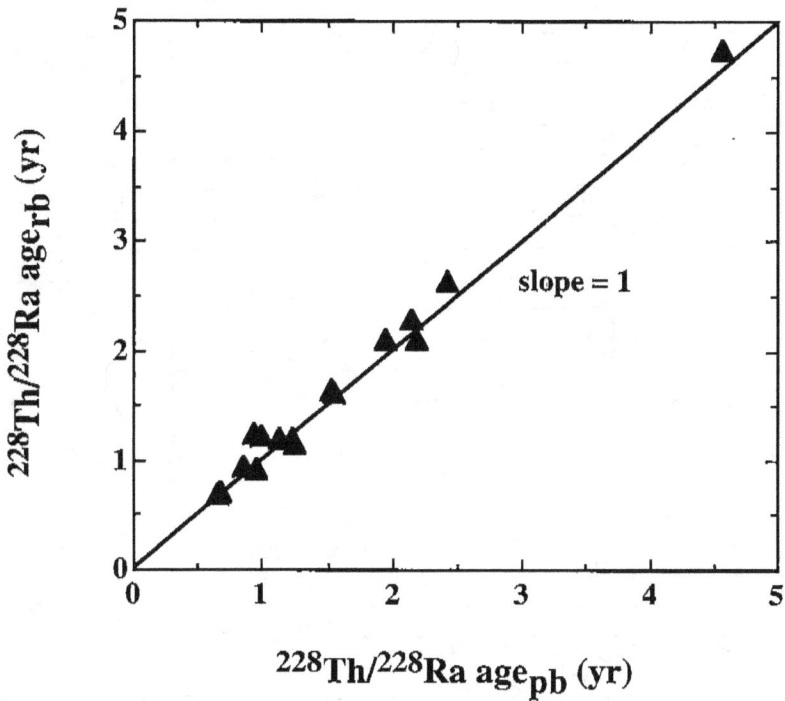

Figure 3.25. Relationship between ^{228}Th/^{228}Ra ages of raw barites (rb) and pure barites (pb) of chimneys. Note that all the data converge along the 1:1 line suggesting that barite purification does not significantly affect the ^{228}Th/^{228}Ra dating.

Table 3.11. Radium-226 activity concentration in chemosynthetic (methanotrophic) Bathymodiolus spp. mussels from seeps. Seep designation "C" denotes carbonate seep and "B" denotes barite seep.

Sample I.D.	Biota[1]	Type	Year[2]	Dive No.[3]	GOM Block	Seep[4]	Ra-226[5] dpm/g
GOM-S-1	MM	Shell	1995	JSL-2634	GC-234	C	0.5 ± 0.4
GOM-S-1	MM	Body	1995	JSL-2634	GC-234	C	1.3 ± 0.8
GOM-S-2	MM	Shell	1995	JSL-2634	GC-234	C	2.3 ± 0.8
GOM-S-2	MM	Body	1995	JSL-2634	GC-234	C	1.1 ± 0.3
GOM-S-8	MM	Shell	1995	JSL-2647	GC-185	C	1.1 ± 0.3
GOM-S-8	MM	Body	1995	JSL-2647	GC-185	C	0.6 ± 0.4
GOM-S-9	MM	Shell	1995	JSL-2647	GC-185	C	0.5 ± 0.4
GOM-S-9	MM	Body	1995	JSL-2647	GC-185	C	0.9 ± 0.4
J-2	MM	Body	1991	JSL-3120	GC-272	C	1.5 ± 0.6
J-6	MM	Shell	1991	JSL-3120	GC-272	C	0.2 ± 0.4
J-6	MM	Body	1991	JSL-3120	GC-272	C	0.9 ± 0.4
L-5	MM	Body	1991	JSL-3116	GC-185	C	BDL
MAC-2	MM	Shell	1990	Alvin-2209	Alaminos Canyon	C	0.4 ± 0.4
MAC-2	MM	Body	1990	Alvin-2209	Alaminos Canyon	C	0.1 ± 0.3
709-1	MM	Shell	1993	JSL-3560	MC-709	C	0.4 ± 0.4
709-1	MM	Body	1993	JSL-3560	MC-709	C	0.4 ± 0.4
GOM-S-44	MM	Shell	1997	JSL-2897	GB-338	B	1.6 ± 0.6
GOM-S-44	MM	Body	1997	JSL-2897	GB-338	B	0.9 ± 0.4
GOM-S-46	MM	Shell	1997	JSL-2897	GB-338	B	1.3 ± 0.3
GOM-S-46	MM	Body	1997	JSL-2897	GB-338	B	0.8 ± 0.4
GOM-S-47	MM	Shell	1997	JSL-2897	GB-338	B	BDL
GOM-S-47	MM	Body	1997	JSL-2897	GB-338	B	0.4 ± 0.8
GOM-S-48	MM	Shell	1997	JSL-2897	GB-338	B	0.8 ± 0.4
GOM-S-48	MM	Body	1997	JSL-2897	GB-338	B	1.3 ± 0.3
GOM-S-49	MM	Shell	1997	JSL-2897	GB-338	B	0.4 ± 0.4
GOM-S-49	MM	Body	1997	JSL-2897	GB-338	B	0.1 ± 0.3
GOM-S-50	MM	Shell	1997	JSL-2897	GB-338	B	0.1 ± 0.3
GOM-S-50	MM	Body	1997	JSL-2897	GB-338	B	0.4 ± 0.5
929-4	MM	Shell	1993	JSL-3559	MC-929	B	BDL
929-4	MM	Body	1993	JSL-3559	MC-929	B	0.2 ± 0.4

[1] MM- methanotrophic mussels Bathymodiolus spp.

[2] Year of collection

[3] Submersible dive number; JSL = Johnson-Sea-Link

[4] Seep type according to predominant geologic products; C = carbonate-dominated seep; B = barite-dominated seep

[5] Radium-226 determination with 2-σ counting error; BDL = below detection limit

Table 3.12. Radium-226 content in heterotrophic fauna from seeps. Seep designation "C" denotes carbonate seep and "B" denotes barite seep.

Sample I.D.	Biota[1]	Type	Year[2]	Dive No.[3]	GOM Block	Seep[4]	Ra-226[5] dpm/g
GS-8	GC	Skeleton	1992	JSL-3300	GC-184	C	0.1 ± 0.3
GS-8	GC	Body	1992	JSL-3300	GC-184	C	0.8 ± 0.4
97-GL1/C1	GC	Skeleton	1997	JSL-2897	GB-338	B	1.0 ± 0.4
97-GL1/C1	GC	Body	1997	JSL-2897	GB-338	B	6.0 ± 2.6
97-GL1/C2	GC	Skeleton	1997	JSL-2897	GB-338	B	0.4 ± 0.3
97-GL1/C2	GC	Body	1997	JSL-2897	GB-338	B	10.7±2.8
GS-1	SF	Whole body	1993	JSL-3300	GC-184	C	0.8 ± 0.4
97-SF2	SF	Whole body	1997	JSL-2897	GB-338	B	1.7 ± 0.4
97-SF3	SF	Whole body	1997	JSL-2897	GB-338	B	2.0 ± 0.5
97-SF1	SF	Whole body	1997	JSL-2897	GB-338	B	3.9 ± 0.6
97-TW1	PY	Skeleton	1997	JSL-2897	GB-338	B	0.5 ± 0.3
97-TW2	PY	Skeleton	1997	JSL-2897	GB-338	B	1.0 ± 0.4

[1] GC- galatheid crab
   SF- starfishes
   PY- polychaetes
[2] Year of collection
[3] Submersible dive number; JSL = Johnson-Sea-Link
[4] Seep type according to predominant geologic products; C = carbonate-dominated seep; B = barite-dominated seep
[5] Radium-226 determination with 2-σ counting error; BDL = below detection limit

74

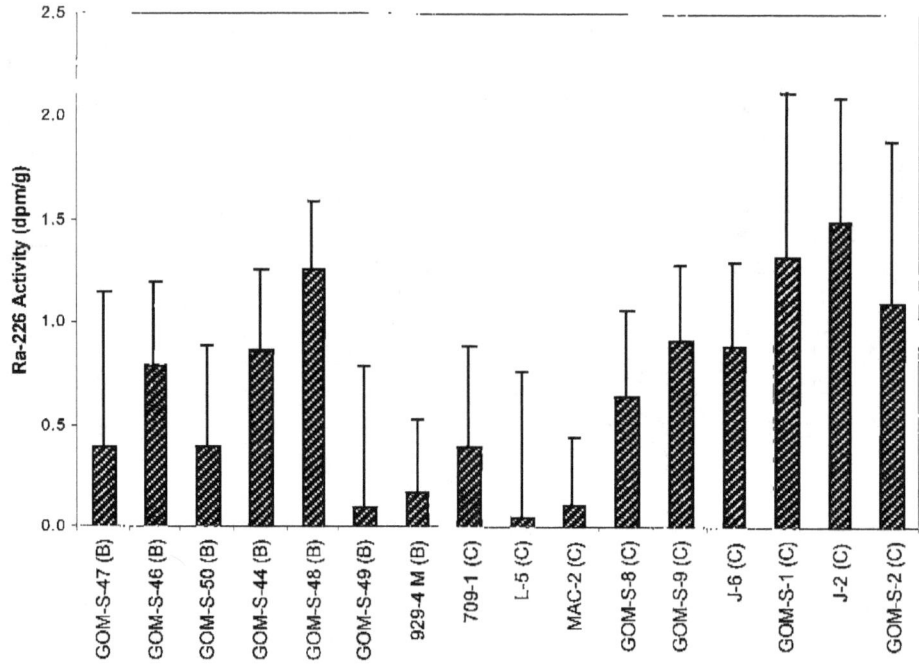

Figure 3.26.- Radium-226 activity concentrations of methanotrophic mussels body tissues. Error bars accompanying data represent the 95% confidence interval for random counting error. "B" and "C" denote mussels collected from barite and carbonate seeps, respectively.

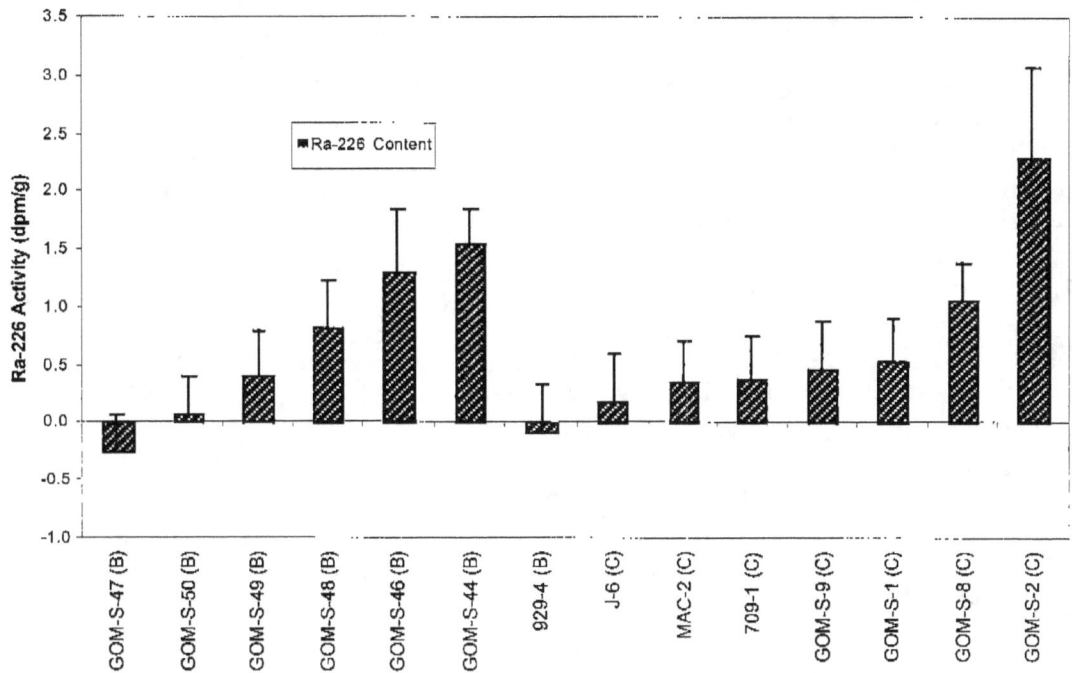

Figure 3.27.- Radium-226 activity concentrations of methanotrophic mussel calcareous shells. Error bars accompanying data represent the 95% confidence interval for random counting error. "B" and "C" denote mussel shells collected from barite and carbonate seeps, respectively.

below detection limit to 1.6 dpm/g. Mussel shell sampled from carbonate seeps (control sites) average 0.8 ±0.7 dpm/g ^{226}Ra (n=7) and range from below detection limit to 2.3 dpm/g. Among shell samples, GOM-S-2 from GC-234 exhibits the highest ^{226}Ra value (2.3 dpm/g). This result is contrary to *a priori* expectations, since the carbonate-bearing seeps were originally hypothesized to be radium depleted relative to the barite-bearing seeps. A possible explanation for this result is that in barite seeps, soluble radium venting from hydrocarbon seeps rapidly coprecipitates with barium and seawater sulfate ions to form barite, so that the seep water is radium depleted when it reaches the benthic fauna. However, an unpaired, two-tailed t-test reveals that there is no significant difference of ^{226}Ra activity at 95% confidence level between mussel shells from barite and carbonate-bearing seeps.

3.3.2 Heterotrophic Fauna

^{226}Ra data from heterotrophic seep fauna are summarized in Table 3.12 and graphed in Figure 3.28. Body tissues of galatheid crabs 97-GL1/C1 and 97-GL1/C2 (B) from barite seeps yield higher ^{226}Ra activities than any other heterotrophic fauna samples (6.0 and 10.7 dpm/g, respectively). The GS-8 crab from a carbonate seep is included for comparison and yields a much lower value of 0.8 dpm/g ^{226}Ra. Since galatheid crabs are presumably interloping scavengers, there may be a component of radium transference from the chemosynthetic barite community fauna; thus, radium is possibly accumulated through the food chain. An alternate explanation for the observed high ^{226}Ra activities is the accumulation of insoluble barite crystals in the GI tract of the crabs associated with their scavenging behavior.

Skeletal elements of the galatheid crabs exhibit the lowest radioactivities among all heterotrophic fauna elements. GS-8 crab from a carbonate seep yields a low ^{226}Ra activity of 0.1 dpm/g representing the lowest value of any body component of the heterotrophic fauna group.

Three starfishes sampled from barite seeps exhibit uniformly high ^{226}Ra activity levels (average 2.5 dpm/g) compared to a single starfish collected from a carbonate seep (0.8 dpm/g). The barite-seep starfishes were second highest of all heterotrophic faunal groups.

^{226}Ra activity levels of two polychaetes sampled at barite seeps average 0.8 dpm/g. No ploychaetes were recovered from carbonate seeps, so no comparison can be made with control fauna in this case. Soft body parts were also unavailable for analyses because polychaetes soft tissues decompose rapidly after harvesting.

3.3.3. Barium-Radium Relationship in Fauna

Representatives of hydrocarbon seep fauna used for barium analysis are listed along with their respective ^{226}Ra values in Table 3.13 and data are graphed in Figure 3.29. The fauna consist of external hard skeletons and whole soft tissues, including galatheid crabs, starfishes, and mussels. The ^{226}Ra

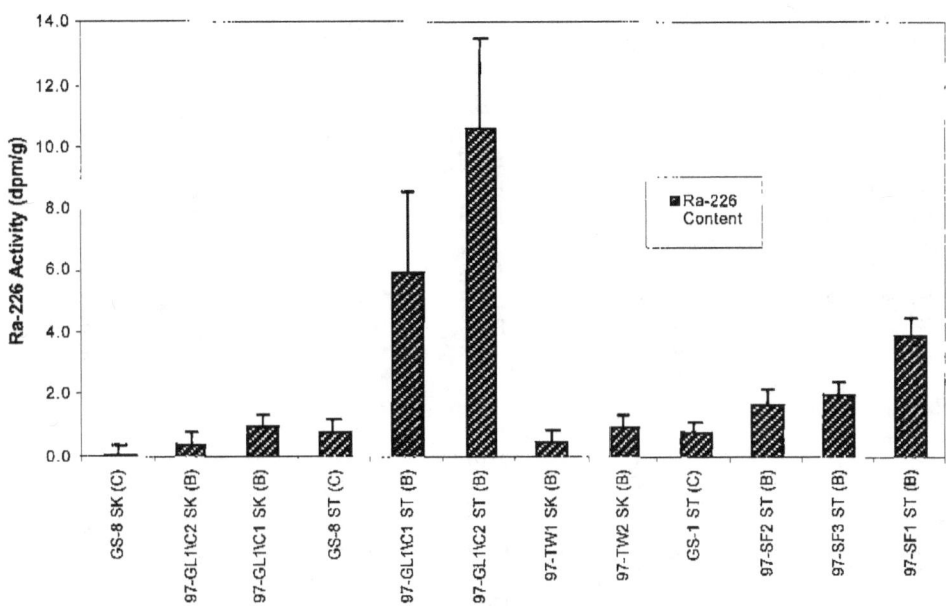

Figure 3.28.- Radium-226 activity concentrations of heterotrophic seep fauna. SK denotes hard skeletal component; ST marks soft tissue component; B and C marks barite and carbonate-bearing seeps, respectively.

Table 3.13. Relationship between barium and radium in selected hydrocarbon-seep fauna.

Sample ID	Biota[1]	Type[2]	Ba (ppm)[3]	Ra-226 (ppt)[4]
Barite Seeps				
Soft Tissues				
GOM-S-50 body	MM	BBC	1	0.18 ± 0.22
GOM-S-47 body	MM	BBC	2	0.01 ± 0.34
GOM-S-48 body	MM	BBC	5	0.57 ± 0.15
97-SF3 starfish body	SF	BBH	281	0.91 ± 0.21
97-SF2 starfish body	SF	BBH	1174	0.78 ± 0.20
97-SF1 starfish body	SF	BBH	3619	1.77 ± 0.25
97-GL1 crab 2 body	GC	BBH	472	4.82 ± 1.27
97-GL1 crab 1 body	GC	BBH	4319	2.72 ± 1.15
Exoskeleton				
GOM-S-44 Shell	MM	BCE	496	0.72 ± 0.27
GOM-S-47 Shell	MM	BCE	96	0.12 ± 0.16
97-GL1 crab1 Shell	GC	BHE	113	0.43 ± 0.17
97-GL1 crab 2 Shell	GC	BHE	138	0.19 ± 0.15
Carbonate Seeps				
Soft Tissues				
J-2 body	MM	CCB	3	0.67 ± 0.27
MAC-2 body	MM	CCB	4	0.05 ± 0.15
GOM-S-8 body	MM	CCB	5	0.29 ± 0.19
GOM-S-9 body	MM	CCB	6	0.41 ± 0.17
929-4 body	MM	CCB	8	0.08 ± 0.16
GOM-S-44 body	MM	CCB	8	0.39 ± 0.18
GOM-S-1 body	MM	CCB	15	0.60 ± 0.36
GOM-S-2 body	MM	CCB	28	0.50 ± 0.13
GS1 starfish	SF	CHB	7	0.34 ± 0.18
Exoskeleton				
MAC-2 Shell	MM	CCE	1	0.16 ± 0.16
GOM-S-8 Shell	MM	CCE	1	0.48 ± 0.15
GOM-S-2 Shell	MM	CCE	1	0.63 ± 0.36
GOM-S-9 Shell	MM	CCE	469	0.21 ± 0.19
GS-8 crab	GC	CHE	15	0.03 ± 0.14

[1] MM- methanotrophic mussels Bathymodiolus spp. ; GC- galatheid crab; SF- starfish; PY- polychaetes

[2] BBC- chemotrophic soft tissues from barite seeps; BBH- heterotrophic soft tissues from barite seeps; BCE- chemotrophic exoskeletons from barite seeps; BHE- heterotrophic exoskeletons from barite seeps; CCB- chemosynthetic soft tissues from carbonate seeps; CHB- heterotrophic soft tissues from carbonate seeps; CCE- chemosynthetic exoskeletons from carbonate seeps; CHE- heterotrophic exoskeletons from carbonate seeps

[3] Values reported in parts per million

[4] Values reported in parts per trillion with 2-σ random counting error

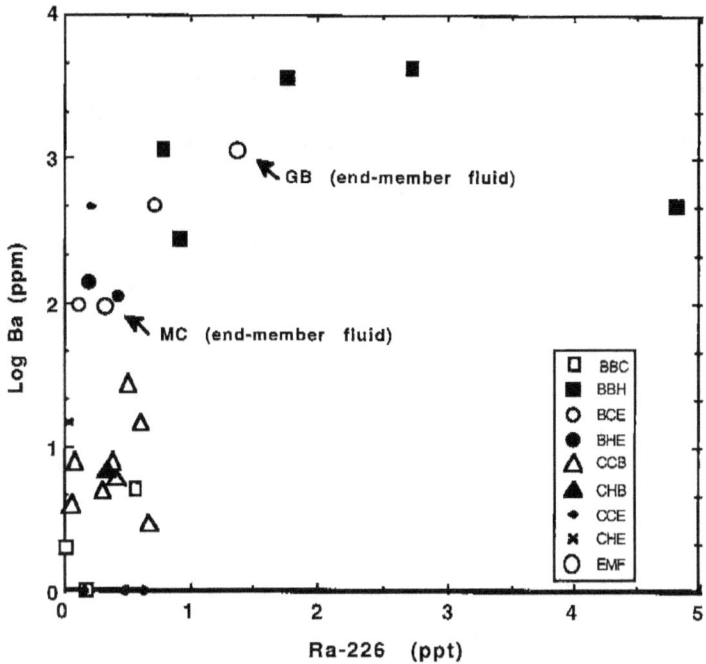

Figure 3.29.- The Relation of Barium and ^{226}Ra in Hydrocarbon Seep Fauna. End member pore fluid values are similar to barite exoskeleton in Ra and Barium content. Radium-226 values are given in ppt (parts per trillion) for order of magnitude comparisons with barium concentrations. Dpm/g ^{226}Ra values may be obtained by multiplying parts per trillion by a factor of 2.22 dpm/ppt.

BBC- chemotrophic soft tissues from barite seeps
BBH- heterotrophic soft tissues from barite seeps
BCE- chemotrophic exoskeletons from barite seeps
BHE- heterotrophic exoskeletons from barite seeps
CCB- chemosynthetic soft tissues from carbonate seeps
CHB- heterotrophic soft tissues from carbonate seeps
CCE- chemosynthetic exoskeletons from carbonate seeps
CHE- heterotrophic exoskeletons from carbonate seeps
EMF-end-member pore-fluid Ba and Ra concentrations

concentrations of the fauna range from 0.01 ppt (parts per trillion) in a mussel shell from a carbonate seep to as high as 4.8 ppt in a galatheid crab from a barite seep. Parts per trillion ^{226}Ra is used in this case to demonstrate orders of magnitude differences between barium and radium. Parts per trillion ^{226}Ra may be converted to dpm/g by multiplying by a factor of 2.22.

Figure 3.29 suggests a log-linear relationship between Ba and ^{226}Ra in fauna from barite seeps. In this region of the figure, Ba increases logarithmically whereas the ^{226}Ra increases linearly. These results seem to be consistent with the pore fluid end members $^{226}Ra/Ba$ values from Mississippi Canyon and Garden Banks barite seeps which are also shown.

4. DISCUSSION

4.1. Sources of Fluids Advecting at Seeps

The geochemistry of pore fluids in marine sediments typically reflects the seawater trapped in the sediments at the time of deposition and modified by diagenesis. The solutes in pore fluids could deviate from the seawater values because of exchange with the clay fraction of the sediments (Presley, 1969). In seepage areas, however, the chemical fingerprints are complicated by the availability of multiple fluid sources advecting through subsurface conduits, complex processes involving fluid interaction with salt diapirs (Aharon et al., 1992a), and microbial activity fueled by hydrocarbons (Aharon, 2000). Extensive in situ diagenesis involving sediment-fluid interaction can be ruled out from the onset because the cores from which the pore fluids were extracted in this study represent surficial sediments less than 50 cm below the seabed. The discussion that follows addresses the question of the fluid source/s and the processes controlling the chemical compositions of pore fluids in the GOM seeps.

4.1.1. Seawater-Derived Fluids

Similar salinities and concentrations of the conservative elements Cl and Na in type I pore fluids and the ambient bathyal seawater (Table 3.1) suggest that these are primarily seawater trapped in the sediment. This contention is further confirmed by the $^{87}Sr/^{86}Sr$ ratios (0.70916) which are identical to the measured deepwater value (0.70917, Table 3.1).

The marked SO_4 deficiency relative to seawater is attributed to its consumption during microbial sulfate reduction within the seep sediments using the carbon-derived hydrocarbons as electron donor (Aharon, 2000). Microbial sulfate reduction using hydrocarbon substrates causes sulfate depletion and simultaneous bicarbonate and hydrogen sulfide enrichments. The occurrence of microbial sulfate alteration in seep sediments is confirmed by the observed inverse linear correlation between dissolved sulfate and hydrogen sulfide (Aharon and Fu, 2000). The slight depletion of Ca (Ef is down to 0.6, Table 3.1 and Fig. 3.4 A), Mg (Ef is down to 0.9, Table 3.1) and Sr (Ef is down to 0.7, Table 3.2 and Fig. 3.4 B) in pore fluids type I is attributed to precipitation of authigenic carbonates because dissolved bicarbonate and carbonate species are generated during the sulfate reduction (Aharon and Fu, 2000). Consequently, the increase in the carbonate alkalinity of the pore fluids triggers carbonate precipitation which scavenges Ca, Mg and Sr. The predicted carbonate deposition in seeps agrees well with the observed authigenic carbonates which are ubiquitous at hydrocarbon seeps from the Gulf of Mexico (Roberts and Aharon, 1994; Ferrell and Aharon, 1994), and elsewhere (e.g., North Sea, Hovland et al., 1987; Pacific northwest, Ritger et al., 1987).

The observed ^{18}O enrichments in type I pore fluids of up to 1⁰/oo relative to a seawater source also require an explanation (Fig. 3.5). Two processes relevant to seeps could shift positively the $\delta^{18}O$ values of seawater-derived fluids, namely (i) sublimation of gas hydrates, and (ii) microbial sulfate reduction. Gas hydrates (clathrates) consist of gas (primarily methane) and water mixed in about 1:6 molar proportion (Kvenvolden, 1988). Because the solid-ice gas hydrates sequester more of the ^{18}O isotope relative to the liquid phase upon sublimation in the host sediment (Hesse and Harrison, 1981), the water fraction of the hydrate would contribute to the elevated $\delta^{18}O$ and simultaneous freshening (i.e., lower salt content) of the pore fluids. For example, a $1^o/oo$ positive shift in pore fluids relative to the overlying seawater (Fig. 3.5 B) can be achieved by mixing a 10% gas hydrate-derived fluid having a $\delta^{18}O$ of $10^o/oo$ (assuming multiple thawing-freezing in a closed system with a starting gas hydrate $\delta^{18}O$ value of $2.6^o/oo$, Davidson et al., 1983) with seawater-derived fluid having a typical bathyal $\delta^{18}O$ value of $0.3^o/oo$ (Table 3.1). Under these circumstances the gas hydrate sublimation will also cause a pore fluid freshening of about 10% relative to bathyal seawater.

Microbial sulfate reduction is another process common in seeps which may alter the $\delta^{18}O$ values of the pore fluids. According to Fritz et al. (1989), bacterial reduction of sulfate is accompanied by oxygen isotope exchange reactions between sulfate and water. Because solute SO_4 is enriched in ^{18}O ($\delta^{18}O = 9.7^o/oo$ SMOW, Faure, 1986) relative to seawater (H_2O), the microbial breakdown of the S-O bonds affords isotope exchange between the sulfate-oxygen and water-oxygen and may cause an ^{18}O-enrichment in the pore fluids. However, it can be estimated that the sulfate reduction effect on the $\delta^{18}O$ of pore fluids is small (at most $0.02^o/oo$) compared with gas hydrate sublimation effects because the amount of oxygen in pore fluid SO_4 is substantially smaller (480 times) than oxygen in water.

The effects of gas hydrate sublimation on the pore fluids type I can be gauged in Figure 3.5 B on the basis of $\delta^{18}O$-chloride inverse relations indicating that ^{18}O enrichments are accompanied by chloride dilution. Observations indicate that gas hydrates are common in the bathyal seeps where type I pore fluids were acquired (MacDonald et al., 1994) and their sublimation have the potential to alter the oxygen isotope fingerprints of seep fluids.

4.1.2 Fluids Derived by Dissolution of Salt Diapirs

The similarity of $\delta^{18}O$ values in type II pore fluids with the $\delta^{18}O$ of ambient bathyal water (Fig. 3.5 A) suggests that the latter is the source for these pore fluids. However, the observed enrichments of Cl, Na, Ca, K and SO_4 (Table 3.1 and Fig. 3.4) indicate that source(s) of solutes other than seawater must be involved in the formation of these pore fluids. Two distinct sources for the elemental enrichments in seep fluids can be discerned: (i) salt diapir dissolution and/or (ii) residual Jurassic seawater (e.g., Louann brine) evaporated at least to the point of saturation with halite and buried along with its cogenetic evaporite (Aharon et al., 1992a). Generally, these two sources can be distinguished on the basis of their Br/Cl and Na/Cl molar ratios as indicated below.

Because Cl is preferentially partitioned over Br into Na, K and Mg-halogen salts during their precipitation, the residual brine will become progressively enriched in Br (White, 1965; Rittenhouse, 1967; Kharaka et al, 1987). Therefore brines formed by subaerial evaporation of sea water will have higher Br/Cl ratios relative to brines formed by dissolution of halite (Rittenhouse, 1967; Carpenter, 1978; Egeberg and Aagaard, 1989). The Na/Cl ratio is another measure to gauge the effect of salt dissolution. Seawater dissolving halite but remaining unmodified by other chemical reactions will have a Na/Cl molar ratio close to 1.0 and substantially higher than normal seawater (0.857) whereas brines evaporated beyond the halite saturation level would have a Na/Cl ratio lower than seawater. Viewed this way, the substantially lower Br/Cl molar ratios of type II pore fluids (0.34×10^{-3} to 1.19×10^{-3}) relative to seawater (1.52×10^{-3}), coupled with their near 1.0 Na/Cl molar ratios (Fig. 4.1), support the view that their Cl and Na were derived from dissolution of subsurface salt diapirs by seawater convective circulation (Jensenius and Munksgaard, 1989). The Ca and SO_4 enrichments in type II pore fluids relative to seawater (Figs. 3.4 A and C) are attributed to dissolution of anhydrite and gypsum disseminated in the halite diapir. The enrichment of K is interpreted to result from dissolution of sylvite (KCl) in the salt, and the deficiency of Mg relative to seawater (Table 3.1) is attributed to the dolomitization as justified by Aharon et al. (1992a).

The $^{87}Sr/^{86}Sr$ ratios of type II pore fluids, ranging from 0.70797 to 0.70897 (n = 3), are significantly lower than the seawater value of 0.70917. These lower ratios can be explained by the scavenging of Sr with lower $^{87}Sr/^{86}Sr$ ratios during salt dissolution. According to Land et al. (1988), most Sr in salt domes occurs in anhydrite inclusions and has a wide range of $^{87}Sr/^{86}Sr$ ratios (from 0.7067 to 0.7095) that are more radiogenic than the presumed coeval Jurassic (Callovian) seawater due to the extensive water-rock interaction during salt deformation. The $^{87}Sr/^{86}Sr$ ratio of the salt under the Green Knoll has not been measured and therefore it is difficult to quantify the contribution of Sr derived from salt dissolution. However, by using a minimum value of 0.7070 for the $^{87}Sr/^{86}Sr$ ratio of Jurassic salt (Burke et al, 1982), the maximum amount of Sr derived from salt dissolution which is required to achieve the observed $^{87}Sr/^{86}Sr$ ratio in type II pore fluids can be estimated from a simple mass balance equation:

$$A \, (^{87}Sr/^{86}Sr)_{salt} + (1-A) \, (^{87}Sr/^{86}Sr)_{sw} = (^{87}Sr/^{86}Sr)_{pf} \qquad (4.1)$$

where A is the fractional contribution of Sr from salt dissolution; salt, sw and pf subscripts are the $^{87}Sr/^{86}Sr$ ratios of the dissolved salt (0.7070), seawater (0.70917) and pore fluids, respectively. Using the least radiogenic $^{87}Sr/^{86}Sr$ ratio of 0.70797 measured in the pore fluids, the equation above yields a 55% Sr contribution from salt dissolution.

4.1.3. Fluids Derived by Advection of Deep-Seated Formation Waters

The linear correlations of Na, Ca, and Sr with Cl in type III pore fluids, and the regression lines passing through the seawater values (Figs. 4.2 A-C), confirm that these pore fluids were formed by mixing of two distinct end members represented by modern seawater at the low end and by Na, Ba, Sr and Ca-rich (but SO_4 depleted) unidentified high end member fluid. This interpretation is further supported by the linear relationships between $^{87}Sr/^{86}Sr$ ratios and the reciprocal of Sr concentrations (Fig. 4.3) because a straight line is expected when fluids are formed by mixing of two component end-members with different strontium isotope signatures (Faure, 1986). The non-linear correlation observed between Ba and Cl (Fig. 4.2 D) indicates that Ba was not conservative during the mixing and was removed from the fluids. This observation is explained by barite precipitation when the Ba-rich end members mixed with the SO_4-rich seawater and is confirmed by the

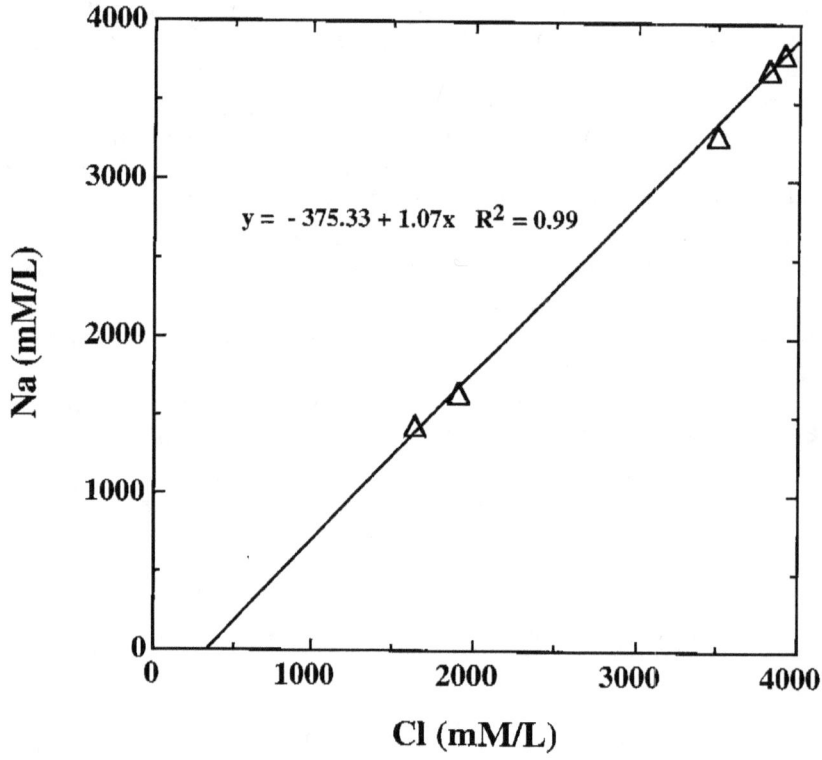

Figure 4.1. Na-Cl relationship in pore fluids type II. The almost 1:1 slope indicates that Cl and Na are derived primarily from dissolution of halite in the salt domes.

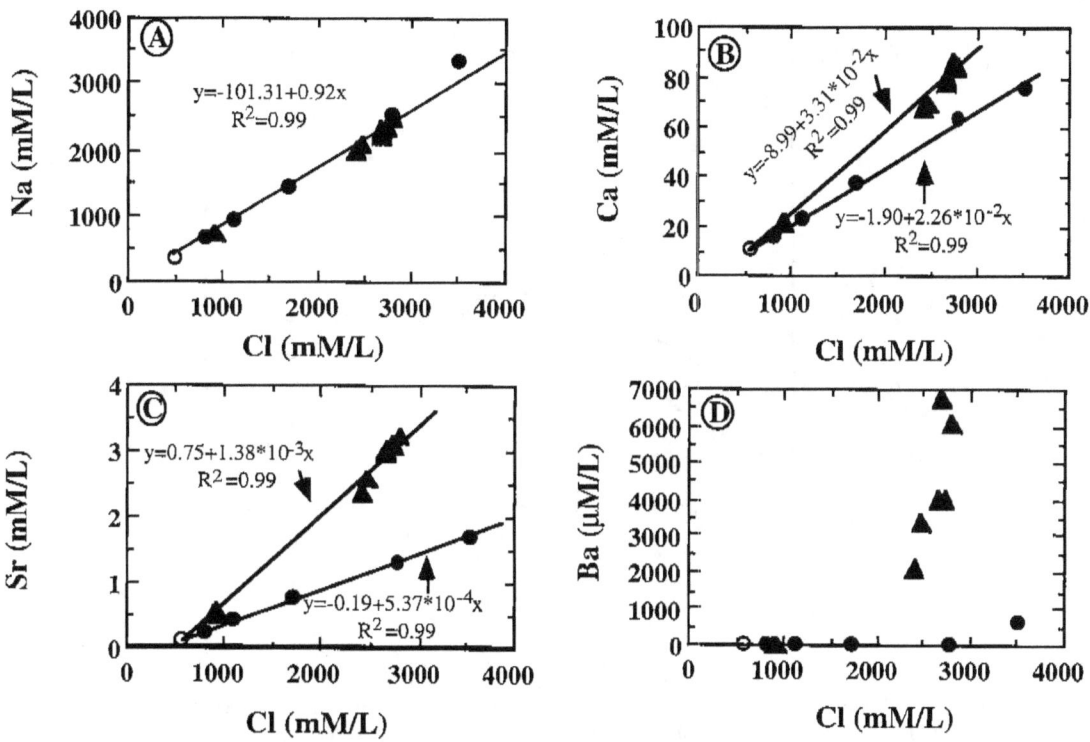

Figure 4.2. Plots of Cl against Na, Ca, Sr and Ba in pore fluids type III. The linear correlations in A, B and C suggest the mixing of seawater with saline end member fluids. The non-linear correlations between Ba and Cl in D result from barite precipitation. Empty circles refer to seawater, solid triangles and solid circles represent pore fluids from Garden Banks and Mississippi Canyon, respectively.

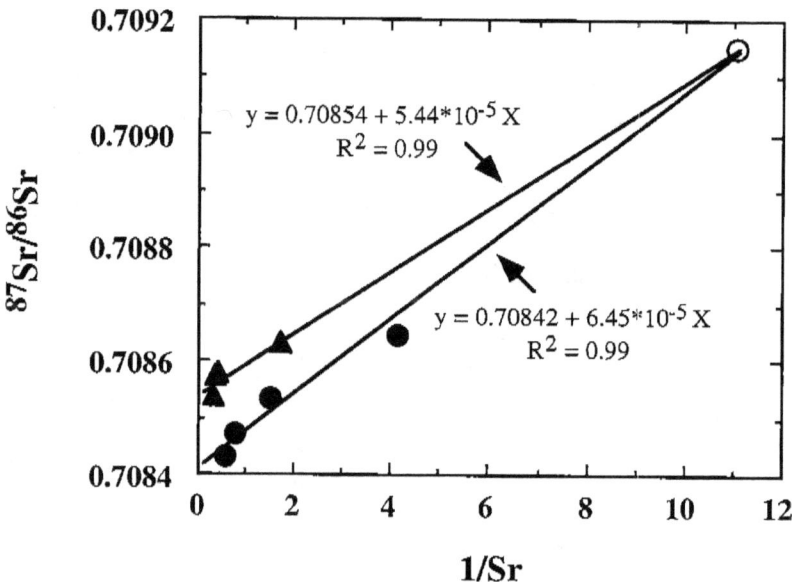

Figure 4.3. Plot of $^{87}Sr/^{86}Sr$ against 1/Sr in pore fluids type III. The empty circle refers to seawater, solid triangles and solid circles represent the pore fluids from Garden Banks and Mississippi Canyon, respectively.

occurrence of barite sands in the cores from which the type III pore fluids were acquired.

In order to decipher the origin of type III pore fluids it is essential to derive the chemical composition of the saline end member. The two regression lines in the plot of $^{87}Sr/^{86}Sr$ against 1/Sr for the pore fluids type III (Fig. 4.3) suggest two distinct saline end-members in Garden Banks and in Mississippi Canyon barite-bearing seeps. It is obvious that the two intercepts in Figure 4.3 should approximately represent the lowest possible $^{87}Sr/^{86}Sr$ ratios for the two end-member fluids. The two intercept values are 0.70854 and 0.70842 which are identical to those of the highest salinity pore fluids (Table 3.1) in Garden Banks and Mississippi Canyon, respectively.

Lower Br/Cl (0.93×10^{-3} and 0.90×10^{-3} in Garden Banks and Mississippi Canyon, respectively, Table 4.1) and higher Na/Cl molar ratios (0.901 and 0.948 in Garden Banks and Mississippi Canyon, respectively) in the possible saline end member fluids relative to seawater (1.52×10^{-3} and 0.857, respectively) suggest that the elevated Cl and Na levels in the saline fluids were acquired by subsurface salt dissolution. Dissolution of salt, however, could not by itself explain the anomalously high levels of Ca, Sr and Ba in the fluids (Table 4.1). The presence of shallow salt diapirs under the sampling areas in Garden Banks 382 and Mississippi Canyon 929, the occurrence of massive barite deposits (Fu et al, 1994; Fu and Aharon 1997), and direct observations of gaseous hydrocarbon and fluid venting during sampling, suggest that these end member fluids were derived from deep-seated formation waters dissolving the Jurassic-age salt during upward transport. The positive relation between pore fluids ^{226}Ra and salinity (Fig. 2.3 B) and its similarity to that found in produced waters from oil and gas fields in the Gulf Coast region (Fu et al, 1996; see below), and the similar negative relationship between pore fluids SO_4 and Ba similar to that found in the formation waters offshore Louisiana (Fig. 4.4) confirms the contention that these hydrocarbon-rich seeping fluids were sourced in deep-seated reservoirs.

Formation waters in the offshore Gulf of Mexico may be transported to the seabed in seeps from two distinct sources, either by dewatering of Cenozoic-age clastic sediments, or by injection from deep-seated Mesozoic-age brines. The two principal types of formation waters differ sufficiently in their chemical constituents and isotope compositions in order to allow a more specific chemical fingerprinting of the fluids advecting in seeps. The chemical and isotope distinctions between the two principal formation waters can be summarized as follows.

(1) Mesozoic and Cenozoic-sourced formation waters are distinguished on the basis of their $\delta^{18}O$ values which are controlled by the temperature and extent of interaction between water and host sediments (Land and Prezbindowski, 1981; Land and Macpherson, 1989). Most formation waters in Mesozoic strata of the Gulf of Mexico exhibit relatively heavy $\delta^{18}O$ values (i.e., >6°/oo SMOW) because extensive oxygen isotope exchange occurred between water and rocks at the high temperatures typical of sediments buried at more than 6 km depth (Land and Prezbindowski, 1981; McGee et al, 1994).

(2) Ba-rich formation waters in the Gulf of Mexico are primarily derived from Cenozoic reservoirs and are produced from dissolution of detrital Potassium-Feldspar containing 0.2 to 0.5 weight percent Ba (Macpherson, 1989).

Table 4.1. Chemical compositions of the two possible saline end member fluids of pore fluids type III.

Components	Saline end member fluids at:	
	Garden Banks	**Mississippi Canyon**
salinity	139	155
Cl	2792	3520
Br	2.6	3.2
SO$_4$	0.5	0.5
Na	2485	3338
K	11	14.8
Ca	84.4	76
Mg	43.2	59.5
Sr	3.2	1.7
Ba	6.1	0.6
Si	1	0.6
DIC	2.4	2.4
$\delta^{13}C$	-3.8	0.8
$^{87}Sr/^{86}Sr$	0.70854	0.70843
$\delta^{18}O$ (H$_2$O)	1.7	0.1

Note: Concentrations are in mM/L, salinity is in permil, $\delta^{13}C$ is in permil (PDB) and $\delta^{18}O$ is in permil (SMOW).

(3) Anomalously high levels of Sr (mean 18.5 mM/L) and Ca (mean 610 mM/L) are generally assigned to Mesozoic formation waters (Macpherson, 1989). Albitization of detrital plagioclase in the Mesozoic reservoirs is considered the principal source of Sr and Ca in Mesozoic formation waters (Macpherson, 1989).

The source/s of the two end member of type III fluids can now be discussed in light of the chemical and isotopic distinctions between the Cenozoic and Mesozoic-derived formation waters. Based on the relationship between $\delta^{18}O$ of formation waters and depth in the sediment (Land and Macpherson, 1989), the $\delta^{18}O$ of pore fluids are expected to be heavier than measured (Table 4.1) if they are derived from Mesozoic strata. The $\delta^{18}O$ values for the possible end-member fluids are 1.7 and 0.1°/oo (SMOW) in Garden Banks and Mississippi Canyon, respectively (Table 4.1) suggesting a Cenozoic-age component in a mixed source.

The relatively high concentrations of Sr and Ca in the fluids (Table 4.1) suggest a partial contribution from a Mesozoic-derived source. Alternative sources for Sr and Ca, such as dissolution of marine carbonates and/or dissolution of anhydrite associated with the salt diapirs, are considered unlikely because the measured levels of SO_4 are incompatible with these sources. Deficiency of SO_4 (0.5 mM/L in Garden Banks and Mississippi Canyon, Table 4.1) argues against Ca and Sr being sourced in carbonates and/or sulfates. If all the Sr and Ca in the end member fluids were derived from Mesozoic strata, the maximum "leakage" of Mesozoic-sourced Sr and Ca-rich formation fluids are estimated to be between 14% and 17% in Garden Banks and between 9% and 12% in Mississippi Canyon. The $^{87}Sr/^{86}Sr$ ratios, which are 0.70854 and 0.70843 for Garden Banks and Mississippi Canyon respectively, are compatible with the values measured in Mesozoic formation waters (Stueber et al., 1984) thus supporting our contention of a Mesozoic source for the Sr (and Ca).

The lower contents of Sr and Ca but higher Cl and Na in the fluids of Mississippi Canyon relative to those of Garden Banks can be explained by a lower contribution from Mesozoic formation waters but a higher proportion from salt dissolution. The higher Ba in Garden Banks end-member fluid could be caused by the more intensive dissolution of K-feldspar in Garden Banks than in Mississippi Canyon. This is consistent with the observation that the saline end-member fluids in Garden Banks contain more Si than in Mississippi Canyon (Table 4.1).

4.2. Radium and Barium in Barite-Bearing Seeps

4.2.1. Source/s of Ra and Ba in the Saline Fluids

Pore fluids of deep-sea sediments are generally enriched in ^{226}Ra and ^{228}Ra by factors of 5 to 100 and 60 to 250 over bottom water, respectively (Somayajulu and Church, 1973; Cochran and Krishnaswami, 1977; Cochran, 1979; Key, 1981). The enrichment of ^{226}Ra in the pore fluids is attributed to two principal factors related to the distinct chemical behavior of U and Th in seawater. First, alpha decay of ^{234}U in the water column produces ^{230}Th which is scavenged by adsorption onto rapidly sinking particulate matter. Second, the removal process results in ^{230}Th activities in the sediment which are in

90

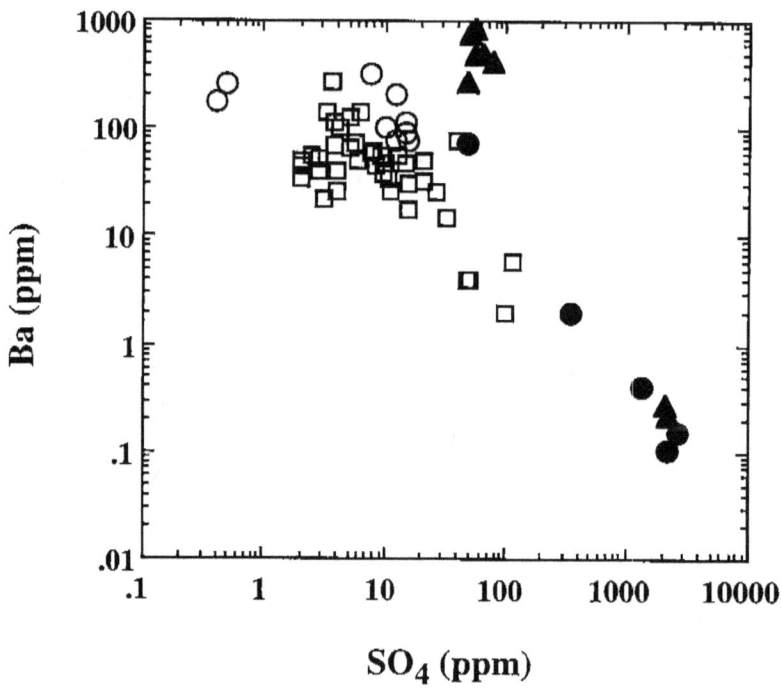

Figure 4.4. Barium-sulfate relationship in formation waters from Miocene and Pleistocene reservoirs offshore Louisiana. Chemistry data of formation waters from Miocene strata (empty circles) and Pleistocene strata (empty squares) are from Carothers et al. (1986) and Land et al. (1988). Note the similarity of the pore fluids type III to the formation waters. Solid circle and solid triangle refer to pore fluids in Mississippi Canyon and Garden Banks.

excess of the amount which can be supported by the coexisting ^{234}U (Cochran,1979). Consequently, the ^{226}Ra resulting from the radioactive decay of excess ^{230}Th in the sediment ends up in the pore fluids by leaching and alpha-recoil processes (Kigoshi, 1971). ^{232}Th in the water column is also scavenged by the falling particulate matter and is buried in the marine sediments (Broecker and Peng, 1982). Consequently the ^{232}Th within the sediments decay to ^{228}Ra which enters the pore fluids by leaching and alpha-recoil processes resulting in a higher concentration of ^{228}Ra in pore fluids than the overlying water column (Cochran,1979).

Although there is a scarcity of ^{226}Ra and ^{228}Ra analyses of pore fluids in deep-sea sediments, the few available data tend to support the model outlined above. For example, determination of ^{226}Ra and ^{228}Ra activities in pore fluids from deep-sea cores in the eastern equatorial Pacific by Somayajulu and Church (1973) and Cochran and Krishnaswami (1977) yielded a range of values from 1 to 15 dpm/L for ^{226}Ra and about 0.43 dpm/L for ^{228}Ra. These values are higher by factors of 8 to 40 and 150, respectively, relative to the ambient Pacific bottom water (0.36 dpm/L for ^{226}Ra and 3×10^{-3} dpm/L for ^{228}Ra).

The ^{226}Ra and ^{228}Ra activities of the pore fluids analyzed in this study, ranging from 27.2 to 36.6×10^2 dpm/L for ^{226}Ra and 63.3 to 24.5×10^2 dpm/L for ^{228}Ra, are by far the highest values reported to date for marine sediments (Table 3.3). Clearly, source(s) of ^{226}Ra and ^{228}Ra other than decay of excess ^{230}Th and ^{232}Th in the sediments must be involved in the interaction with these fluids.

Barium in seawater is typified by surface water depletions (~7 ppb) and deep water enrichments (~25 ppb) and has a nutrient-like profile that suggest Ba transport in biological debris (Wolgemuth and Broecker, 1970). Barite continuously forms in the water column and is an ubiquitous minor phase in deep-sea sediments (Church, 1979). The fallout of pelagic barite into unsaturated sediments causes partial dissolution of the barite and Ba enrichment in the normal marine pore fluids (40 to 50 ppb) (Church, 1979). The Ba concentrations in the pore fluids from barite-bearing seeps are 839 ppm and 83 ppm in the Garden Banks and Mississippi Canyon end-member fluids (Table 4.1), respectively, which are higher by orders of magnitude relative to normal oceanic pore fluids reported above. These pore fluids were interpreted to represent a mixture of advecting, highly saline, fluids sourced in the deep subsurface with seawater on the basis of elemental and isotope chemistry.

It is reasonable to assume that the anomalously high ^{226}Ra, ^{228}Ra activities and Ba concentrations in the pore fluids are derived from deep-seated highly saline formation waters advecting to the seafloor. This interpretation regarding the source of Ra in the pore fluids is supported by the significant positive relationship between salinity and Ra observed in the fluid samples (Fig. 3.2) which is remarkably similar to that derived for formation waters produced by onshore and offshore oil and gas rigs, and produced waters discharged in the nearshore marine habitats (Fig. 4.5). Similarly, the identification of the Ba source in deep-seated formation waters is supported by the observed overlap between the pore fluid and produced waters Ba and SO_4 data (Fig. 4.4).

92

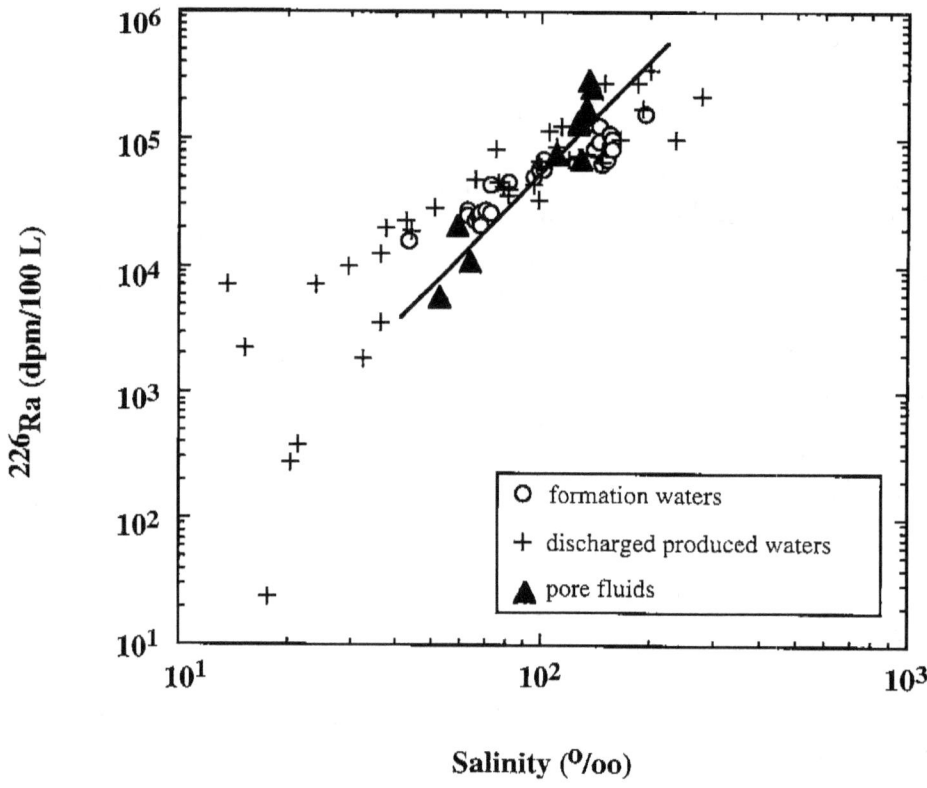

Figure 4.5. ^{226}Ra-salinity relationship in formation waters and discharged produced waters from the Gulf Coast region. Formation water data (open circles) are from Kraemer and Reid (1984). Discharged produced waters data (crosses) are recalculated from Rabalais et al. (1991) assuming that ^{226}Ra activities represent 2/3 of the total radium reported by these authors. Note the overlapping of the pore fluid data (solid triangles) with the field defined by the formation water.

The enrichment of Ra in the saline waters can be explained by the process of cations competition with Ra for ion exchange sites resulting in a greater proportion of Ra ions remaining in solution (Tanner, 1964). However, the exact source of radium in highly saline formation waters is still poorly known. For example, on the basis of radium-salinity relationship in formation waters from the US Gulf Coast region, Kraemer and Reid (1984) argued that Ra enrichment in these waters is derived from interaction of the fluids with the reservoir matrix. Specifically, the most likely sources are the clay minerals and the sand-sized quartz which contain adsorbed U and Th. In contrast, Kronfeld et al. (1993) and Kronfeld (1995) suggest on the basis of ^{226}Ra anomalies determined in saline hot springs and borings from the Jordan Rift Valley that high Ra levels in formation fluids result from leaching of U-rich source rocks. The close association of high concentrations of Ra with wells developed on the flanks of piercement-type salt domes found in parts of the Texas Gulf Coast caused Cech et al. (1988) to speculate that the salt domes may be one of the Ra sources. Due to a scarcity of available geochemical and subsurface geophysical data in the study area, the source for the Ra in the venting fluids is presently unknown. The high radium levels in the fluids advecting to the sea floor are likely to be related to a number of factors, including: (i) leaching of salt dome and salt sheets, (ii) leaching of deep-seated, kerogen-rich source rocks, (iii) desorption from clay minerals and silicate-rich sands, and (iv) leaching from subsurface uranium deposits (Cook, 1980). The interaction of rocks, salt domes, and uranium-bearing deposits as the fluids migrate through fault conduits has not been well documented in the literature and further study is needed to better understand the mechanisms controlling the distribution of Ra, and particularly the role of salt domes.

4.2.2 The Residence Time of Fluids in Barite-Bearing Seeps

Two time intervals can be discerned concerning the advecting fluids. One is the fluid traveling time (FTT) which is the time elapsed since the fluid left the subsurface source until trapped in the sediment. The other is the fluid residence time (FRT) which is the time period since the fluid was trapped in the sediments until it was sampled.

The high concentration of ^{228}Ra in fluids from barite-bearing seeps (Table 3.3) suggests that the total time, including FTT and FRT, must be less than 20 years. This is because 91% of the ^{228}Ra would have decayed away within 20 years due to its short half life (5.75 yr). Because the Ra isotope composition in the subsurface source is unknown, it is impossible to derive the exact FTT. However, the FRT can be estimated according to the following equation:

$$(^{228}Ra/^{226}Ra)_t = (^{228}Ra/^{226}Ra)_0 e^{-\lambda t} \tag{4.2}$$

where $(^{228}Ra/^{226}Ra)_t$ is the measured activity ratio of the fluid in GB-382 (Table 3.3); t is the residence time of the fluid in the sediments; $(^{228}Ra/^{226}Ra)_0$ is $^{228}Ra/^{228}Ra$ activity ratio of the fluid at the time it was trapped in the sediment; and λ is the decay constant of ^{228}Ra ($\lambda = 0.121/yr$). In this calculation it is assumed that ^{228}Ra decays exponentially with time but that ^{226}Ra remains constant due to its long half life (1,600 yr.).

94

The initial $^{228}Ra/^{226}Ra$ activity ratio of the barite chimneys could be used as a measure of $(^{228}Ra/^{226}Ra)_0$ for the advecting fluids. Thus the average initial $^{228}Ra/^{226}Ra$ activity ratio of chimneys are 1.09 ±0.07 and 0.71 ±0.08 for the fluids in Garden Banks and Mississippi Canyon, respectively (Table 3.6). The FRT calculated by this method range from 0.6 to 2.9 years indicating that the fluid seepage in the study areas is recent. This conclusion is consistent with our observations of pervasive active fluid seepage during the submarine sampling and the dating of barite chimney-ages of <7 years (Table 3.6).

4.3. Ages and Growth Rates of Barite Deposits

The following observations emerge from Figure 4.6 summarizing the radiometric ages of barite chimneys and crusts acquired in this study: (i) in general, the crusts are older than the chimneys; (ii) crusts from both Garden Banks and Mississippi Canyon areas have a similar age range, from 9.0 to 23.1 years old, and (iii) the chimneys from Mississippi Canyon yield ages from 2.5 to 6.5 years which are slightly older than the chimneys from Garden Banks which range from 0.4 to 2.5 years. The interpretation that barite deposition in the Garden Banks and Mississippi Canyon sites is a relatively recent event is substantiated by the fact that very little or no sediment cover was observed on top of these barite deposits.

Concerning the age difference between the chimneys and the crusts, the question that needs to be addressed is why all the chimneys are younger than the crusts. Two possibilities are proposed here. First, based on the growth rates (see below), the construction of a chimney should be rapid and most chimneys were probably built within 5 years (assuming the height is less than 30 cm and average growth rate is about 7 cm/yr). Because of the friable nature of these chimneys and the possible ocean bottom current erosion, the chimneys may collapse within a short period of time after their formation. Therefore, the life span of a chimney from its initial formation to its toppling was probably very short. This may be the main reason why all of the chimneys dated here are very young (< 8 yrs). Second, it is noted that the surface of most crusts is older than the bottom (Table 3.8) allowing to postulate a time-sequence for their formation. During the early stage of fluid seepage, the Ba-, and Ra-rich fluids mix with sulfate-rich seawater and precipitate barite which forms the upper part of the crust. The later seeping fluids are probably trapped below the fledgling crust surface and the Ba and Ra-rich fluids react with the dissolved sulfate in the pore fluids and precipitate barite which forms the lower part of the crusts. Because of sampling depth limitation with the submersible robot arm, only surficial crusts were collected. Therefore, the barite precipitation events deciphered here should represent the earliest events occurring in the formation of the crusts which may explain why the crusts are older than the chimneys.

Alternatively, the observed age gap between chimneys and crusts may have resulted from sampling biases. A more systematic sampling is needed in future studies to fully understand the complete history of the barite deposits.

4.3.1. Growth Rates of Chimneys

The $^{228}Th/^{228}Ra$ age profiles obtained from hardened chimneys #6, 8, and 11 (Figs. 3.17, 3.18, and 3.19) are used to reconstruct the growth history of the chimneys. Growth rates were obtained from the slopes of the regression lines

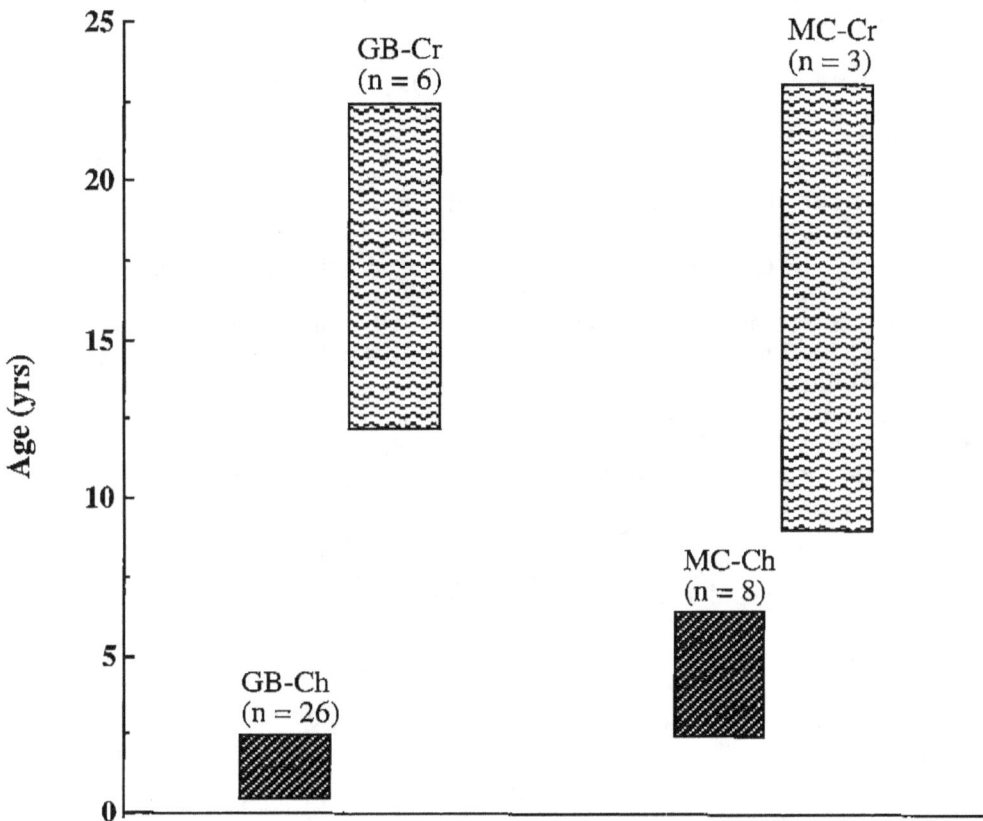

Figure 4.6. Ages of barite chimneys and crusts in the Gulf of Mexico. Notes: All the ages are corrected to the sampling time (July 20, 1993). The ages of chimneys are obtained from $^{228}Th/^{228}Ra$ method on pure barites and hardened chimneys. The ages of crusts are obtained from $^{210}Pb/^{226}Ra$ method on pure barites.

GB-Ch: Chimneys in the Garden Banks.
GB-Cr: Crusts in the Garden Banks.
MC-Ch: Chimneys in the Mississippi Canyon.
MC-Cr: Crusts in the Mississippi Canyon.

in coordinates of $^{228}Th/^{228}Ra$ ages vs. the distance from the bottom of the chimneys (Figs. 4.7, 4.8 and 4.9). In these plots a constant linear growth is assumed in each sampling interval (2 to 3 cm) and the age is assigned to the midpoint of each interval. The growth rates determined by this method are 9.3 cm/yr for chimney #6, 8.9 cm/yr for chimney #8, and 4.4 cm/yr for chimney #11. These growth rates indicate that the buildup of a chimney is very rapid. The growth rates obtained here are similar to the growth rate of about 6 cm/yr for barite-rich hydrothermal chimneys at Juan de Fuca Ridge (Grasty et al., 1988; Kim and McMurtry, 1991; Reyes et al., 1995), but greater than the value of 1.2 cm/yr calculated for a hydrothermal sulfide chimney at the same ridge (Kadko et al., 1985).

Regional differences in growth rates may occur between sites. The two chimneys from Garden Banks (chimney #6 and chimney #8) have similar growth rates and yield an average value of 9.13 ±0.28 cm/yr whereas the growth rate obtained from chimney #11 in Mississippi Canyon is about 4.4 cm/yr. The growth rate in Garden Banks is thus twice that in Mississippi Canyon. Because these barite chimneys formed by the mixing of sulfate-rich seawater with the Ba/Ra-rich seeping fluids, the difference in growth rate may be controlled either by distinct Ba concentrations in the seeping fluids and/or by different fluid seepage rates. Indeed, the end member fluid in Garden Banks contains a higher concentration of Ba than Mississippi Canyon (Table 4.1), and this could explain the faster growth rate of chimneys in Garden Banks. Alternatively, the chimney growth rates may be controlled by the fluid seepage rate. The higher the fluid seeping rate, the more Ba could be vented out resulting in more barite precipitation within a certain period of time. The higher growth rate found in the chimneys from Garden Banks may therefore suggest that the fluid seepage rate in Garden Banks is higher than in Mississippi Canyon.

4.3.2 Initial $^{228}Ra/^{226}Ra$ in the Barites

The ^{228}Ra isotope decays much faster than ^{226}Ra and therefore the latter can be assumed to have remained constant in the short life span of the barites. Thus the initial $^{228}Ra/^{226}Ra$ can be calculated according to the following equation:

$$(^{228}Ra/^{226}Ra)_t = (^{228}Ra/^{226}Ra)_0 e^{-\lambda t} \tag{4.3}$$

where $(^{228}Ra/^{226}Ra)_t$ is the measured ratio in the barite, t is the age as determined by the $^{228}Th/^{228}Ra$ dating method, $(^{228}Ra/^{226}Ra)_0$ is the initial ratio, and λ is the decay constant of ^{228}Ra ($\lambda^{228}Ra = 0.121/yr$). The decay constant of ^{226}Ra is ignored in the equation because of its long half life (1,620 yrs).

The initial $^{228}Ra/^{226}Ra$ of the chimneys determined by eq. 4.3 above are listed in Tables 3.6 and 3.7. The initial $^{228}Ra/^{226}Ra$ for the crusts were not calculated because most crusts contain ^{228}Ra below the detection limit. The initial $^{228}Ra/^{226}Ra$ of the chimneys in Garden Banks range from 0.9 to 1.2 (mean = 1.09 ±0.08, n = 24) whereas the ratios in Mississippi Canyon range from 0.6 to 0.8 (mean = 0.71 ±0.08, n = 7). The broad negative relation occurring

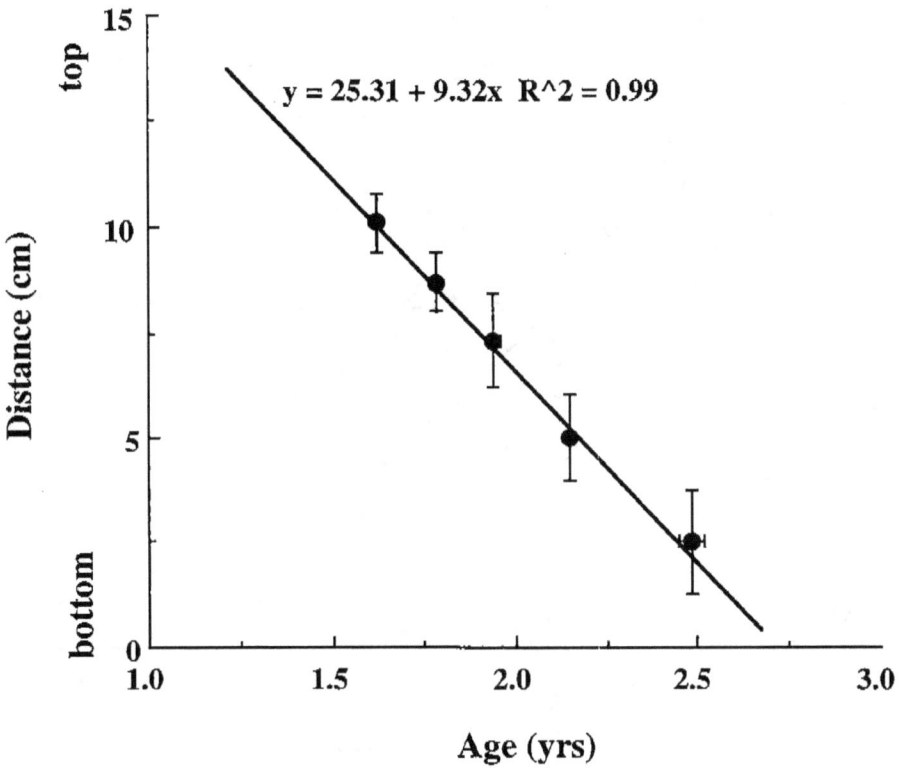

Figure 4.7. Vertical age profile for chimney #6, Garden Banks block 382. Growth rate determined on the basis of slope is 9.32 cm/yr.

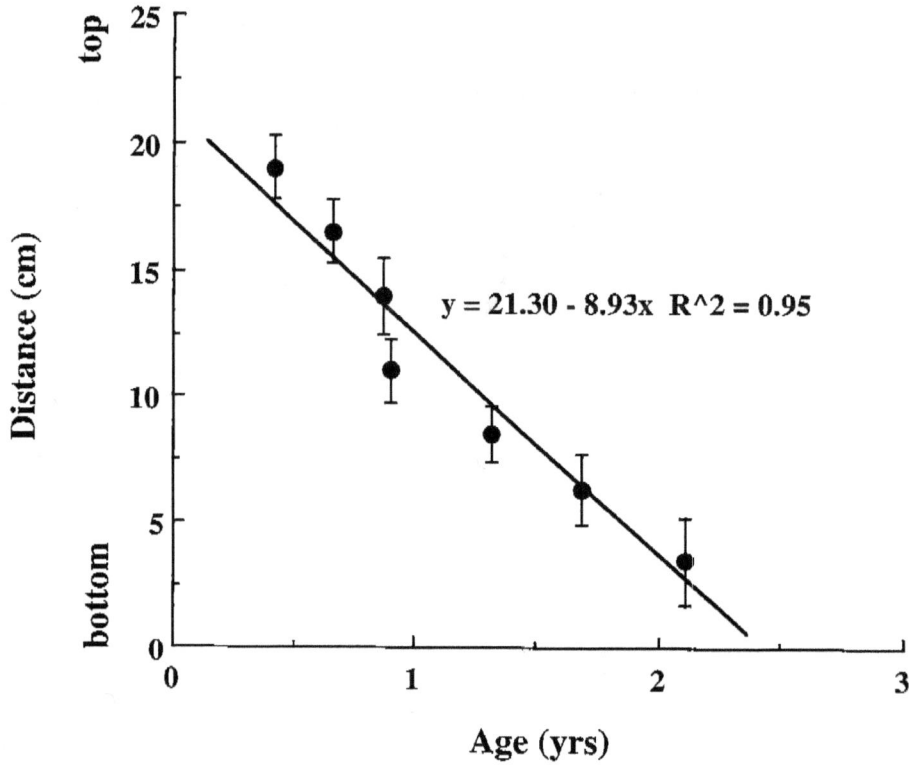

Figure 4.8. Vertical age profile for chimney #8, Garden Banks block 382. Growth rate determined on the basis of slope is 8.93 cm/yr.

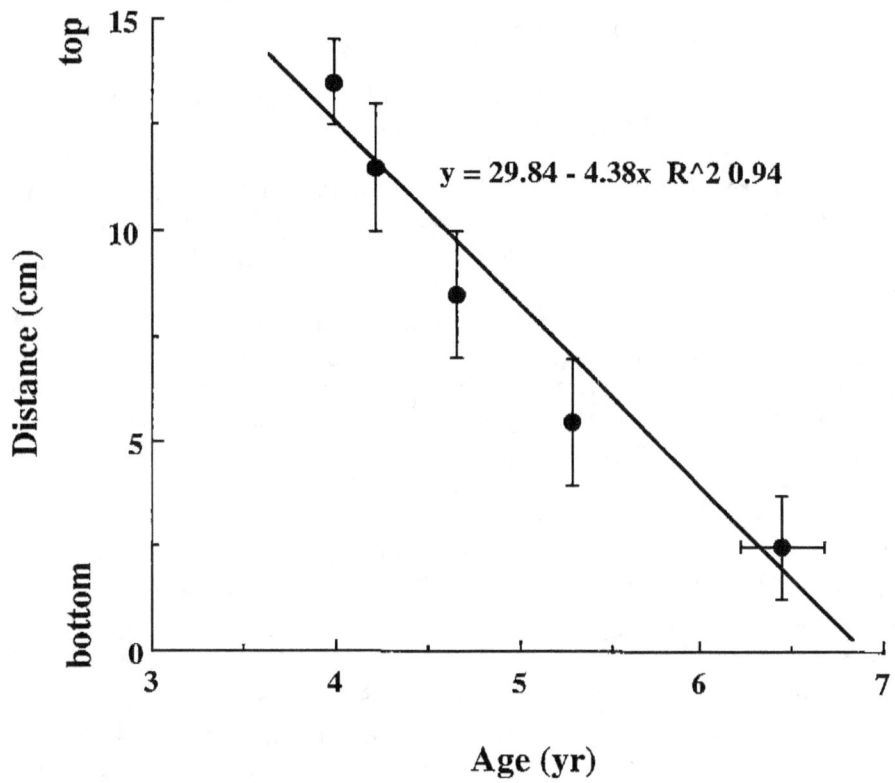

Figure 4.9. Vertical age profile for chimney #11, Mississippi Canyon block 929. Growth rate determined on the basis of slope is 4.38 cm/yr.

between the initial $^{228}Ra/^{226}Ra$ and the ages of the chimneys (Fig. 4.10) leads to the following three observations: (i) the initial $^{228}Ra/^{226}Ra$ ratios are variable; (ii) there appears to be regional differences in the initial $^{228}Ra/^{226}Ra$ between Garden Banks (0.9 to 1.2) and Mississippi Canyon (0.6 to 0.8), and (iii) a broad negative relationship exist between the initial $^{228}Ra/^{226}Ra$ and the ages of the chimneys.

Regional and temporal variations of the initial $^{228}Ra/^{226}Ra$ (from 0.2 to 1.0) have also been found in the hydrothermal sulfides and barite-enriched deposits occurring in the mid-oceanic hydrothermal vents (Stakes and Moore, 1991; Kadko and Moore, 1988). It is generally accepted that Ra in the hydrothermal deposits is primarily leached out from the basalts and the variations of initial $^{228}Ra/^{226}Ra$ are caused by differences in either fluid residence time, depth of generation of hydrothermal fluids, or temperature fluctuations near the basalts (Stakes and Moore, 1991; Kadko and Moore, 1988).

Concerning the cause(s) of the regional difference in initial $^{228}Ra/^{226}Ra$ found in the Gulf of Mexico barites, two possibilities are proposed. First, fluids in different areas may have originated from different sources. Viewed this way, the fluid source under Garden Banks area may have higher $^{228}Ra/^{226}Ra$ than under Mississippi Canyon area implying different Th/U ratios in the respective sources. Second, the subsurface fluid sources may have the same $^{228}Ra/^{226}Ra$ under the two areas, but the fluid migration time is different. Because of its short half life (5.57 yr), the ^{228}Ra concentration in the fluid decreases exponentially with migration time, but ^{226}Ra concentration can be considered to remain constant due to its long half life (1,620 yr). Hence, the longer the fluid migration time, the lower the $^{228}Ra/^{226}Ra$ in the seepage fluids would be and in turn would result in a lower initial $^{228}Ra/^{226}Ra$ values in the barite. If migration time is the controlling factor, the average initial $^{228}Ra/^{226}Ra$ value of 1.09 in Garden Banks and 0.71 in Mississippi Canyon will correspond to fluids in Mississippi Canyon travelling 3.5 years longer than the fluids in Garden Banks. The fluid migration time could be controlled by either the length of the pathway and/or the migrating rate which is reflected by the seepage rate. Therefore, the fluids in Mississippi Canyon are either derived from a deeper source, their migration rate is lower than the fluids in Garden Banks, or the source in the former is overlain by a thicker sediment sequence resulting in a longer fluid migration time.

As previously indicated, the chemistry, isotopes and radioactivity (^{226}Ra and ^{228}Ra) of the end member fluids in the two areas are different, suggesting that fluids in the two areas may be derived from different sources. Alternatively, different growth rates of chimneys (8.9 to 9.3 cm/yr in Garden Banks and 4.4 cm/yr in Mississippi Canyon) may reflect distinct fluid migration times.

Another implication concerning the initial $^{228}Ra/^{226}Ra$ is that the presence of ^{228}Ra in the barites indicates that the maximum migration time for the fluids in both areas should be less than 20 years, otherwise 91% of the ^{228}Ra would have decayed due to its short half life (5.75 yrs).

$^{228}Ra/^{226}Ra$ could also be used to date barites if the initial ratio is known. However, because the initial $^{228}Ra/^{226}Ra$ of the barites vary, $^{228}Ra/^{226}Ra$ can not be used to calculate the exact age. A plot of the ages versus the

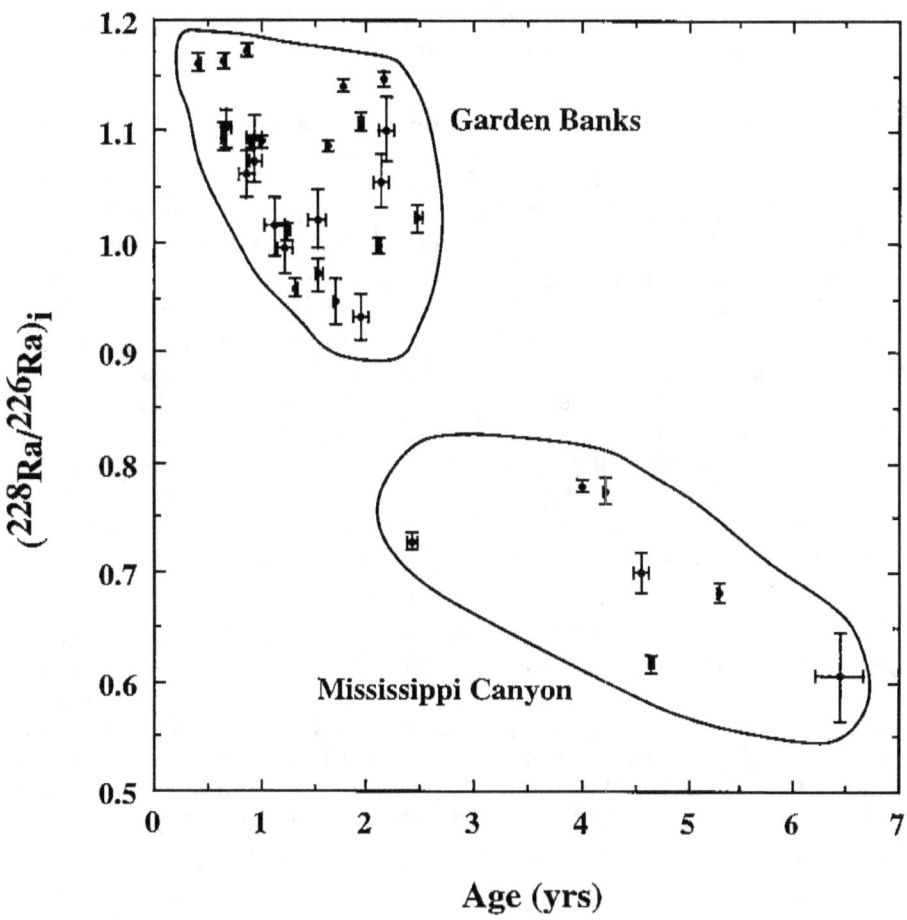

Figure 4.10. Initial $^{228}Ra/^{226}Ra$ versus age of barite chimneys.

^{228}Ra/^{226}Ra for the chimneys exhibit two negative trends (Fig. 4.11) where high ^{228}Ra/^{226}Ra ratios correspond to younger ages. One negative trend is for the chimneys in Garden Banks and the other trend is for the chimneys in Mississippi Canyon. Therefore, the ^{228}Ra/^{226}Ra may be used to estimate whether the sample is old or young but not to obtain an accurate age.

4.3.3. ^{226}Ra Activity in the Barites and Its Source/s

Relatively young barites are often radioactive because Ra is commonly coprecipitated with Ba during the formation of barite. Radioactive barites forming in different environments have been documented by previous studies. For example, high activity of ^{226}Ra has been reported in marine barites sampled in cores taken from the Northeast Equatorial Pacific (Borole and Somayajulu, 1977; Paytan et al., 1996). Radium-enriched barite sinters were reported at a cold spring site in northwestern Canada (Cecile and Jones, 1979, Cecile et al., 1984). More recently, abundant radioactive barite-sulfide deposits have been discovered at hydrothermal vents from deep-sea spreading centers (Lalou & Brivhet, 1982, 1987; Grasty et al., 1988; Moore and Stakes, 1990; Reyes et al., 1995). The overall ranges of radium activity in barites reported previously, along with the values obtained in this study, are summarized in Figure 4.12. Because the activity of ^{228}Ra is strongly controlled by the age of the sample, only ^{226}Ra activities are used here for comparison.

The specific ^{226}Ra activities of the Gulf of Mexico barites range from about 1,000 to 4,000 dpm/g and are comparable with the barite-rich hydrothermal deposits found at the deep-sea spreading centers but are two to four orders of magnitude higher than those of marine barites and sulfide-rich hydrothermal deposits (Fig. 4.12). Some barites from Mississippi Canyon (e.g., sample Ch#11-F/1, Table 3.6) contain by far the highest values (about 4,000 dpm/g) reported to date. Barites deposited in the same area of the Gulf of Mexico seem to have similar ^{226}Ra activities, but there appears to be regional differences. For example, the ^{226}Ra activities of the chimneys and crusts in Garden Banks range from 1100 to 1700 dpm/g, whereas the chimneys and crusts in Mississippi Canyon range from 2700 to 4000 dpm/g. Therefore, the ^{226}Ra activities of barites in Mississippi Canyon are higher by a factor of two relative to those in Garden Banks.

Two important questions need to be addressed concerning the ^{226}Ra in the Gulf of Mexico barites: (i) the source/s of ^{226}Ra in the barites, and (ii) the cause(s) of differences in ^{226}Ra activities between barites from Garden Banks and from Mississippi Canyon.

Seawater can be precluded as the source for ^{226}Ra in the barites because it contains trace amounts of ^{226}Ra (0.001-0.01 dpm/L, Chung, 1980). The ^{226}Ra in marine barites is commonly attributed to uptake from pore fluids which are generally enriched in ^{226}Ra by factors of 100 to 1500 (1 to 15 dpm/L) over that in near bottom water (e.g. Borole and Somayajulu, 1977; Cochran, 1979; Key, 1981; Paytan et al., 1996). The enrichment of marine pore fluids in ^{226}Ra are ascribed to two processes related to the distinct chemical behavior of U and Th in the seawater. First, alpha decay of ^{234}U in the water column produces ^{230}Th which is scavenged by adsorption onto rapidly sinking particulate matter. Second, the removal process results in ^{230}Th activities in the sediment which

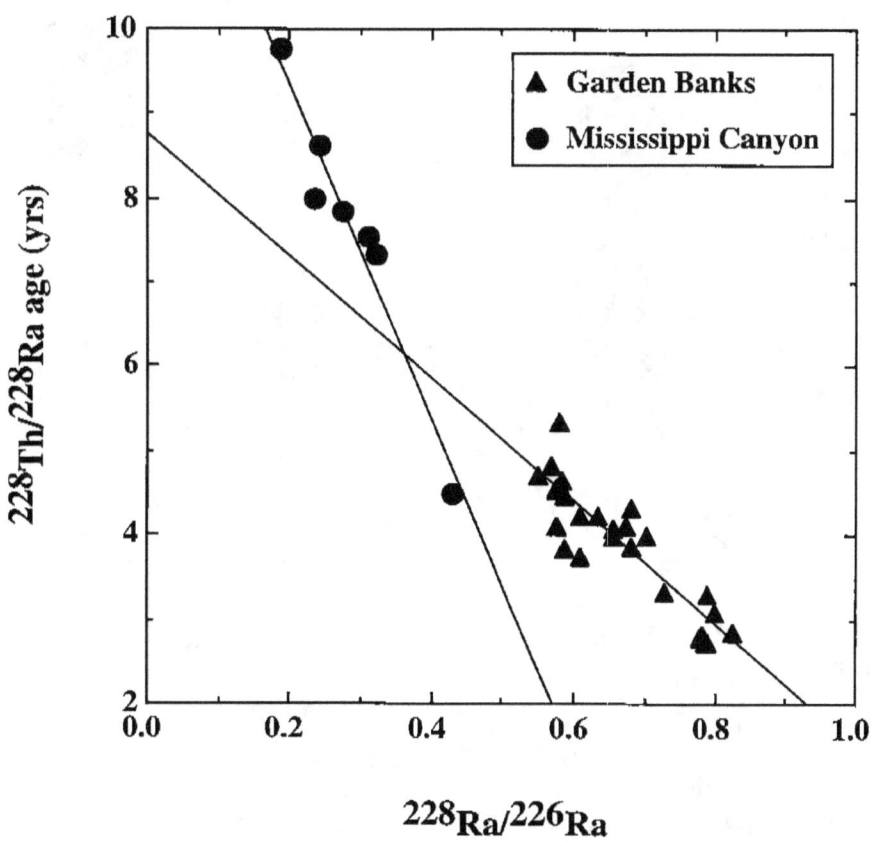

Figure 4.11. ^{228}Ra/^{226}Ra AR versus ^{228}Th/^{228}Ra ages (yrs) of chimneys. These relationships can be used to quantitatively estimate the ages of samples.

104

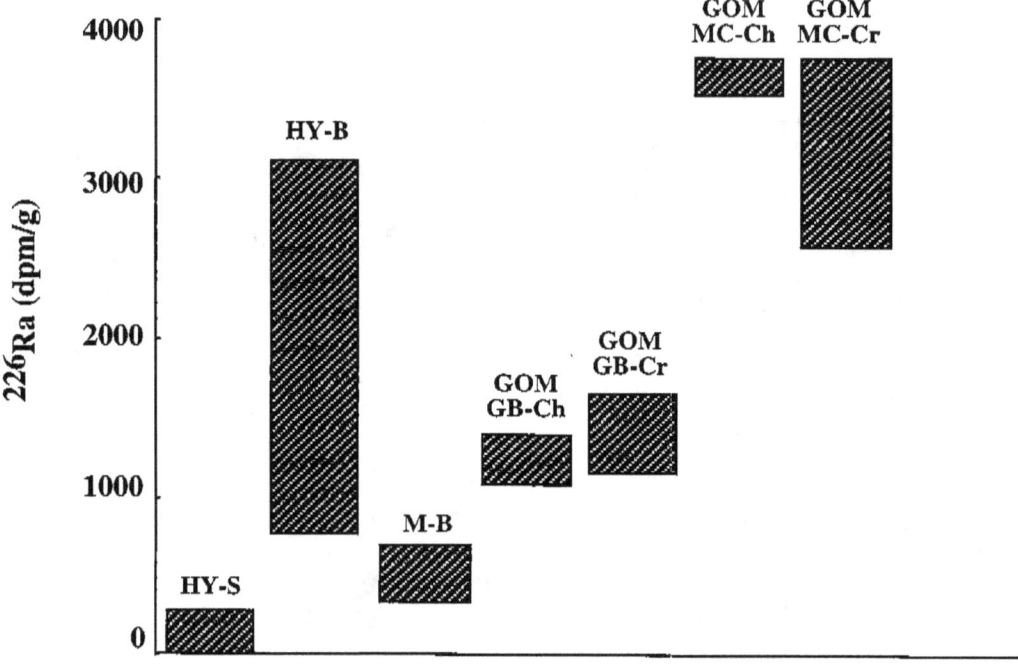

Figure 4.12. ^{226}Ra activities in barites formed in different depositional environments.

Gulf of Mexico
    GOM GB-Cr: Barite crusts from Garden Banks.
    GOM GB-Ch: Barite chimneys from Garden Banks.
    GOM MC-Cr: Barite crusts from Mississippi Canyon.
    GOM MC-Ch: Barite chimneys from Mississippi Canyon.
M-B: Marine barites (Borole and Somayajulu, 1977; Paytan et al., 1996).
HY-B: Barite-rich hydrothermal deposits (Grasty et al., 1988; Moore and Stakes, 1990; Reyes, 1993; Reyes et al., 1995). HY-S: Sulfide-rich hydrothermal deposits (Finkel et al., 1980; Lalou and Brichet, 1982; Kadko et al., 1985; Kim and McMurtry, 1991).

are in excess of the amount which can be supported by the coexisting ^{234}U (Cochran, 1979). Consequently, the ^{226}Ra resulting from the radioactive decay of excess ^{230}Th in the sediment ends up in the pore fluids by leaching and alpha-recoil processes (Kigoshi, 1971). Concerning the Gulf of Mexico barites, normal marine pore fluids can be ruled out as the source of ^{226}Ra because most barites, especially the barite chimneys, form above the water/sediment interface, and because ^{226}Ra activities in pore fluids from non-seep sediments are low (<16 dpm/L).

Basalt is generally considered as the source of ^{226}Ra for hydrothermal deposits in deep-sea spreading centers (MacDonald et al., 1980; Dymond et al., 1983; Tivey and Delaney, 1986; Kadko and Moore, 1988; Stakes and Moore, 1991; Kim and McMurtry, 1991; Stuben et al., 1994). This mechanism, however, can be dismissed here because there are no surficial basalts and no evidence of hydrothermal venting has been reported from the Gulf of Mexico.

Because Ra-rich fluid seepage is pervasive in the study areas (Fu et al., 1996), it is reasonable to propose that the ^{226}Ra in the barites is derived from fluids which originated as deep-seated formation waters. The ^{226}Ra activity of barites in Mississippi Canyon is higher than in Garden Banks (Table 3.6). By contrast, the ^{226}Ra activity in the pore fluids from Mississippi Canyon are generally lower than in Garden Banks (Table 3.3). Therefore, the difference of ^{226}Ra activity in the pore fluids can not explain the ^{226}Ra activity variation in the barites between the two areas. In order to understand the process causing the difference of ^{226}Ra activity in the barites, the homogeneous distribution law of Henderson and Kracek (1927) is applied in which the ratio of the concentrations of Ra to Ba in the precipitated crystals is proportional to the ratio of the concentrations in the final solution:

$$(Ra/Ba)_{crystal} = D \ (Ra/Ba)_{solution} \tag{4.4}$$

where D is the homogeneous distribution coefficient of Ra and Ba; $(Ra/Ba)_{crystal}$ and $(Ra/Ba)_{solution}$ are $^{226}Ra/Ba$ ratios in units of dpm/mg in barites and fluids, respectively.

It is obvious from equation 4.4 that the radioactivity in the barites are controlled by (i) the partition coefficient D, and (ii) the Ra/Ba ratio, instead of the absolute Ra concentration in the fluids. The coefficient D in the two areas is considered to be constant because of the similar temperature and pressure (water depths are 510 and 640 m in Garden Banks and Mississippi Canyon, respectively). Therefore, the difference in ^{226}Ra activities of the barites between Garden Banks and Mississippi Canyon should be controlled by the Ra/Ba ratio in the fluids. The calculated Ra/Ba ratio for the most concentrated fluids in Mississippi Canyon and Garden Banks are 9.2 and 2.7 dpm/mg, respectively (Table 4.2). Thus, the ^{226}Ra activities of barites in Mississippi Canyon are predicted to be 3.4 times that in Garden Banks. This value is close to the observed value of 2.7 for the barites (Table 4.2). Therefore, the barite ^{226}Ra activity differences between Mississippi Canyon and Garden Banks are attributed to the different Ra/Ba ratios of the fluids in the two areas.

106

Table 4.2. ²²⁶Ra/Ba ratios in barites and fluids.

Sampling area	Sample name	Barite deposits		Sample name	End member fluids		
		²²⁶Ra (dpm/g BaSO$_4$)	²²⁶Ra/Ba (dpm/mg Ba)		²²⁶Ra (dpm/L)	Ba (mg/L)	²²⁶Ra/Ba (dpm/mg Ba)
	Ch#2-a	1452	2.469	3566-1-21	2492	919	2.712
	Ch#2-b	1184	2.014				
	Ch#9-T/a	1279	2.175				
	Ch#9-M/a	1246	2.119				
	Ch#9-B/a	1339	2.277				
	Ch#9-T/b	1229	2.090				
	Ch#9-M/b	1346	2.289				
	Ch#9-B/b	1174	1.997				
Garden Banks	Ch#10-T/a	1125	1.913				
	Ch#10-M/a	1332	2.265				
	Ch#10-B/a	1250	2.126				
Block 382	Ch#10-T/b	1345	2.287				
	Ch#10-M/b	1211	2.060				
	Ch#10-B/b	1302	2.214				
	93-7-7/l	1352	2.299				
	93-8-5/3/l	1545	2.628				
	93-8-8/3/u	1502	2.554				
	93-8-7/2/u	1203	2.046				
	93-8-7/2/l	1725	2.934				
	93-8-7/3	1271	2.162				
	Average		2.246±0.245				
Mississippi Canyon	Ch#11-F/l	3945	6.709	2559-2-32	739	80	9.238
	Ch#11-F/2	3697	6.288				
	93-1-3/l	3797	6.458				
Block 929	93-4-4/1/u	2701	4.594				
	93-4-4/1/l	3940	6.701				
	Average		6.150±0.888				

Note: Pore fluids 2559-2-32 and 3566-1-21 are representatives of end member fluids in Mississippi Canyon and Garden Banks, respectively (see text). Their ²²⁶Ra activities are from Table 3.3.

4.3.4. The Source of Sulfate in the Barites

Sulfur ($\delta^{34}S$) and oxygen ($\delta^{18}O$) isotope compositions are commonly used as indicators of the source of SO_4^{2-} because they preserve the identity of the sulfate in the fluids from which the barites precipitated (Church, 1970; Sakai, 1971; Cecile et al., 1983). The following are the most common sources of sulfate attributed to marine barites.

(1) Barites precipitated from normal seawater have similar oxygen and sulfur isotope compositions to those of the coeval seawater sulfate which varied through the geological time (Cecile et al., 1983). The $\delta^{34}S$ and $\delta^{18}O$ compositions of modern seawater sulfate are constant within narrow limits and are represented by a mean $\delta^{34}S$ value of 20.3°/oo CDT and a mean $\delta^{18}O$ value of 9.7°/oo SMOW, respectively (Cecile et al., 1983; Faure, 1986). The constancy and oceanic uniformity are due to the rapid mixing rate of the oceans and the long residence time of sulfate in seawater (i.e., 12.3 Ma, Drever, 1982). In modern pelagic sediments most large barites (>5 μm), interpreted to be precipitated from seawater (Church, 1970), match or are slightly heavier in both oxygen and sulfur isotope compositions relative to modern seawater sulfate.

(2) Barites formed in anoxic environments display heavier $\delta^{34}S$ and $\delta^{18}O$ values than those of the coeval seawater sulfate. The enrichments of ^{34}S and ^{18}O of barites are ascribed to the reduction of sulfate ions by anaerobic bacteria such as Desulfovibrio (Berner, 1971). During bacterial reduction, sulfates containing ^{16}O and ^{32}S isotopes are preferentially metabolized (Rafter and Mizutani, 1967; Sakai, 1971; Mizutani and Rafter, 1973; Claypool et al., 1980; Cecile et al., 1983). Thus, barites precipitated from a residual sulfate reservoir will display heavier $\delta^{34}S$ and $\delta^{18}O$ values than those of the coeval seawater sulfate. This process has been used to explain the heavier $\delta^{34}S$ and $\delta^{18}O$ values of barite off the California coast (Goldberg et al., 1969; Sakai and Krouse, 1971), barite concretions from the Japan Sea (Sakai, 1971), and barite nodules and rosettes of Late Devonian age in Nevada (Rye et al., 1978).

(3) Barites can also form by oxidation of sulfides. Since most sulfides have highly negative $\delta^{34}S$ values, barites formed by this process often exhibit light sulfur isotope compositions. The $\delta^{18}O$ of the barites formed by this process varies depending on the $\delta^{18}O$ values of dissolved oxygen (O_2) and the water (H_2O) from which the barites precipitated. This is because three of the four sulfate oxygens are derived from dissolved oxygen (O_2) and the forth one from water (H_2O) during the oxidation of sulfides (Lloyd, 1968). Smaller barites (<5 μm) in modern pelagic sediments usually show lighter $\delta^{34}S$ values than modern seawater sulfate and were explained by this sulfide oxidation process (Church, 1970).

(4) Barites formed by mixing of barium-rich hydrothermal fluids with sulfate-rich cold seawater are common in submarine hydrothermal vent sites (e.g. Peter and Scott, 1988; Kusakabe et al., 1990). In this case, the $\delta^{34}S$ of barites are controlled by the mixing of the following sources: (i) seawater sulfate ($\delta^{34}S$ = 20.3°/oo CDT); (ii) sulfides and sulfate leached from basalt ($\delta^{34}S$ of about 0°/oo CDT), and (iii) residual seawater sulfate after thermal chemical sulfate reduction occurred at high temperatures ($\delta^{34}S$ > 20.3°/oo CDT).

Therefore, the $\delta^{34}S$ values of hydrothermal vent barites depend on the proportions of the above sources in the mixture of the fluid from which the barites precipitated (Zierenberg et al., 1984; Bertine and Keene, 1987; Kusakabe et al., 1990). The $\delta^{18}O$ values of hydrothermal barites are controlled primarily by the ambient temperature which determines both the degree of sulfate reduction and the extent of oxygen isotope exchange between dissolved sulfate and water (Lloyd, 1968; Bertine and Keene, 1987; Kusakabe et al., 1990; Urabe and Kusakabe, 1990).

Concerning the GOM barites, it is important to note that both $\delta^{34}S$ and $\delta^{18}O$ of the chimneys, listed in Table 3.5, are isotopically similar to modern sea water sulfate. Therefore it is apparent that seawater sulfate has been the chief contributor to the formation of the barite chimneys. Modern seawater can be dismissed as a source for the crusts because of their substantially heavier $\delta^{34}S$ and $\delta^{18}O$ values relative to modern seawater sulfate. The possibility that the crusts formed by oxidation of sulfides is also ruled out because this process should yield lighter rather than heavier $\delta^{34}S$ values. Sulfate reduction at high temperature could cause enrichments of ^{34}S and ^{18}O in barites because sulfates containing ^{16}O and ^{32}S isotopes are preferentially reduced there (Lloyd, 1968). Enrichment of ^{18}O in barites can also be attributed to isotope exchange between dissolved sulfate and water, accelerated at higher temperatures, and cause the oxygen isotope composition of sulfate to shift toward the equilibrium sulfate-seawater value of 38°/oo SMOW (Lloyd, 1968; Zierenberg et al., 1984; Bertine and Keene, 1987; Kusakabe et al., 1990; Urabe and Kusakabe, 1990). Regarding the GOM barites, however, the temperature factor seems to be insignificant in controlling the $\delta^{34}S$ and $\delta^{18}O$ of the barites because our direct observations indicate relatively cold (8.6°C) and practically invariable bottom-water temperatures.

The observed enrichments of ^{34}S and ^{18}O in the GOM barite crusts (Fig. 3.11) are likely caused by bacterial reduction of seawater sulfate. This interpretation is corroborated by the following two lines of evidence. First, SEM analyses reveal that the crusts consist of up to 8% by volume pyrite. During bacterial sulfate reduction to H_2S, the gas may escape from the system or react with ferrous iron to form pyrite. Therefore the presence of pyrite in the crusts is a good indicator of sulfate reduction. Second, the $\delta^{13}C$ of calcite in the crusts ranges from -21 to -36°/oo PDB (Table 3.5). These light isotope values suggest that the carbonate-carbon is derived from the microbial degradation of organic phases (most likely thermogenic methane). As previously discussed, reduced carbon is oxidized to produce HCO_3^- during microbial sulfate reduction which is precipitated subsequently as authigenic carbonate with light $\delta^{13}C$ inherited from the fossil fuel- derived carbon. Thus, the light $\delta^{13}C$ values of calcite strongly indicate the occurrence of sulfate reduction during the formation of the barite crusts.

The enrichments in ^{34}S and ^{18}O relative to the seawater in samples from inner side of chimneys (Table 3.5 and Fig. 3.12) suggest that sulfate reduction also occurred during the formation of the chimneys interior. However, the sulfate reduction rate and intensity occurring in the chimneys must be lower than that occurring in the crusts. This is because the enrichments in ^{34}S and ^{18}O relative to the seawater in chimneys are much smaller than those in the crusts (Fig. 3.11). For example, the $\delta^{34}S$ of barite crusts are as high as 62.3°/oo (CDT, Table 3.5), which indicates that 95% of seawater sulfate has been reduced based on the values of $\delta^{34}S$ and the concentration of sulfate in pore fluids. In contrast, the highest $\delta^{34}S$ value in chimneys is 21.6°/oo (CDT) (Table 3.5) suggesting that only about 5% of seawater sulfate has been reduced.

4.3.5. The Source of Major (Ba) and Trace Elements (Sr and Ca) in the Barites

The mechanism for the formation of barite from normal seawater is problematic because modern oceans are commonly undersaturated with respect to barite due primarily to the low concentration of Ba (e.g., the average concentration of Ba in seawater is about 14 ppb, while the saturation value is 44 to 50 ppb, Church and Wolgemuth, 1972). Two barium sources have been proposed to explain the occurrence of barite in normal marine sediments. One source of Ba is from dissolution of biologically-derived inorganic and organic compounds in sulfate-rich micro-environments (Church, 1970; Dehairs et al., 1980). The other source is from barium-rich brine seeps (Hanor, 1982).

Our direct observations during submersible dives indicate a close association of barite deposits with gaseous hydrocarbon seeps. In addition, high concentrations of Ba (up to 1,173 ppm) were measured in the pore fluids sampled from barite-bearing seeps (Table 3.3) and all these pore fluids are supersaturated relative to barites. Therefore it is evident that the most likely source of Ba for the GOM barites is the fluids advecting to the seafloor and derived from formation waters ascending through fault conduits.

Sr and Ca are generally the next most abundant elements after barium in the barite due to their similar ionic radii (1.13 Å for Sr^{2+}, 0.99 Å for Ca^{2+} and 1.35 Å for Ba^{2+}). However, compared with barites from hydrothermal and marine settings, the GOM barites are anomalously enriched in Sr and Ca by a factor of about 15 and 28, respectively (Fig. 4.13). This suggests that the Sr and Ca of the GOM barites must be derived from a source other than the Gulf of Mexico seawater. As shown in the results, in addition to Ba the pore fluids (pore fluids type III) sampled from barite deposition sites are also highly enriched in Sr (up to 250 ppm) and Ca (up to 3000 ppm) relative to modern GOM bottom waters (7.4 ppm and 389 ppm for Sr and Ca, respectively, Aharon et al, 1992). It is therefore self-evident that the Sr and Ca are derived from venting fluids. This interpretation is strongly supported by the similar $^{87}Sr/^{86}Sr$ ratios in the barites to those in the venting fluids. As shown in Figure 3.13, $^{87}Sr/^{86}Sr$ ratios of barites (including chimneys and crusts) from Garden Banks (0.70857-0.70861) are slightly higher than those from Mississippi Canyon (0.70845-0.70849). However, their values are very close to the saline end member fluids in each area (The $^{87}Sr/^{86}Sr$ ratios for the saline end member fluids in Garden Banks and Mississippi Canyon are 0.70854 ±0.00001 and 0.70843 ±0.00001, respectively). The slightly higher $^{87}Sr/^{86}Sr$ ratios in barites than the end member fluids may result from the addition of Sr from seawater (0.70917). The contribution of Sr from seawater in the formation of barite can be estimated from the following simple mass balance equation:

$$A\ (^{87}Sr/^{86}Sr)_{sw} + (1-A)\ (^{87}Sr/^{86}Sr)_f = (^{87}Sr/^{86}Sr)_{br} \qquad (4.5)$$

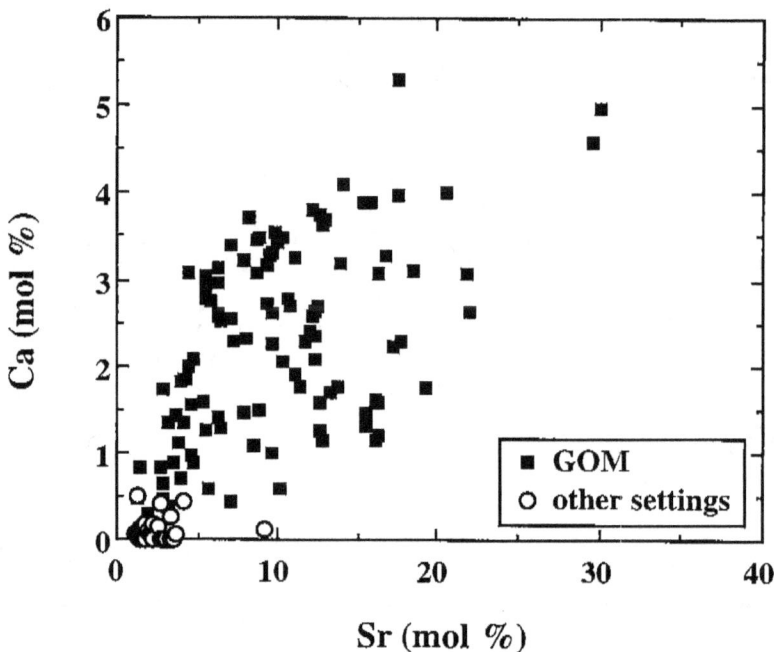

Figure 4.13. Compositions of Ca and Sr in barites from GOM and barites from other settings (hydrothermal, marine and continental settings). Note: Compared with barites from other settings, the GOM barites are enriched in Sr and Ca by a factor of about 15 and 28, respectively. The data for hydrothermal barites are from Hofmann and Baumann (1984), Kalogeropoulos and Mitropoulos (1983), Hannington and Scott (1988), and Bertine and Keene (1987) and the data for marine and continental barites are from Church (1970) and Hanor (1966).

where A is the fractional contribution of Sr from seawater; sw, f and br subscripts are the $^{87}Sr/^{86}Sr$ ratios of seawater (0.70917), end member fluids (0.70854 and 0.70843 for Garden Banks and Mississippi Canyon, respectively) and barites, respectively. Using the highest $^{87}Sr/^{86}Sr$ ratios in the barites (0.70861 and 0.70849 for Garden Banks and Mississippi Canyon, respectively, Table 3.5), the equation above yields the maximum amounts of Sr from seawater of 11% and 8% for the barites in Garden Banks and Mississippi Canyon, respectively.

4.3.6. Depositional Model of the Barites in the Gulf of Mexico

The isotope compositions of barites presented above allow us to delineate a model of their origin (Fig. 4.14). In general, the GOM barites formed by the mixing of sulfate-rich seawater with Ba, Sr, and Ca-rich formation fluids advecting with the hydrocarbons. The chimneys formed at or above the sediment/water interface whereas the crusts formed below the sediment/water interface. The latter precipitated from residual seawater sulfate left over from a pool of pore water sulfate consumed by sulfate-reducing bacteria in a closed or semiclosed system (Fig. 4.14).

Since the chimneys formed in oxidizing environments at or above the sediment/water interface, they preserve the sulfur and oxygen isotope compositions of seawater sulfate. Slightly heavier $\delta^{34}S$ and $\delta^{18}O$ values measured in some samples from the inside of the chimneys may have resulted from weak bacterial sulfate reduction in the micro-environments.

The sulfur and oxygen isotope compositions of the barite crusts clearly place their formation in anoxic environments below the sediment/water interface where extensive sulfate reduction occurred. Therefore, it is reasonable to suggest that the extensive bacterial sulfate reduction in the pore fluids preceded the Ba, Sr, and Ca-rich fluids venting through the sediments. Prior to the formation of the crusts, the pore fluids must have been enriched in H_2S, HCO_3^- with light $\delta^{13}C$ and impoverished in SO_4 with heavier $\delta^{34}S$ and $\delta^{18}O$ due to sulfate reduction using an organic carbon substrate. When the Ba, Sr, and Ca-rich fluids vented through the sediments and mixed with the pore fluids, light $\delta^{13}C$-calcite and heavy $\delta^{34}S$ and $\delta^{18}O$ barites co-precipitated due to the supersaturation of the fluid with respect to both calcite and barite. This model explains why most calcite and barite in the crusts are interlocked showing mosaic textures. Pyrite could have precipitated either before or after the fluid venting through the sediments, depending on whether the source of ferrous iron was from sediments or from the venting fluids. Sulfate reduction using thermogenic methane is inferred on the basis of $\delta^{13}C$ of carbonates in the crusts (-21 to -36°/oo PDB, Table 3.5). This is consistent with the submersible observations that intensive gaseous hydrocarbon venting occurs in barite depositional areas.

4.4. The Impact of Ra and Ba-Rich Venting Fluids on the Benthic Habitat

4.4.1. Fluxes of Radium/Barium-Rich Fluids from Point Sources

The fluxes of the radium and barium-rich fluids from which the Gulf of Mexico barite precipitated are important. The following approach is used to

112

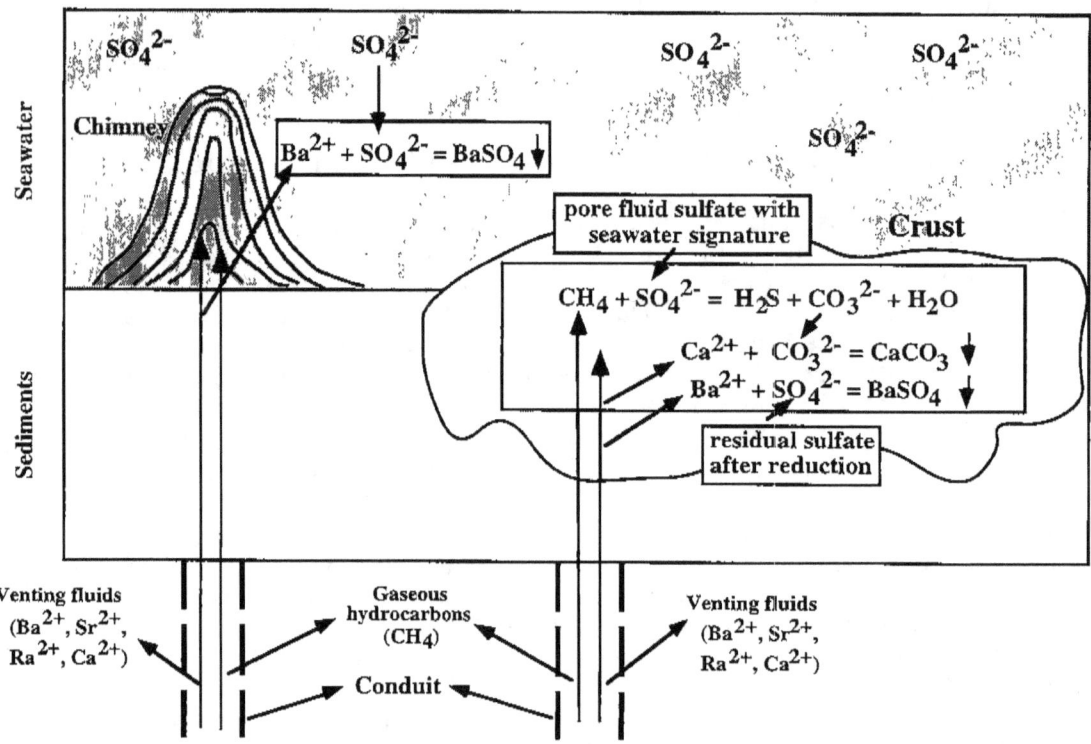

Figure 4.14. Depositional model of GOM barites. Note that chimney and crust are not shown to scale.

estimate the radium and barium fluxes from a point source. Radium fluxes are derived first.

Given the radioactivity of fluid seepage and the growth rate of a radioactive barite chimney, the flux of radium in dpm/yr can be determined according to the following equation:

$$F = (V\rho A_{Ra_i})/t \qquad (4.6)$$

where F is the average flux of radium in dpm/yr; V is the volume of the barite deposit in cm^3; ρ is the density of the barite deposit in gm/cm^3; t is the duration of growth (Ra-rich fluid emission) in years; and Ra_i is the average total initial radium activity in dpm/g scavenged by the barite. The Ra_i is the summation of the two dominant radium isotopes, ^{226}Ra and ^{228}Ra. During the initial fluid emission at t = 0, this value can be calculated from the actual measurements of Ra activities as follows:

$$A_{Ra_i} = {}^{226}Ra_i + {}^{228}Ra_i \qquad (4.7)$$

where $^{226}Ra_i$ and $^{228}Ra_i$ are the initial activities in dpm/g of the two Ra isotopes. Due to the long half life of ^{226}Ra (1,620 yrs) and the young ages of the barite deposits (< 30 yrs), the measured ^{226}Ra values can be used as $^{226}Ra_i$. $^{228}Ra_i$ can be obtained from the following equation:

$$^{228}Ra_i = {}^{226}Ra_i({}^{228}Ra/{}^{226}Ra)_i \qquad (4.8)$$

where $({}^{228}Ra/{}^{226}Ra)_i$ is the initial $^{228}Ra/{}^{226}Ra$ activity ratio of the barite deposits.

Equation (4.6) can be used to calculate the radium fluxes of the barite deposits. For illustrative purposes, let's assume that a barite deposit forming on top of a point-source emission site has a truncated conical-shape form (Fig. 4.15), which is typical to the observed morphologies of the chimneys and the crusts blanketing mud-volcanoes in the Gulf of Mexico. For a truncated conical-shape barite chimney, the radium flux in dpm/yr units from a point source can be determined by the following equation:

$$F = [1/3\pi h(r_1^2+r_2^2 + r_1r_2)\rho A_{Ra(i)}]/t \qquad (4.9)$$

Where r_1 and r_2 are the radii of the base and the top, respectively, of a truncated conical barite feature in cm and h is the height of the chimney in cm (Fig. 4.15).

Because the term h/t in equation (4.9) equals the average growth rate (G) of the chimney, this equation can be rearranged into:

$$F = 1/3\pi G(r_1^2+r_2^2 + r_1r_2)\rho A_{Ra(i)} \qquad (4.10)$$

where G is the vertical average growth rate in cm/yr.

Using equation (4.10) and the parameters in Table 4.3, fluxes of radium emission from three barite chimneys are calculated and their values are

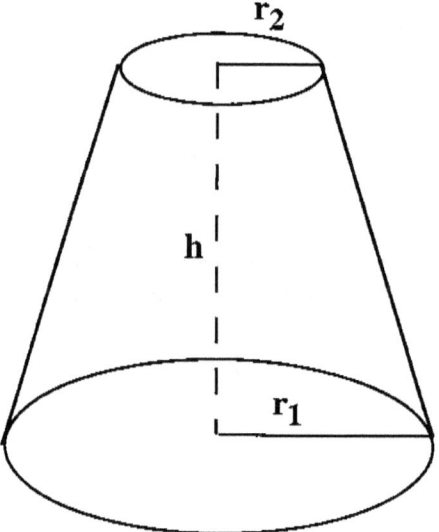

Figure 4.15. Dominant morphological truncated conical-shaped barite chimneys used in the modeling of radium fluxes (see text).

Table 4.3. Fluxes of radium-rich fluids calculated from barite chimneys.

Chimney name	Top radius (cm)	Bottom radius (cm)	Growth rate (cm/yr)	Density (gm/cm³)	Ra$_i$ (dpm/gm)	Ra Flux (dpm/yr)	Fluid flux (L/yr)
Garden Banks block 382							
Ch#6	2.0	4.0	9.3	2.6	2000	1.4×10^6	270
Ch#8	2.0	3.5	8.9	2.6	2132	1.2×10^6	230
Mississippi Canyon block 929							
Ch#11	2.5	7.0	4.4	2.6	3987	3.5×10^6	2920

Note: Ra$_i$ is the mean total initial radium activity in dpm/gm scavenged by the barite (see text).

1.2×10^6 and 1.43×10^6 dpm/yr in Garden Banks and 3.5×10^6 dpm/yr in Mississippi Canyon. The highest total radioactivity ($A^{226}Ra + A^{228}Ra$) measured in pore fluids from barite areas are 5.2×10^3 and 1.2×10^3 dpm/L (Table 3.3) in Garden Banks (GB-382) and Mississippi Canyon(MC-929), respectively. Thus, leakage of 230 to 270 L/yr of fluids in GB-382 and 2920 L/yr of fluids in MC-929 from a single point source are required to account for the radium present in the barite chimneys (Table 4.3).

4.4.2. Leakage of Radium/Barium-Rich Fluids in the Benthic Habitat

In the following we derive estimates of Ba and Ra fluxes into the benthic habitat of the Louisiana upper slope using the preceding fluid fluxes from point sources amounting to a mean of 250 L/yr in Garden Banks and 2,920 L/yr in Mississippi Canyon. Here we assume that pore fluids in barite-bearing seeps are saturated with respect to barite and therefore in chemical equilibrium with the sediments.

The annual discharge estimates of Ba and Ra from barite-bearing seeps are listed in Table 4.4. Annual fluxes from the Mississippi River are also listed for comparison purposes. With the exception of the areal coverage of seeps, to be discussed below, all other data are self-explanatory. Although leakage of hydrocarbons from the deep reservoirs on the upper Louisiana slope has been known for over two decades (see MacDonald et al., 1993 for a review), their areal extent is still debated. Using the imagery data reported by MacDonald et al. (1993) we estimate that about 5% of the upper Louisiana slope area of 15,552 km^2 is covered by bottom hydrocarbon seeps, and only 0.1% by barite-bearing seeps (i.e., 1/50 of seeps, amounting to 16 km^2). On the basis of submersible observations we also estimate a density of 5 point sources per square meter(Fig. 1.2 B).

Viewed this way, the annual fluxes of Ba using either Garden Banks or Mississippi Canyon fluid rates yield comparable values (i.e., 2.3×10^{10} and 2.1×10^{10} g/yr, respectively) and are of the same order of magnitude as the total annual Ba discharge from the Mississippi River (4.1×10^{10} g/yr). Calculations of the total Ra fluxes (i.e., $^{226}Ra + ^{228}Ra$) yield a similar picture, namely close agreement between Garden Banks and Mississippi Canyon rates (1.2×10^{14} and 2.8×10^{14} dpm/L) which amount to fluxes having the same order of magnitude as the Mississippi River (1.5×10^{14} dpm/L). The considerably slower fluid flow rates in seeps relative to the River are compensated by the much greater concentration of the Ba and Ra elements in the seepage fluids (Table 4.4). Another major difference between the seep sources and the river source is that the former delivers the Ba and Ra directly to the benthic habitat whereas the latter gets dispersed from the surface. A future comprehensive survey of Ba and Ra concentrations in bottom waters is required in order to estimate the proportion scavanged by the barites and the leftover leakage into the bottom waters.

Although our flux estimates carry the uncertainty of the areal coverage of barite-bearing seeps, we feel that the values are likely to be conservative. The assumptions regarding the parameters of the model can be tested by future empirical observations and the veracity of the estimates can now be challenged by future studies.

117

Table 4.4. Annual discharge estimates based on data from barite-bearing seeps in the Garden Banks and Mississippi Canyon produced in this study. Discharges from the Mississippi River into the Gulf of Mexico are shown for comparison purposes.

[1] Source	[2] F_{fluid} (L/yr)	[3] C_{Ba} (mg/L)	[4] $A_{226\text{-}Ra}$ (dpm/L)	[5] $A_{228\text{-}Ra}$ (dpm/L)	[6] F_{Ba} (g/yr)	[7] $F_{226\text{-}Ra}$ (dpm/yr)	[8] $F_{228\text{-}Ra}$ (dpm/yr)	[9] F_{Ra} (dpm/yr)
Garden Banks	250	1,173	3,656	2,453	2.3×10^{10}	7.3×10^{13}	4.9×10^{13}	1.2×10^{14}
Mississippi Canyon	2,920	91	739	491	2.1×10^{10}	1.7×10^{14}	1.1×10^{14}	2.8×10^{14}
Mississippi River	507×10^{12}	8×10^{-2}	0.18	0.12	4.1×10^{10}	9.1×10^{13}	6.1×10^{13}	1.5×10^{14}

[1] Garden Banks: GB-382 and GB-338; Mississippi Canyon: MC-929.

[2] Seeps fluid fluxes data from Table 4.3; Mississippi River discharge is the 46 year mean of 507 km^3/yr (Dinnel and Wiseman, 1986).

[3] Ba concentration in seep pore fluids from Table 3.4; Mississippi River data from Buerkert (1997).

[4,5] Ra activities in seep pore fluids from Table 3.3; Mississippi River data from Krest (1995).

[6,7,8] $F = F_{fluid} \times C$ (or A): Annual discharges from seeps are estimated over the Louisiana upper slope area of 15,552 km^2 assuming a barite-seep distribution of 0.1% of area and a density of 5 point-sources per square meter (see text).

[9] Total radium flux (^{226}Ra + ^{228}Ra).

117

^{226}Ra and ^{228}Ra activities of the saline fluids advecting on Garden Banks and Mississippi Canyon are highly anomalous as they exceed by a factor of up to 2.8×10^4 and 5.5×10^5, respectively, the values reported from the Gulf of Mexico ambient deep water (Table 3.3). This observation suggests that Ra in the fluids venting on the sea floor may diffuse freely into the water column and may contribute to the reported radium enrichment in the Gulf of Mexico relative to the inflowing Caribbean Sea waters (Reid, 1979, 1984; Reid et al., 1979; Key, 1981).

The studies conducted by Reid (1979) and Key (1981) have indicated that: (i) the top 100 m of central Gulf of Mexico waters have a mean specific ^{226}Ra activity higher by up to 0.11 dpm/L relative to the Caribbean Sea, (ii) the average near-bottom ^{226}Ra for the Gulf of Mexico (0.132 ± 0.002 dpm/L) is statistically indistinguishable from the inflowing Caribbean Sea waters (0.123 ± 0.008 dpm/L), but the detailed analyses hint that Gulf of Mexico samples might be slightly higher than that of Caribbean, and (iii) the increase of ^{226}Ra activity with depth is greater in the Gulf of Mexico than in the Caribbean Sea. The excess ^{226}Ra in the Gulf of Mexico was attributed by these authors (op. cit.) to either deep (about 600 m) injection of Ra produced after the water influx from the Caribbean Sea, or to the relatively long residence time of deep water in the Gulf of Mexico allowing for accumulation of Ra diffusing upward from the sediment. In a subsequent time-series study, Reid (1979, 1984) and Reid et al. (1979) also found a significant increase of both ^{226}Ra and ^{228}Ra activities from 1973 to 1976 in the upper 100 m of the Gulf of Mexico (i.e., from 0.072 ± 0.007 to 0.091 ± 0.007 dpm/L for ^{226}Ra and from 0.051 ± 0.006 to 0.062 ± 0.003 dpm/L for ^{228}Ra), that was attributed to a Ra flux from sediments on the northern Gulf of Mexico shelf.

The impact of these Ra-rich fluids leakage from seeps into the overlying water column of the Gulf of Mexico is not presently known with certainty because of the absence of Ra and daughter isotopes determinations in the water column above seeps. However, gullies filled with highly radioactive coarse barite sediment and occurrence of Ra-rich barite chimneys over extensive areas of the slope suggest that the phenomena might be widespread on the sea floor (Fig. 1.2). Therefore, previously unknown leakage of Ra-rich fluids on the sea floor may be one of the major factors controlling the Ra (and Ba) budget in both bottom and surface waters of the Gulf of Mexico. Fluid venting is likely to be periodic and with variable intensity because fault-related seeps are not continually active (Roberts et al., 1990). Hence leakage periodicity may have contributed to the temporal variability of ^{226}Ra and ^{228}Ra in the near-surface Gulf of Mexico observed by Reid (1979, 1984) and Reid et al. (1979). The knowledge of the impact of radioactive fluids leakage on benthic marine habitats is presently in its infancy. But the observation of extensive dead fields of methanotrophic mussels surrounding the seeps in GB-382 and GB-338 and the presence of mussels engulfed in highly radioactive barite sands (Fig. 1.2 D) suggest that harmful effects of excessive radioactivity on the benthic fauna are likely (see below). Further investigations along the line of this study should be important to the overall assessment of the Ra (and Ba) budget in the Gulf of Mexico in general, and for evaluation of the environmental impact of natural radium discharges on the offshore habitats in particular.

It needs to be stated that recent studies by Moore (1996, 1997) indicate that submarine groundwater discharge may be responsible for the ^{226}Ra enrichments to coastal waters and such fluxes may contribute to the ^{226}Ra in the global ocean. The results of this study indicates that natural discharges of Ra through faults intersecting the seafloor may be another source of ^{226}Ra in the ocean and further studies are needed to assess this problem.

4.4.3. The Impact of Radium/Barium-Rich Fluid Venting on the Benthic Fauna

A total of 42 faunal samples were assayed for ^{226}Ra activities which range widely from below detection limits to 10.7 dpm/g (Tables 3.11 and 3.12). A simple student-t test reveals that only soft-body galatheid crabs from barite seeps are significantly different from the rest of the seep faunal elements. This result can be explained by a number of conjectures. The most likely explanation is that the scavenging behavior of these crabs results in the ingestion of radium-rich barite material and consequent deposition of resistent particles in the GI tract of the crabs. Although it is beyond the scope of this study, future investigations should include separation of GI tracts from whole soft tissue in all seep fauna, including methanotrophic mussels, so that this relationship can be clearly delineated.

The observation that calcareous shells and soft tissue bodies of the methanotrophic mussels from barite and carbonate seeps are statistically indistinguishable with regard to their ^{226}Ra content leads to the following plausible explanations.

The high concentrations of Ba present in the venting fluids of barium-radium-rich sites may cause rapid precipitation of $BaSO_4$ when the venting fluids come into contact with seawater sulfate. The accompanying soluble ^{226}Ra is consequently rapidly co-precipitated with highly insoluble barite; thus, the seep water is possibly relatively Ra depleted (up to 98% removal efficiency according to Hanslik and Mansfield, 1990) when it reaches the mussels surrounding the barite deposits. In contrast, natural hydrocarbon seep emissions contain barium concentrations well below the K_{SP} for barite; Hence, available ^{226}Ra does not coprecipitate with $BaSO_4$ because it does not precipitate in these sites. "Free" radium present in carbonate seeps emission fluid is, therefore, possibly available for uptake by fauna at carbonate-seep sites. It was not possible to test this conjecture because all available fluids consisted of interstitial pore fluids and did not necessarily represent epibenthic venting fluids issuing directly from the vents.

The extremely high concentrations of Ba in the venting fluids of barium seeps may competitively interfere with the biological uptake of relatively low concentration Ra in the venting fluids. Barium is present in the radium-rich barite formations at g/g concentration levels, while coprecipitated ^{226}Ra is present at the parts per trillion (picograms/g) level. This is representative of the relative abundances of soluble elemental barium and radium in aqueous venting fluids (Fig. 3.29). If the biokinetics of uptake can be assumed to follow first order processes, the rate of uptake before equilibrium levels are reached will be proportional to the elemental concentration of each ionic species. Given a relative abundance ratio of ^{226}Ra/Ba of approximately 10^{-12}, biouptake of Ba should be greatly enhanced over that of ^{226}Ra in agreement with our observations (Fig. 3.29). In addition, the discrimination factor (DF) for radium with respect to barium in marine organisms is different and largely dependent on the effective ionic radius of the respective element. According to Szabo (1967), the sequence of selectivity in Mollusca and Crustacea is found to be as follows:

Element: Ra>   Ba>   Sr>   Ca>   Mg
(DF)   (19)   (18)   (1.2)   (1.0)   (0.1)

where DF is the Discrimination Factor which, for example, when calculated with respect to Ba is as follows:

$$DF_{(Ra/Ba)}= [(C_{Ra}/C_{Ba})_{org}/(C_{Ra}/C_{Ba})_{sw}] \tag{4.11}$$

where C= concentration of the respective chemical element in the organism (org) or sea water (sw) as denoted by subscripts.

Fairly high levels of Sr and Ca are also known to be present in the pore fluids of barium-radium-rich seeps (Table 3.1), and these elements may also selectively compete for biological radium uptake by virtue of their respective smaller discrimination factors.

Marine Mollusca have been extensively studied for radium and other radionuclides. A comprehensive literature review of ^{226}Ra results from marine animals worldwide has been completed by Iyengar and Narayana (1990) for the International Atomic Energy Agency. ^{226}Ra activities in molluscan soft parts were found to range from 0.005 dpm/g to 0.1 dpm/g wet weight. These authors also found molluscan shell ^{226}Ra activities to range from 0.03 dpm/g to 0.3 dpm/g. These values overlap with some of the lowest ^{226}Ra activities measured in seep mussels studied here (Table 3.11).

Alam et al. (1999) studied radionuclide concentrations in marine mussel Perna viridis and estuarine mussel Modiolus striatulus H. from the southern coast of Bangladesh. For the whole soft tissues of three size groups of the marine mussels, the averages were 0.3, 0.2, and 0.2 dpm/g, respectively. For the shells, the averages were 0.8, 0.6, and 0.6 dpm/g, respectively. The three size groups of the estuarine mussels yielded average values of the whole soft tissue of 0.2, 0.1, and 0.1 dpm/g and 0.7, 0.5, and 0.06 dpm/g, respectively, for the shells.

Rabalais et al. (1991) found that oysters deployed closest to nearshore Gulf of Mexico oil well discharge points contained soft body total radium concentrations ranging from 1.1 dpm/g to 4.3 dpm/g dry weight as compared to 0.2 dpm/g (lower limit of detection) for control oysters. The author reported that, in general, ^{226}Ra concentrations in most cases constitute approximately 2/3 of the total radium. The adjusted ^{226}Ra concentration range would then be 0.7 dpm/g to 2.9 dpm/g. All mussel soft body tissues in Rabalais' study ranged from 0.1 dpm/g (lower limit of detection) to 4.3 dpm/g. By comparison, mussel soft tissues from barite seeps range from 0.1 dpm/g to 1.3 dpm/g while mussel soft tissues from carbonate seeps range from below detection limit to 1.5 dpm/g which are somewhat lower than that of the oysters deployed by Rabalais.

In a bioaccumulation study near produced water discharges in low-energy, brackish environments of southeastern Louisiana (St. Pé, 1990), one of three deployed oysters exhibited an elevated ^{226}Ra activity (6.9 dpm/g) which exceeds by far all the mussel soft tissues measured in this study (Table 3.11).

Table 4.5 summarizes the comparison data. The data taken from Iyengar and Narayana (1990) was originally reported on a wet-weight basis. Soft tissues were assumed to contain 90% water in order to adjust the data to a dry weight basis. The Crustacea soft body parts from the barite seeps stand out with respect to their high ^{226}Ra content relative to all other comparable fauna (Fig. 4.16).

Rabalais et al. (1991) found that oysters deployed closest to nearshore Gulf of Mexico oil well discharge points contain soft body total barium concentrations occasionally exceeding 3200 ppm. The highest barium content found in mussel soft bodies from this study was 28 ppm (Table 3.11). However, one galatheid crab whole soft body collected from a barite seep site yielded a Ba value of 4319 ppm and also one of the highest ^{226}Ra levels (2.72 dpm/g). Again, these high values are likely to reflect barite crystals harbored in the GI tract of the galathean crab and not necessarily soft tissue concentrations of barium and radium.

4.5 Radiation Consequences of Radium Leakage from Seeps on the Benthic Fauna

4.5.1. Radium Metabolism and Radiation

Radium is a skeletal seeker because of its chemical similarities to calcium. Therefore its presence in the body long after initial uptake is due to sequestration in the skeleton of vertebrates or calcareous exoskeleton of invertebrate animals, such as molluscs. Concomitantly, radium is absorbed from the G.I. tract (International Commission on Radiological Protection, 1973), which accounts for its potential oral radio-toxicity (Raabe, 1994). Additionally, ^{226}Ra's ability to radioactively decay into a noble gas, ^{222}Rn, become airborne, diffuse throughout the entire organism, and subsequently transmutate into short lived alpha-emitting daughters (^{218}Po and ^{214}Po, Fig. 2.3) increases the potential for internal cellular injury. These radioactive decay products diffuse throughout the entire organism via radon gas and subsequently irradiate sensitive cells remotely located from the original site of deposition in radium contaminated organisms. The primary mode of potential cellular damage resulting from internal deposition of radium is alpha particle radiation resulting in cellular energy deposition of about 24 MeV (3.84×10^{-16} Joules) per atom of ^{226}Ra and its three short lived alpha emitting daughters (where the assumption is made that no ^{222}Rn gas escapes from the contaminated organism). Under conditions of chronic intake, radium becomes very uniformly distributed in calcareous body parts (International Commission on Radiological Protection, 1973).

In addition to potential cellular damage due to internally deposited radium, a potentially significant hazard is posed by external gamma rays emitted by authigenic radium and its radioactive daughters. The gamma radiation from radium and its daughters is sufficiently penetrating so that cells may suffer electromagnetic ionizing radiation damage in addition to that caused by internally deposited radionuclides.

Biological radiation damage depends on the absorption of energy from ionizing radiation, whether deposited by an external or internal source. The amount of cellular damage from radiation is approximately proportional to the concentration of absorbed energy per unit mass of tissue. For this reason, the

Table 4.5. Radium-226 Activities (dpm/g) in Marine Molluscans and Crustaceans

Organism	Iyengar and Narayana (1990)	Alam ct al. (1999)	This Study[c]	Rabalais et al. (1991)
Mollusca				
Soft parts	0.048 – 0.834	0.02 – 0.3	0.02 – 1.5	0.1– 2.7
Shells	0.03 – 0.031	0.6 – 0.8	BDL[a] – 2.3	NR[b]
Crustacea				
Soft parts	BDL[a] – 0.18	NR[b]	6.04 – 10.7	NR[b]
Exoskeletons	0.032 – 0.204	NR[b]	0.42 – 0.95	NR[b]

[a]BDL: below detection limit
[b]NR: did not report data
[c]Barite Seeps

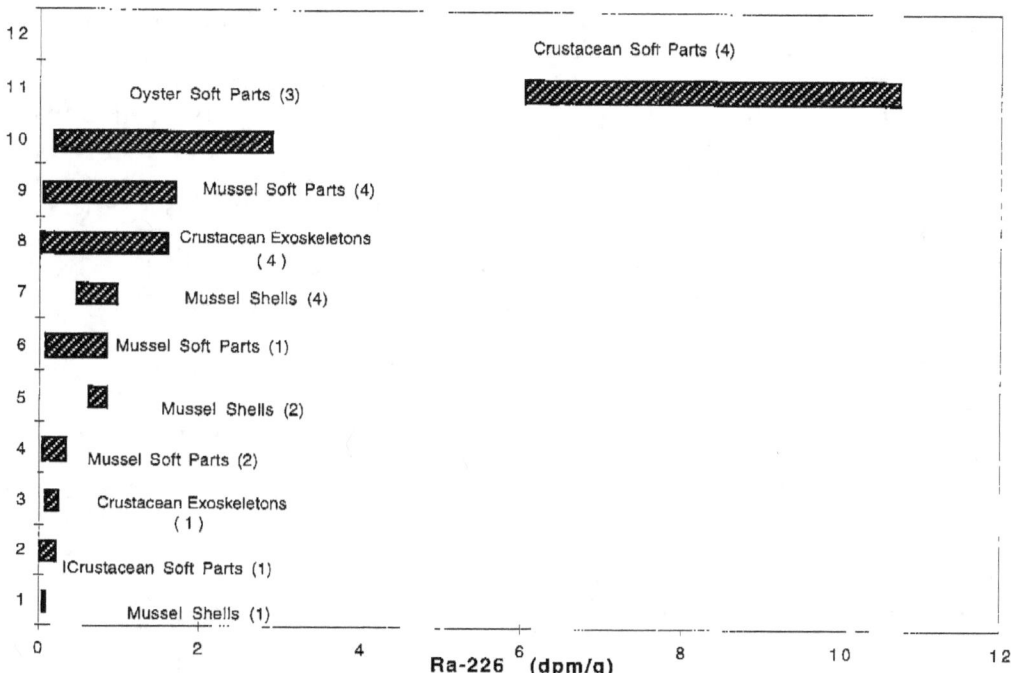

Figure 4.16.-A comparison of ^{226}Ra activity ranges from literature with results from barite seeps. Wet weights from Iyengar and Narayana (1990) were converted to a dry weight basis by assuming a soft tissue water content of 90%.
(1)- Iyengar and Narayana (1990)
(2)- Alam et al. (1999)
(3)- Rabalais et al. (1991)
(4)- Barite Seeps, this study

basic unit of radiation dose is expressed in terms of absorbed energy per unit mass of tissue. The SI unit for radiation absorbed dose is the gray (Gy) and is defined as an absorbed dose of one joule per kilogram of tissue (Cember, 1996). The gray is universally applicable to all types of ionizing radiation-irradiation due to external fields of gamma rays, x-rays, neutrons as well as charged particle emissions due to internally deposited radioisotopes.

The "rad" (radiation absorbed dose) is still widely in use in the U.S. and will be briefly defined for comparison purposes here. Before the introduction of the SI units, the radiation dose was measured by a unit called the "rad". One rad is an absorbed radiation dose of 100 ergs per gram of tissue. One Gy is equal to 100 rad. Although the gray is the newer unit and will eventually replace the rad, the rad nevertheless continues to be widely used. Since one centigray (cGy) equals one rad, it is convenient to utilize this unit division of the Gy.

Somatic sensitivity to acute (delivered all at once) radiation dose varies greatly among phylogenetic groups and tends to increase with phylogenetic heirarchy. For mammals, the acute dose LD_{50} is approximately 400-500 cGy. For molluscs, the acute dose LD_{50} is approximately 2000 cGy (Bacq and Alexander, 1961).

Genetic effects (mutations caused in chromosomes) manifested by radiation-produced mutations in germinal cells being carried on to future generations remains a topic of much debate among experts (BEIR V, 1990) . There are no reliable data available for calculating a genetically deleterious radiation dose to molluscs in natural environments. Therefore, no attempt can be made to estimate genetic effects from radiation measurements conducted during this study.

4.5.2. Chemical and Radiation Flow of Radium Into Benthic Fauna

Figure 4.17 represents a conceptual model for chemical and radiation flow derived from radium into seep fauna as a synthesis of interelationships suggested by our observations.

^{226}Ra and ^{228}Ra resulting from the ^{238}U and ^{232}Th decay series, respectively (Fig. 2.3) are highly mobile in concentrated brines and are transported along with soluble barium via formation waters through subsurface faulting zones to the seafloor where it coprecipitates with barium sulfate and consolidates into radioactive barite deposits. About 2% (Ritcey, 1990) to 30% (our own experiments) of radium does not coprecipitate with $BaSO_4$ under ideal and realistic conditions, respectively, and is available in soluble form for intake by seep fauna (Fig. 4.17 A). Because the Bathymodiolus spp. mussels are methanotrophic symbiont-bearing and not filter-feeders, radium cannot be ingested and subsequently absorbed through the digestive tract. However, water circulation through the gills would provide a mode for internal absoption of radium from the point source effluent. The radium would then be available for incorporation into soft tissues and/or calcareous shells by replacement of Ca in the carbonate lattice. Radium in the barite would also dissolve slightly into interstitial pore fluids along with barium. It seems apparent that pore fluid constituents such as radium and barium are incorporated at their respective pore fluid concentrations in mussel shells (Fig. 3.29).

Heterotrophic fauna such as galatheid crabs would also be capable of internalizing radium via gill circulation and absorption of radium through the large surface area provided by the gills. An additional source of radium to scavenging heterotrophs is radium intake into the G.I. tract via fine barite

A. Chemical Flow of Radium into Fauna

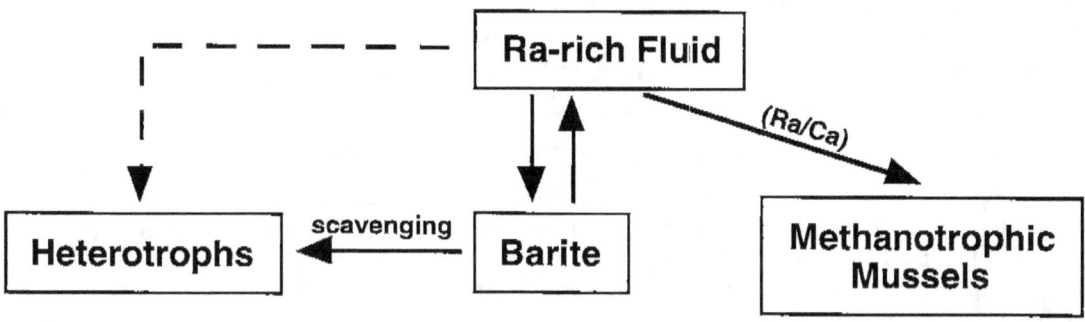

B. Radiation Flow to Fauna

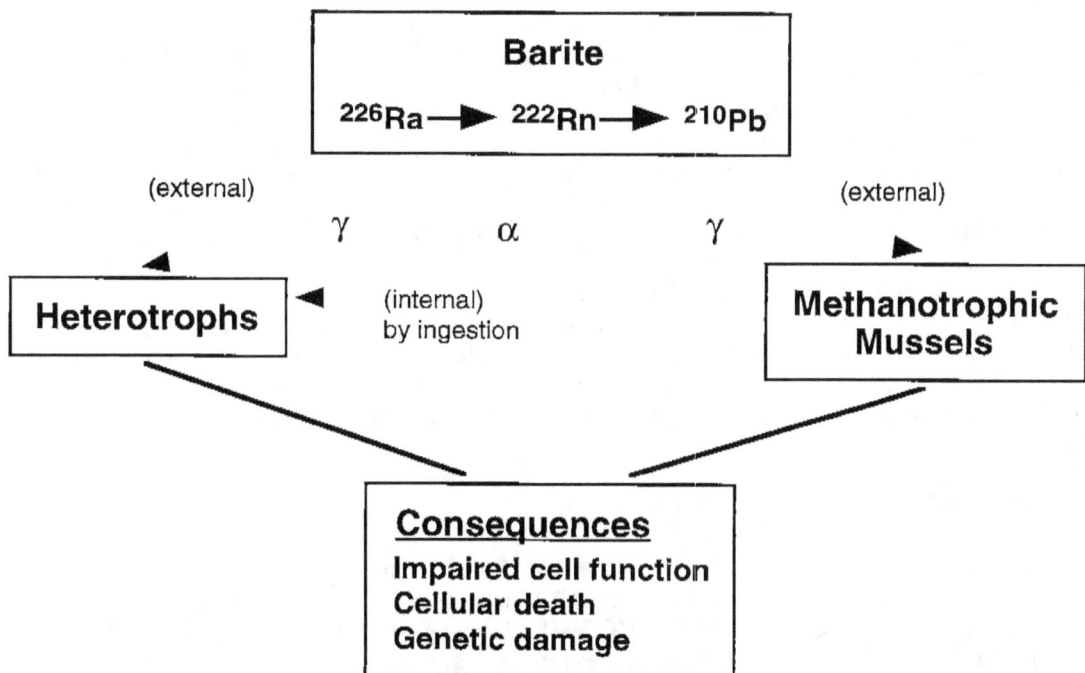

Figure 4.17. Conceptual model depicting the chemical and radiation flow derived from radium-rich barite deposits into fauna (methanotrophic mussels; heterotrophs, including galatheid crabs, starfishes, and polychaetes) inhabiting the barite-rich seeps (see text).

sand particles. The extent to which barite dissolves in the digestive tracts of these animals is not certain. However, *in vitro* barite remains resistant to acid or akaline conditions and is sparingly soluble.

Figure 4.17 B is a conceptual model of ionizing radiation energy flow to seep fauna. Radium coprecipitated in the barite radioactively decays to its respective daughter products by emissions of alpha and beta particles. The ^{226}Ra decay chain of short lived daughters produces the majority of its gamma ray emissions up through the radionuclide ^{210}Pb. The ^{228}Ra decay series emits a nearly equal amount of gamma rays as ^{226}Ra decay chain if activities are equivalent (dpm/dpm). The external gamma rays easily penetrate through the shells of the mussels and the heterotrophs in near proximity to the barite chimneys and barite sand infilling the gulleys (Fig. 1.2). The gamma rays account for the majority of the dose received by the mussels and heterotrophs.

Radiation consequences are primarily from externally emitted penetrating gamma rays from the radium incorporated in barite deposits. The most likely consequences include impaired function of affected cells, possible cellular death, and stochastic genetic damage. Impaired cell function may or may not lead to cell death. If enough cells are affected, a threshold is reached where effects are manifested at the whole organism level with consequences ranging from temporary mild organismal impairment to death of the affected individual. These types of effects are termed non-stochastic effects and are proportional in severity to the radiation dose received (Cember, 1996). This effect parallels morbid effects from other types of noxious agents such as poisonous chemical exposure. For example, a small amount of cyanide will not have any significant effects until a certain cellular threshold level is reached.

Genetic damage (mutations) at the DNA level may also result in impaired cell function and cell death as well as eventual organismal death. These type of effects are termed stochastic effects and are independent of the radiation dose received (Cember, 1996). However, the probability of an effect increases with radiation dose and may manifest itself in one organism but not in another, even though both received identical radiation doses.

Genetic damage to germinal cells has been shown to propagate into future generations as mutations, usually being of a deleterious nature. However, most expressive mutations are lethal if they are dominant, and are therefore usually not passed on to successive generations as dominant alleles (Cember, 1996).

4.5.3. Radiation Risk Assessment

External dose rates to sessile epifauna (Bathymodiolus spp. mussels) located in radium-rich barite seeps were calculated using the computer program MICROSHIELD Version 5.0. The MICROSHIELD program uses the "point kernel" technique to estimate dose rates from external gamma rays generated by radioactive geometric volumes. Radioactive sources were specified as the measured radioactivities of ^{226}Ra, ^{228}Ra, and their radioactive decay products in conical geometric volumes approximating the actual shape and dimensions of barite chimneys found in the barite seep sites (Figure 1.2).

The point kernel technique of dose estimation is not trivial. This method of dose estimation involves dividing up volumetric sources (in this case, a truncated cone) into differentially small sources which can be treated independently as point sources. The resulting differential doses to the target (mussel) become an integrand or "kernel" inside an integral, which then gives total target dose due to the entire radioactive volumetric source. The mathematical concept is a special case of a Green's function. A rigorous treatment of this method is found in Chilton et al. (1984).

Table 4.6 lists the mean activities of ^{226}Ra and ^{228}Ra radionuclides in the barite deposits measured in this study. For calculation purposes, the irradiated target (mussel) was assumed to be at a position of 1 cm from the geometric surface of the cone (barite chimney); Both chimney and mussel were immersed in a water medium.

Internal dose contributions from ^{226}Ra incorporated into mussel soft tissues would normally be calculated based on alpha emssion energy transmitted from radium and its short-lived daughters to the unshielded tissues of the whole organisms at 24 MeV per ^{226}Ra atom deposited. Actual calculations based on measured ^{226}Ra levels in barite-seep mussels reveal that the internal dose rate is insignificant compared to external dose rates received by the mussels. This inference is supported by the observation that there is no significant difference of internal ^{226}Ra between control mussels (collected at carbonate-bearing seeps) and radium-rich, barite-bearing seep mussels (Table 3.11).

The average absorbed external dose rates generated by radium-rich barite chimneys and crusts are listed in Table 4.7. Accordingly, the estimated hourly radiation dose rates are 6.4 µGy and 12.8 µGy for Garden Banks and Mississippi Canyon, respectively. Age dating data have shown that a _Bathymodiolus_ spp. mussel of an average size lives for at least 25 years (Nix et al., 1995). Assuming that the biota spend 100% of their time near a chimney, the maximum external lifetime dose based on the highest total Ra value in the barite deposits back to the time of collection is estimated to be 11.2 cGy/y (11.2 rad/y) or 280 cGy (280 rad) per average mussel lifetime of 25 years.

About 10 mGy/day threshold is necessary before detrimental effects to aquatic organisms is noticeable (IAEA, 1992). The largest possible dose to the mussels (without regard to possible radon gas dissolved in bottom water) is estimated to be 0.0128mGy/day or 112 mGy/year which is much smaller than the cited threshold. Therefore, radiation exposures from radiation sources both external and internal to the fauna may pose an insignificant radiation hazard to the methanotrophic mussels. The effect on gametes and subsequent generations of mussels may be insignificant as well.

It should be noted for purposes of comparison that the 25 year cumulative dose of 2800 mGy (280 rad) is a potentially lethal dose if received all at once in an acute exposure, and is greater than the mean dose received by Hiroshima survivors (Gofman, 1981). This dose would result in approximately 8.4% excess cancers in an irradiated population of humans (BEIR V, 1990). This dose rate and lifetime dose would definitely be of concern both somatically and genetically if applied to a human population. However, due to the complexity of radiation interactions between species, it is impossible to speculate at this time what the long term effects on seep mussels would be.

A potentially significant source of radiation exposure to seep organisms could be contributed from dissolved ^{222}Rn in the surrounding bottom waters. Laboratory tests of sampled barites reveal that barite can emanate (or lose) as much as 3% of its radon gas in secular equilibrium with radium to the environment. Internally deposited ^{222}Rn and its alpha emitting decay products in biological tissues is potentially damaging. Since no direct measurements of radon gas dissolved in water could be carried out during this

Table 4.6. ^{226}Ra and ^{228}Ra mean activities in barite deposits with 2-σ random counting error

Location	Number	^{226}Ra Mean dpm/g	^{228}Ra Mean dpm/g
Garden Banks	28	2796 ± 414	1872 ± 564
Mississippi Canyon	4	7146 ± 3168	2568 ± 1644

Table 4.7. External dose rates to seep fauna calculated from Microshield 5.0

Location	^{226}Ra Dose Rate :μGy/h	^{228}Ra Dose Rate : μGy/h	Total Dose Rate :μGy/h
Garden Banks	3.4 (0.34 mrad/h)	3.0 (0.30 mrad/h)	7.4 (0.74 mrad/h)
Mississippi Canyon	8.7 (0.87 mrad/h)	4.1 (0.41 mrad/h)	12.8 (1.28 mrad/h)

study, there is a need to know the extent to which radon is present in chemosynthetic ecosystems before assessing the radon radiation hazards.

5. CONCLUSIONS AND RECOMMENDATIONS

1. Three chemical types of pore fluids associated with hydrocarbon seeps occur in the deepwater Gulf of Mexico. Two are derived from the ambient seawater and their chemical compositions are altered by microbial interactions and by dissolution of sub-seafloor salt diapirs. The third type, highly enriched in Ba and Ra, is derived from deep-seated formation waters and its advection on the seafloor through fault conduits associated with salt diapirism impacts adversely the ambient benthic habitats.

2. Formation-water-derived fluids emerging on the seafloor are anomalously enriched in Ra and Ba relative to seawater by factors of up to 4.5×10^4 and 15×10^4, respectively. Their migration time from the source to the seafloor is established to be < 20 years on the basis of the relatively short-lived ^{228}Ra isotope content.

3. Barite ($BaSO_4$) deposits consist of chimneys, crusts blanketing mud volcanoes, and unconsolidated sands infilling gulleys. The chimneys are dominated by the mineral celesto-barite (i.e., Sr-rich barite), whereas the crusts consist of both barite and calcite. The Gulf of Mexico seep barites are anomalously enriched in Sr, Ca and Ra by comparison with barites from normal marine settings elsewhere.

4. Sulfur, oxygen and strontium isotope compositions indicate that the Gulf of Mexico seep barite deposits form by the mixing of sulfate-rich seawater with Ba-, Sr-, and Ca-rich formation fluids seeping with gaseous hydrocarbons, primarily thermogenic methane. The chimneys are erected vertically above the seafloor whereas the crusts drape mud volcanoes and/or form pavements at the sediment/water interface.

5. Both ^{226}Ra and ^{228}Ra are "orphans" in the sense that their respective parents ^{238}U and ^{232}Th are practically absent in the fluids and barites. The "orphan" property of Ra affords radiometric dating of the barites by ^{210}Pb/^{226}Ra and ^{228}Th/^{228}Ra daughter/parent isotope pairs. The assays indicate that chimney ages range from 0.5 to 6.5 years whereas the crust ages range from 9.0 to 23.1 years. The growth rates of the chimneys vary from 4.4 cm/yr to 9.1 cm/yr. These results indicate that the Ba-Ra-rich fluid expulsion on the seafloor, triggering barite deposition, is a rapid and recent event. At this point we cannot discern whether or not the intensified emissions are related to disturbances in subsurface hydrology triggered by exploration and production from deepwater platforms. This question must be addressed responsibly in future studies.

6. Fluid fluxes from point sources in the Garden Banks and Mississippi Canyon, estimated on the basis of material mass balance, are 250 L/yr and 2920 L/yr, respectively. Assuming that the Ba-Ra-rich seeps cover about 0.1% of the Louisiana upper slope, the annual fluxes of Ba and Ra are estimated to be of the same order of magnitude as their annual discharges from the Mississippi River. Although our flux estimates carry the uncertainty of the areal coverage of barite-bearing seeps, the values reported here are likely to be conservative. The assumptions regarding the parameters of the model can be tested by future empirical observations and the veracity of our estimates can be

challenged by future studies. Additional local and regional surveys should also address the question of Ra and Ba dispersion from the seeps into the water column in view of data suggesting an "unexplained" increase in the downstream Ra concentrations in the Gulf of Mexico (Reid, 1979; Key, 1981).

7. The uptake of Ba and Ra by the fauna inhabiting the barite-bearing seeps was found to be proportional to the Ba/Ra ratio in the pore fluids. Mussels harboring methanotrophic endosymbionts average 0.6 dpm/g and 0.5 dpm/g ^{226}Ra for soft tissues and calcareous shells, respectively, which are significantly higher than those reported for shallow marine mussels. Vagrant, heterotrophic, fauna living around the seeps yield ^{226}Ra and Ba up to 10.7 dpm/g and 4319 ppm, respectively. The considerably higher levels of Ra and Ba in the heterotrophs are probably acquired through ingestion of barite particles.

8. The largest possible radiation dose to fauna from Ra-rich barites (0.0128 mGy/day) is substantially lower than the threshold of detrimental radiation effects for aquatic animals. However, the cumulative radiation dose and consequential genetic effects over a mean lifespan of 25 years for mussels could be substantial. These estimates have not considered the radiation exposure derived from ^{222}Rn gas dissolved in the surrounding bottom waters because of absence of data. There is a need to determine the level of radon in the ambient seeps in order to properly assess the impact of radon radiation hazards.

6. REFERENCES

Aharon, P. (2000) Microbial processes and products fueled by hydrocarbons at submarine seeps *In* Microbial Sediments R.E. Riding and S.M. Awramik (Eds.) Springer-Verlag Berlin, Heidelberg. pp. 270-281.

Aharon, P., Graber, E.R. and Roberts, H.H. (1992) Dissolved carbon and $\delta^{13}C$ anomalies in the water column caused by hydrocarbon seeps on the northwestern Gulf of Mexico slope. Geo-Marine Lett. 12: 33-40.

Aharon, P, H.H. Roberts, and R. Snelling (1992a) Submarine venting of brines in the deep Gulf of Mexico slope: Observations and geochemistry: Geology 20: 483-486.

Aharon, P., Schwarcz, H.P. and Roberts, H.H. (1997) Radiometric dating of submarine hydrocarbon seeps in the Gulf of Mexico. Geol. Soc. Am. Bull. 109: 568-579.

Aharon, P., and B. Fu. (2000) Microbial sulfate reduction rates and sulfur and oxygen isotope fractionations at oil and gas seeps in deepwater Gulf of Mexico. Geochim. Cosmochim. Acta 64: 233-246.

Alam, M.N., Chowdhurry, M.I., Kamal, S., Matin, A.K., and Ferdousi, G.S. (1999) Radionuclide concentrations in mussels collected from the southern coast of Bangladesh. J. Environ. Radioactivity 47: 201-212.

Bacq, Z.M. and P. Alexander (1961) Comparative Radiosensitivity of Living Organisms. In: Fundamentals of Radiobiology, 2nd Ed., Pergamon Press, Oxford, pp. 299-309.

BEIR V Report (1990) Health effects of exposure to low levels of ionizing radiation. National Academy Press, Washington D.C., pp. 71-134.

Bence, A.E. and A.L. Albee (1968) Empirical correction factors for the electron microanalysis of silicates and oxides: J. Geol. 76: 382-403.

Berner, R.A. (1971) Principles of chemical sedimentology: McGraw-Hill, N.Y., 240pp.

Bertine, K.K. and J.B. Keene (1987) Submarine barite-opal rocks of hydrothermal origin: Science 188: 150-152.

Bloch, S. and Key, R.M. (1981) Modes of formation of anomalously high radioactivity in oil field brines. Am. Assoc. Petrol. Geol. Bull. 65(1): 154-159.

Boothe, P.N. and Presley, B.J. (1985) Long term fate of drilling mud barite on the Texas-Louisiana continental shelf and slope. EOS, Am. Geophys. Union 66 (51): 1329.

Borole, D.V. and B.L.K. Somayajulu (1977), Radium and lead-210 in marine barite: Marine Chem. 5: 291-296.

Boulegue, J., A.M. Kersabiec, and F. Vidot (1990) Trace metals (Ba, Sr, Mn, Cu) in interstitial waters, Leg 116: Proc. Ocean Drill. Progr. Sc. Res. 116: 117-125.

Breit, G.N., E.C. Simmons and M.B. Goldhaber (1985) Dissolution of barite for the analysis of strontium isotopes and other chemical and isotopic variations using aqueous sodium carbonate: Chem. Geol. 52: 333-336.

Broecker, W.S. and Peng, T.H. (1982) Tracers in the Sea. LDGO Press, Palisades, New York, pp. 169.

Buerkert, T.M. (1997) Barium in water and foraminiferal shells: Indicators of present and past oceanographic conditions in the Gulf of Mexico. Unpublished PhD Dissertation, Louisiana State University, pp. 96.

Burke, W.H., R.E., Denison, E.A., Hetherington, R.B., Koepnick, H.F., Nelson and J.B., Otto (1982) Variations of seawater $^{87}Sr/^{86}Sr$ throughout Phanerozoic time: Geology 10: 516-519.

134

Carney, R.S. (1994) Consideration of the oasis analogy for chemosynthetic communities at Gulf of Mexico hydrocarbon vents: Geo-Marine Lett. 14: 149-159.

Carothers, W.W., Cocker, J.D., Law, L.M. and Kharaka, Y.K. (1986) Application of stable isotopes to the origin and migration of oil-field waters in Pleistocene reservoir rocks, offshore Texas. In: Selected Papers in the Hydrologic Sciences (ed. Subitzky, S.), US Geol. Survey Water Supply Paper 2310: 117-127.

Carpenter, A.B. (1978) Origin and chemical evolution of brines in sedimentary basins, in K.S. Johnson and J. Russell, eds., 13th Annual Forum of Geology of Industrial Minerals: Oklahoma Geological Survey Circular 79: 60-77.

Cech, I., M. Lemma, C.W. Kreitler and H.M. Prichard (1988) Radium and radon in water supplies from the Texas Gulf Coastal aquifer: Water Res. 22(1): 109-121.

Cecile, M.P., and L.D. Jones (1979) Note on a radioactive barite sinter, Bonnet Plume map-area, District of Mackenie: *In* Current Research, part B, Geological Survey of Canada, paper 79-1B, p. 416.

Cecile, M.P., M.A. Shakup, and H.R. Krouse (1983) The isotopic composition of western Canadian barites and the possible derivation of oceanic sulfate $\delta^{34}S$ and $\delta^{18}O$ age curves: Can. J. Earth Sciences 20: 1528-1535.

Cecile, M.P., W.D. Goodfellow, L.D. Jones, H.R. Krouse and M.A. Shakur (1984) Origin of radioactive barite sinter, Flybye springs, Northwest Territories, Canada: Can. J. Earth Sciences 21: 383-395.

Cember, H. (1996) Introduction to Health Physics. 3rd. ed. McGraw-Hill New York, NY, pp.733.

Chilton, A,B, Shultis, J.K., and R.E. Faw (1984) Principles of Radiation Shielding. Prentice-Hill, Inc., Englewood Cliffs, NJ, pp. 175-177.

Chung, Y. (1980) Radium-barium-silica correlations and a two-dimentional radium model for the world ocean. Earth Planet. Science Lett. 49: 309-318.

Church, T.M. (1970) Marine barite. Unpublished PhD Dissertation: University of California, San Diego, 100 p.

Church, T. M. and K. Wolgemuth (1972) Marine barite saturation. Earth Planet. Science Lett. 15: 35-44.

Church, T.M. (1979) Marine barite. In: Marine Minerals, (ed. Burns, R.G.), Mineral. Soc. Am. Short Course Notes, Washington DC, v. 6, ch. 7, p. 175-210

Clark, J.R. and Patrick, J.M. (1987) Toxicity of sediment-incorporated drilling fluids. Marine Pollution Bull. 18 (11): 600-603.

Claypool, G.E., W.T. Holser, I.R. Kaplan, H. Sakai, and I Zak (1980) The age curves of sulfur and oxygen isotopes in marine sulfate and their mutual interpretation: Chem. Geol. 28: 199-260.

Cline, J.D. (1969) Spectrophotometric determination of hydrogen sulfide in natural waters. Limnol. Oceanogr. 14: 454-458.

Cochran, J.K. and S. Krishnaswami (1977), Ra-226 and Ra-228 in sediment pore water: EOS, Am. Geophys. Union Trans. 58(12): 1153.

Cochran, J.K., (1979) The geochemistry of ^{226}Ra and ^{228}Ra in marine deposits: Unpublished Ph.D dissertation, Yale University, 260 p.

Cochran, J.K. (1982) The oceanic chemistry of the U and Th series nuclides. *In* M. Ivanovich and R.S. Harmon (eds), Uranium Series Disequilibrium: Application to environmental problems: Claredon Press, Oxford, p. 384-430.

Cook, L.M (1980) The uranium district of the Texas Gulf Coastal Plain: In Natural Radiation Environment III (ed T.F. Gessel and W.M. Lowder), . U.S. Department of Energy, Washington, D.C, pp. 1602-1922

Costlow, J.D. and 12 co-authors (1983) Drilling discharges in the marine environment. National Academy Press, Washington D.C., pp. 180.

Davidson, D.W., D.G. Leaist, and R. Hesse (1983) Oxygen-18 enrichment in the water of a clathrate hydrate: Geochim. Cosmochim. Acta 47: 2293-2295.

Dehairs, F., R. Chesselet, and J. Jedwab (1980) Discrete suspended particles of barite and the barium cycle in the open ocean: Earth Planet. Science Lett. 49: 528-550.

Dinnel, S.P. and Wiseman, W.J. (1986) Fresh water on the Louisiana and Texas shelf. Cont. Shelf Res. 6 (6): 765-784.

Drever, J.I., 1982, The geochemistry of natural waters: Prentice Hall, New Jersey, 437 pp.

Dymond, J., R. Cober, L. Gordon, P. Biscaye and G. Mathieu, (1983) ^{226}Ra and ^{222}Rn contents of Galapagos Rift hydrothermal waters-the importance of low-temperature interactions with crustal rocks: Earth and Planet. Science Lett. 64: 417-429.

Egeberg, P.K., and P. Aagaard (1989) Origin and evolution of formation waters from oil fields on the Norwegian shelf: Applied Geochem. 4: 131-142.

Environmental Health Criteria 107 (1990) Barium. World Health Org., Geneva, 148 pp.

EPA (1980) EPA/600/4-80-032 & EPA 903.1: Prescribed Procedures for Measurement of Radioactivity in Drinking Water. U.S. Government Printing Office, 133 pp.

Faure, G. (1986) Principles of Isotope Geology: John Wiley & Sons, New York, 531 pp.

Ferrell, R.E. and P. Aharon (1994) Mineral assemblages occurring around hydrocarbon vents in the northern Gulf of Mexico: Geo-Marine Lett. 14: 74-80.

Finkel, R.C., J.D. Macdougall, and Y.C. Chung (1980) Sulfide precipitates at 21°C on the East Pacific Rise: ^{226}Ra, ^{210}Pb and ^{210}Po: Geophys. Res. Lett. 7: 685-688.

Fritz, P., G.M. Basharmal, R.J., Drimmie, J. Ibsen and R.M. Qureshi (1989) Oxygen isotope exchange between sulfate and water during bacterial reduction of sulfate: Chem. Geol. 79: 99-105.

Fu, B., Aharon P., Byerly G.R., and Roberts, H.H. (1994) Barite chimneys on the Gulf of Mexico slope: initial report on their petrography and geochemistry: Geo-Marine Lett. 14: 81-87.

Fu, B. and Aharon, P. (1995) Oxygen and sulfur isotopes and elemental chemistry of barite deposits associated with hydrocarbon seeps in the deep Gulf of Mexico. Geol. Soc. Am. Abstracts with Programs 27: A97.

Fu, B. , P. Aharon, D.L. Van Gent, and L.M. Scott (1996) Anomalously high ^{226}Ra in fluids advecting to the sea floor: A new radioactive source in the Gulf of Mexico. Gulf Coast Assoc. Geol. Soc.Trans. 46: 125-131.

Fu, B. and P. Aharon (1997) Origin and depositional model of barite deposits associated with hydrocarbon seeps on the Gulf of Mexico slope, offshore Louisiana: Gulf Coast Assoc. Geol. Soc. Trans. 47: 13-20.

Fu, B. (1998) A Study of Pore Fluids and Barite Deposits from Hydrocarbon Seeps: Deepwater Gulf of Mexico. Unpublished PhD Dissertation, Louisiana State University, 243 pp.

Gofman, J.W. (1981) Radiation and Human Health. A comprehensive investigation of the evidence relating low-level radiation to cancer and other diseases. Sierra Club, San Francisco. pp. 908.

Goldberg, E.D., B.L.K. Somayajulu, J. Galloway, I.R. Kaplan, and G. Faure (1969) Differences between barites of marine and continental origins: Geochim. Cosmochim. Acta 33: 287-289.

Graber, E.R. and Aharon, P. (1991) An improved microextraction technique for measuring dissolved inorganic carbon (DIC), $\delta^{13}C$ (DIC) and $\delta^{18}O$ (H_2O) from milliliter-size water samples. Chem. Geol. (Isotope Geosc. Sec.) 94: 137-144.

Grasty, R.L, C.W. Smith, J.M. Franklin and I.R. Jonasson (1988) Radioactive orphans in barite-rich chimneys, Axial Caldera, Juan de Fuca Ridge: Can. Mineral. 26: 627-636.

Hannington, M.D. and R. Scott (1988) Mineralogy and geochemistry of a hydrothermal silica-sulfide-sulfate spire in the caldera of axial seamount, Juan de Fuca ridge: Can. Mineral. 26: 603-625.

Hanor, J.S. (1966) The origin of barite: Unpublished Ph.D Dissertation, Harvard University, 257 pp.

Hanor, J.S. (1982) Problems concerning the geochemistry and genesis of ratiform barite-pyrite ore deposits in Arkansas, in McFarland, J. D., ed., Contributions to the Geology of Arkansas: Ark. Geol. Comm. Misc. Publ. 18: 27-32.

Hanslik, E. and A. Mansfield (1990) Removal of radium from drinking water in The environmental behaviour of radium. IAEA Technical Report Series No. 310(2): 229-268.

Henderson, L.M. and F.C. Kracek (1927) The fractional precipitation of barium and radium chromates: J. Am. Chem. Soc. 47: 738-749.

Hesse, R. and W.E. Harrison (1981) Gas hydrates (clathrates) causing pore-water freshening and oxygen isotope fractionation in deep-water sedimentary sections of terrigenous continental margins: Earth Planet. Science Lett. 55: 453-462.

Hofmann, R. and A. Baumann (1984) Preliminary report on the Sr isotopic composition of hydrothermal vein barites in the Federal Republic of Germany: Mineralium Deposita 19: 166-169.

Horwitz, W. (1980) Fish and other marine products. In: Official methods of analysis of the association of official analytical chemists, 13th ed. Association of Official Analytical Chemists. p. 285-290.

Hovland, M., M. Talbout, H. Qvale, S. Olausson, and L. Aasberg (1987) Methane related carbonate cements in pockmarks of the North Sea: J. Sedim. Petrol. 57: 881-892.

International Atomic Energy Agency (IAEA) (1992) Effects of Ionizing Radiation on Plants and Animals at Levels Implied by Current Radiation Protection Standards. Technical Reports Series No. 332, IAEA, Vienna.

International Commission on Radiological Protection. (1973) Alkaline Earth Metabolism in Adult Man. Publication 20; Pergamon Press, New York

Iyengar, K. and R. Narayana. (1990) Uptake of radium by marine animals In The environmental behaviour of radium. International Atomic Energy Agency. Technical Report Series No. 310(1): 467-485.

Jackson, T.J., Wade, T.L., McDonald, T.J., Wilkinson, D.L. and Brooks, J.M. (1994) Polynuclear aromatic hydrocarbon contaminants in oysters from the Gulf of Mexico (1986-1990). Env. Poll. 83 (3): 291-298.

Jahnke, R.A. (1988) A simple, reliable, and inexpensive pore-water sampler: Limnol. and Oceanogr. 33(3): 483-487.

Jarmul, D. (1984) Drilling mud poses minimal risk. Geotimes 29 (1): 14.

Jensenius, J. and N.C. Munksgaard (1989) Large scale hot water migration systems around salt diapirs in the Danish central trough and their impact on diagenesis of chalk reservoirs: Geochim. Cosmochim. Acta 53: 79-88.

Kadko, D., R. Koski, M. Tatsumoto, and R. Bouse (1985) An estimate of hydrothermal fluid residence times and vent chimney growth rates based on ^{210}Pb/Pb ratios and mineralogical studies of sulfides dredged from the Juan de Fuca Ridge: Earth Planet. Science Lett. 76: 35-44.

Kadko, D. and W.S. Moore (1988) Radiochemical constraints on the crustal residence time of submarine hydrothermal fluids: Endeavour Ridge: Geochim. Cosmochim. Acta 52: 659-668.

Kalogeropoulos, S.I. and P. Mitropoulos (1983) Geochemistry of barite from Milos island: Neues Jahrbuch fuer Mineral. Monatsh. 1: 13-21.

Kesler, S.E., L.M. Jones and J. Ruiz (1988) Strontium and sulfur isotope geochemistry of the Galeana barite district, Nuevo Leon, Mexico: Econ. Geol. 83: 1907-1917.

Key, R.M. (1981) Examination of abyssal sea floor and near-bottom water mixing processes using Ra-226 and Rn-222. Unpublished Ph.D Dissertation, Texas A & M University, 227 pp.

Kharaka, Y.K., A.S., Maest, W.W., Carothers, L.M., Law, P.J., Lamothe, and T.L., Fries (1987) Geochemistry of metal-rich brines from central Mississippi Salt Dome basin, U.S.A.: Applied Geochem. p. 543-562.

Kigoshi, K. (1971) Alpha-recoil thorium-234: Dissolution into water and the uranium-234/uranium-238 disequilibrium in nature: Science 173: 47-48.

Kim, K.H. and G.M. McMurtry (1991) Radial growth rates and ^{210}Pb ages of hydrothermal massive sulfides from the Juan de Fuca Ridge: Earth Planet. Science Lett. 104: 299-314.

Kraemer, T.F. and Reid, D.F. (1984) The occurrence and behavior of radium in saline formation water of the U.S. Gulf coast region. Chem. Geol. (Isotope Geosc. Sec.) 2: 153-174.

Krest, J.M. (1995) ^{228}Ra and ^{226}Ra as indicators of sea water-sediment interactions in the Mississippi and Atchafalaya mixing zones. Unpublished MS Thesis, University of South Carolina, pp. 60.

Kronfeld, J., Minster, T. and Ne'eman, E. (1993) ^{238}U-series disequilibrium in the Upper Cretaceous oil shales of Israel as the primary source for the Dead Sea ^{226}Ra anomaly. Terra Nova 5: 563-567.

Kronfeld, J. (1995) Oil shale brines and radium anomalies (Israel). Geol. Soc. Am. Abstracts with Programs 27: A97.

Kusakabe, M., S. Mayeda, and E. Nakamura (1990) S, O and Sr isotope systematics of active vent materials from the Mariana backarc basin spreading axis at 18°N: Earth Planet. Science Lett. 100: 275-282.

Kvenvolden, K.A. (1988) Methane hydrate: A major reservoir of carbon in the shallow geosphere. Chem. Geol. 71: 41-51.

Lalou, C. and E. Brichet (1982) Ages and implications of East Pacific Rise sulfide deposits at 21°C: Nature 300: 169-171.

Lalou, C. and E. Brichet (1987) On the isotopic chronology of submarine hydrothermal deposits. Chem. Geol. 65: 197-207.

Land, L.S., and D.R. Prezbindowski (1981) The origin and evolution of saline formation water, Lower Cretaceous carbonates, south-central Texas: J. Hydrol. 54: 51-74.

138

Land, L.S., Macpherson, G.L. and Mack, L.E. (1988) The geochemistry of saline formation waters, Miocene, offshore Louisiana. Gulf Coast Assoc. Geol. Soc. Trans. 38: 503-511.

Land, L.S. and G.L. Macpherson (1989) Geochemistry of formation water, Plio-Pleistocene reservoirs, offshore Louisiana: Gulf Coast Assoc. of Geol. Soc. Trans. 39: 421-430.

Land, L.S., Macpherson, G.L. and Mack, L.E. (1988) The geochemistry of saline formation waters, Miocene, offshore Louisiana. Gulf Coast Assoc. Geol. Soc. Trans. 38: 503-511.

LaRock, P. J.H. Hyun, S. Boutelle, W.C. Burnett, and C.D. Hull (1996) Bacterial mobilization of polonium: Geochim. Cosmochim. Acta 60(22): 4321-4328.

Lloyd, R.M. (1968) Oxygen isotope behavior in the sulfate-water system: J. Geophys. Res. 73: 6099-6110.

MacDonald, K.C., K. Becker, F.N. Speiss and R.D. Ballard (1980) Hydrothermal heat flux of the 'black smoker' vents on the East Pacific Rise': Earth Planet. Science Lett. 48: 1-7.

MacDonald, I.R., Guinasso, N.L., Ackleson, S.G., Amos, J.F., Duckworth, R., Sassen, R. and Brooks, J.M. (1993) Natural oil slicks in the Gulf of Mexico visible from space. J. Geophys. Res. 98 (C9): 16,351-16,364.

MacDonald, I.R., Guinasso, N.L., Sassen, R., Brooks, J.M., Lee, L. and Scott, K.T. (1994) Gas hydrate that breaches the sea floor on the continental slope of the Gulf of Mexico. Geology 22: 699-702.

Macpherson G.L. (1989) Lithium, boron and barium in formation waters and sediments, northwestern Gulf of Mexico sedimentary basin. Unpublished Ph.D dissertation, University of Texas at Austin, 286 p.

Manker, J.P. and Rickman, D.A. (1994) Toxic metal concentrations and distributions in sediments along the Louisiana/Texas coast. Geol. Soc. Am. Abstr. with Progr., Southeastern Sec. 26 (14): 26.

McGee, D.T., P.W. Bilinski, P.S. Gary, D.S. Pfeiffer, and J.L. Sheiman (1994) Geological models and reservoir geometries of Auger Field, deepwater Gulf of Mexico: GCS-SEPM Foundation 15th Annual Res. Conf., Submarine Fans and Turbidite Systems, p. 245-256.

Mendelssohn, I.R., Flynn, K.M. and Wilsey, B.J. (1990) The relationship between produced water discharges, and plant biomass and species composition in three Louisiana marshes. Oil and Chem. Poll. 7(4): 317-335.

Mizutani, Y. (1971. An improvement in the carbon reduction method for the oxygen isotopic analysis of sulfates. Geochem. J. 5: 69-77.

Mizutani, Y. and T.A. Rafter (1973) Isotopic behavior of sulfate oxygen in the bacterial reduction of sulfate: Geochem. J. 6: 183-191.

Moore, W. and D. Stakes, (1990), Ages of barite-sulfide chimneys from the Mariana Trough: Earth Planet. Science Lett. 100: 265-274.

Moore, W.S. (1996) Large groundwater inputs to coastal waters revealed by ^{226}Ra enrichments: Nature 380: 612-614.

Moore, W.S. (1997) High fluxes of radium and barium from the mouth of the Ganges-Brahmaputra River during low river discharge suggest a large groundwater source: Earth Planet. Science Lett. 150: 141-150.

Nix, E.R., Fisher, C.R., Vodenichar, J. and Scott, K.M. (1995) Physiological ecology of a mussel with methanotrophic endosymbionts at three hydrocarbon seep sites in the Gulf of Mexico. Mar. Biol. 122: 605-617

Orr, J.C. (1988) ^{222}Rn, ^{226}Ra, and ^{228}Ra as tracers for the evolution of warm core rings. Unpublished Ph.D dissertation. Texas A & M University, 211 p.

Paytan, A., W.S. Moore, and M. Kastner (1996), Sedimentation rate as determined by ^{226}Ra activity in marine barite: Geochim. Cosmochim. Acta 60(22): 4313-4319.

Peter, J.M. and S. Scott (1988) Mineralogy, composition, and fluid-inclusion microthermometry of seafloor hydrothermal deposits in the southern trough of Guaymas basin, Gulf of California: Can. Mineral. 26: 567-587.

Presley, B.J. (1969) Chemistry of interstitial water from marine sediments. Unpublished Ph.D dissertation, University of California at Los Angeles, 225 pp.

Prichard, H.M., Gesell, T.F. and Mewyer, C.R. (1980) Liquid scintillation analysis for radium-226 and radon-222 in potable water: In Liquid Scintillation Counting-Recent Applications and Development (eds. Peng, C.T., Horrocks, D.L. and Alpen, E.L.), Academic Press, N.Y., v. 1, p. 347-355.

Raabe, O.G. (1994) Dose reconstruction from bioassay measurements of long-lived residual activity In Internal Radiation Dosimetry (ed. Raabe, O.G.), Medical Physics Publishing, Madison, W.I. p. 495-515.

Rabalais, N.N., McKee, B.A., Reed, D.J. and J.C. Means (1991) Fate and effects of nearshore discharges of OCS produced waters. Volume I. Executive Summary. OCS Study/MMS 91-0004. U.S. Dept. of the Interior, Minerals Management Service, Gulf of Mexico OCS Regional Office, New Orleans, Louisiana, 48 pp.

Rabalais, N.N., B.A. McKee, D.J. Reed, and J.C. Means (1991) Fate and effects of nearshore discharges of OCS produced waters: Volume III. Appendices. OCS study/MMS 91-0006. U.S. Dept. of the Interior, Minerals Management Service, Gulf of Mexico OCS Regional Office, New Orleans, Louisiana, 225 p.

Rafter, T.A. and Y. Mizutani (1967) Oxygen isotopic composition of sulfate, Part 2. Preliminary results on oxygen isotopic variation in sulfates and the relationship to their environment and to their δ^{34}S values: New Zealand J. Science 10: 816-840.

Raloff, J. (1991) NORM: The new hot waste. Science News 140: 264-267.

Reid, D.F. (1979) The near-surface distribution of radium in the Gulf of Mexico and Caribbean Sea: Temporal and spatial variability and hydrographic relationship: Ph.D dissertation. Texas A & M University, 245 p.

Reid, D.F., W.S. Moore and W.M. Sackett (1979) Temporal variation of ^{228}Ra in the near-surface Gulf of Mexico: Earth Planet. Science Lett. 43: 227-236.

Reid, D.F. (1984) Radium variability produced by shelf-water transport and mixing in the western Gulf of Mexico: Deep-Sea Res. 31(12): 1501-1510.

Reyes, A. O. (1993) ^{228}Th/^{228}Ra ages of hydrothermal chimney samples from the Endeavour Segment of the Juan de Fuca Ridge. Unpublished Master Thesis, University of South Carolina, 118 pp.

Reyes, A.O., W.S. Moore, and D.S. Stakes (1995) ^{228}Th/^{228}Ra ages of a barite-rich chimney from the Endeavour Segment of the Juan de Fuca Ridge: Earth Planetary Science Letters 131: 99-113.

Ritger, S., B. Carson, and E. Suess (1987) Methane-derived authigenic carbonates formed by subduction-induced authigenic carbonates along the Oregon/Washington margin: Geol. Soc. Am. Bull. 98: 147-156.

Ritcey, G. M. (1990) Weathering processes in uranium tailings and the migration of contaminants. In The Environmental Behaviour of Radium. IAEA Technical Report Series No. 310 (2): 27-82.

Rittenhouse, G. (1967), Bromide in oilfield waters and its use in determining possibilities of origins of these waters: Am. Assoc. Petrol. Geol. Bull. 51: 2430-2440.

Roberts, H.H., P. Aharon, R. Sassen, R. Carney, J. Larkin, and R. Sassen (1990) Sea floor responses to hydrocarbon seeps, Louisiana Continental Slope: Geo-Marine Lett. 10: 232-243.

Roberts, H.H. and P. Aharon (1994) Hydrocarbon-derived carbonate buildups of the northern Gulf of Mexico continental slope: A review of submersible investigations. Geo-Marine Lett. 14(2):135-148.

Roberts, H.H. and Carney, R.S. (1997) Evidence of episodic fluid, gas, and sediment venting on the Northern Gulf of Mexico continental slope. Econ. Geol. 92: 863-879.

Robinson, P. (1980) Determination of calcium, magnesium, manganese, strontium, sodium and iron in the carbonate fraction of limestones and dolomites: Chem. Geol. 28: 135-146.

Rye, R.O., D.R. Shawe, and F.G. Poole (1978) Stable isotope studies of bedded barite at East Northumberland Canyon in Toquina Range, central Nevada: J. Res. U.S. Geol. Surv. 6: 221-229.

Sakai, H. (1971) Sulfur and oxygen isotopic study of barite concretions from banks in the Japan Sea off the Northeast Honshu, Japan: Geochem. J. 5: 79-93.

Sakai, H., and H.R. Krouse (1971) Elimination of memory effects in $^{18}O/^{16}O$ determination in sulfate: Earth Planet. Science Lett. 11: 369-373.

Schroll, E. (1987) Die Standardgesteinsreferenzprobe Dolomit/Topla IU-EA-ADT. Bundesversuchs und Forschungsanstalt Arsenal Report, 23 pp.

Somayajulu, B.L.K. and T.M. Church (1973) Radium, thorium, and uranium isotopes in the interstitial water from the Pacific Ocean sediments: J. Geophys. Res. 78: 4529-4531.

Stakes , D. and W.S. Moore (1991) Evolution of hydrothermal activity on the Juan de Fuca Ridge: Observations, mineral ages, and Ra isotope ratios: J. Geophys. Res. 96(B13): 21,739-21,752.

Stuben, D., N.E., Taibi, G.M. McMurtry, J. Scholten, P. Stoffers and D. Zhand (1994), Growth history of a hydrothermal silica chimney from the Mariana backarc spreading center (southwest Pacific, 18°13'N): Chem. Geol. 113: 273-296.

Stueber, A.M., P. Pushkar, and E.A. Hetherington (1984) A strontium isotopic study of Smackover brines and associated solids, southern Arkansas: Geochim. Cosmochim. Acta 48: 1637-1649.

St. Pé, K.M. (1990) An assessment of produced water impacts to low-energy, brackish water systems in Southeast Louisiana. Louisiana Department of Environmental Quality, Water Pollution Control Division, Baton Rouge, Louisiana, 204 pp.

Szabo, B.J. (1967) Radium content in plankton and seawater in the Bahamas. Geochim. Cosmochim. Acta 31: 1321-1331.

Tanner, A.B. (1964) Physical and chemical controls on distribution of radium-226 and radon-222 in ground water near Great Salt Lake, Utah In Proceedings of International Symposium on the Natural Radiation Environment (e.d., J.C. Adams and W.M. Lowder): University of Chicago Press, Chicago, Illinois, p. 253-276.

Tivey, M.K. and J.R. Delaney (1986) Growth of large sulfide structures on the Endeavour Segment of the Juan de Fuca Ridge: Earth Planet. Science Lett. 77: 303-317.

Urabe, T. and M. Kusakabe (1990) Barite silica chimneys from the Sumisu Rift, Izu-Bonin Arc: possible analog to hematitic chert associated with Kuroko deposits: Earth Planet. Science Lett. 100: 283-290.

Van Gent, D.L., B. Fu, P. Aharon, and L.M. Scott (1995) Radium decay series dating of barite deposition in the Gulf of Mexico: Initial results. *In* Environmental Issues and Solutions in Petroleum Exploration, Production, and Refining. Sept. 25-27, New Orleans, LA. IPEC Proc. (ed. K.L. Sublette), Penwell Publ. p. 821-829.

White, D.H. (1965) Saline waters in sedimentary rocks: Am. Assoc. Petrol. Geol. Mem. 4: 342-366.

Wolgemuth, K. and Broecker, W. S. (1970). Barium in seawater. Earth Planet. Science Lett. 8: 372-378.

Zierenberg, R.A., W.C. III Shanks and J.L. Bischoff (1984) Massive sulfide deposits at 21°N, East Pacific Rise: Chemical composition, stable isotopes, and phase equilibrium: Geol. Soc. Am. Bull. 95: 922-929.

The Department of the Interior Mission

As the Nation's principal conservation agency, the Department of the Interior has responsibility for most of our nationally owned public lands and natural resources. This includes fostering sound use of our land and water resources; protecting our fish, wildlife, and biological diversity; preserving the environmental and cultural values of our national parks and historical places; and providing for the enjoyment of life through outdoor recreation. The Department assesses our energy and mineral resources and works to ensure that their development is in the best interests of all our people by encouraging stewardship and citizen participation in their care. The Department also has a major responsibility for American Indian reservation communities and for people who live in island territories under U.S. administration.

The Minerals Management Service Mission

As a bureau of the Department of the Interior, the Minerals Management Service's (MMS) primary responsibilities are to manage the mineral resources located on the Nation's Outer Continental Shelf (OCS), collect revenue from the Federal OCS and onshore Federal and Indian lands, and distribute those revenues.

Moreover, in working to meet its responsibilities, the **Offshore Minerals Management Program** administers the OCS competitive leasing program and oversees the safe and environmentally sound exploration and production of our Nation's offshore natural gas, oil and other mineral resources. The MMS **Royalty Management Program** meets its responsibilities by ensuring the efficient, timely and accurate collection and disbursement of revenue from mineral leasing and production due to Indian tribes and allottees, States and the U.S. Treasury.

The MMS strives to fulfill its responsibilities through the general guiding principles of: (1) being responsive to the public's concerns and interests by maintaining a dialogue with all potentially affected parties and (2) carrying out its programs with an emphasis on working to enhance the quality of life for all Americans by lending MMS assistance and expertise to economic development and environmental protection.